A THEOLOGY OF ELECTION

A Theology of Election

ISRAEL and the CHURCH

By

JAKÓB JOCZ, D.Litt., Ph.D.

With a Preface by
The Right Reverend F. D. COGGAN, D.D.
Bishop of Bradford

NEW YORK
THE MACMILLAN COMPANY

First published 1958

Printed and bound in England by
Hazell Watson and Viney Ltd
Aylesbury and Slough

ACKNOWLEDGEMENTS

This book, like every other book, has a history. It is the result of years of searching, and was written under inward compulsion. The author is specially indebted to his wife for typing the script and showing infinite patience; to Mr Charles Johnson, F.R.S., and Mrs Rita Barns for reading the MS. and offering valuable advice; to his good friend and brother, E. P. E. Lipson, for compiling the Index; and to the S.P.C.K. for expert advice and invaluable help in the production of this book.

J. J.

PREFACE

THE study of the relation of Christian and Jew, of Church and Synagogue, down the centuries is full of interest and for the Christian at times full of shame. The well-known statues of the Church and Synagogue at Strasbourg, the former standing upright with Cross in one hand and chalice in the other, and the latter in a dejected attitude with bandaged eyes, broken staff, and the Tables of the Law falling from her left hand, are moving in their mute appeal to the Christian mind and conscience. There is much to-day for which we may thank God and in regard to which we may take courage in the matter of the relationships existing between Christians and Jews. The Council of Christians and Jews exists "to combat all forms of religious and racial intolerance; to promote mutual understanding and goodwill between Christians and Jews; and to foster co-operation in educational activities and in social and community service." It is doing a noble work. Jew and Christian are engaged in various tasks of research together, and each learns from and contributes to the other. The writer of this preface owes much to the learned and devout Herbert Loewe and would fain acknowledge his debt to him and other Jewish scholars. There is a drawing together and an increasing appreciation of mutual indebtedness. If the Church believes, as indeed she does, that Christianity is the legitimate flowering of Judaism, she can but realize her eternal indebtedness to the "bud" from which she came. And it is of deep interest and significance that to-day many of the greatest of Israel's scholars are realizing, in the words of Dr Jocz, that "Jesus is not only tied to the Jews by bonds of blood, but also by spiritual tradition. . . . It is the merit of scholars like M. Buber and J. Klausner that they have rediscovered for the Jewish people the spiritual link between them and the Nazarene. The fact that much in the New Testament is genuinely Jewish is gradually bearing in upon the Jewish consciousness."

The climate of opinion has indeed changed from the day when the Jew spat at the mention of the name of Jesus, and the "Christian", with a strange marriage of ignorance and piety which begat "a fanaticism eager-eyed for superstition and blind to God", killed vast numbers of Jews who would not forcibly be converted to Christianity.

In the light of such facts as these, Dr Jakób Jocz's book is to be warmly welcomed, and will be read by Jews and Christians alike with deep interest. Dr Jocz writes as a convinced and learned Christian, with a love for the Jewish people due not only to the fact that he is a Jew himself but also due to his conviction that "there is no difference between believing Jews and Gentiles; their difference is only in function but not in quality. Before God they are all saved by grace and grace alone. Israel from henceforth includes both Jews and Gentiles."

His book is a welcome addition, written against the background of a wide knowledge of Jewish and Christian thought, to the already extensive literature of Jewish-Christian debate.

DONALD BRADFORD

CONTENTS

CHAPTER I

INTRODUCTION

WHEN discussing historic Israel we are immediately placed in the centre of the problem of revelation. In the Bible Israel and revelation are correlatives and presuppose one another. It is from this fact that we will have to proceed in elucidating the meaning of election.

It has generally been understood that Israel's function was to act as a channel for the transmission of "divine truth". St Paul tells us that Israel was entrusted with the "oracles of God" (Rom. 3. 2). These "oracles" are usually identified with the Canon of Scripture which we call the Bible. To it the Church turns for her rule of life and for doctrine. But when we look closer into the record of the Bible, we soon discover that the "oracles"—λόγια τοῦ θεοῦ—are not concerned with the "truth" but with God, and that the God of the Bible is non-transmittable in terms of "truth". The "words" of the Bible are ordinary men's words which point to him who alone gives meaning to all human speech. He alone is the Word who in the Second Person of the Holy Trinity became both visible and audible to man. The Incarnate Word the human mind cannot comprehend or the tongue repeat it: to hear it means to meet *him*. To the Church, "God's Word" can only mean the Word which he spoke in Jesus Christ.[1] Revelation therefore in the Christian context can never mean "teaching", "doctrine", "truth", or "law", but must always mean God's stepping into history to encounter man. Revelation must primarily be described in terms of action and not of thought. Revelation in Christ means: God interferes, enacts, challenges, confronts, judges, saves, kills and makes alive. Here impersonal nouns are changed into transitive verbs. Revelation in the Bible is not a question of philosophical discussion but an encounter with the burning Presence of the living God.[2] This encounter with God takes place by the miracle of the Word. There is no real analogy between the human word and God's Word, for God's Word is always an act. The history of revelation is therefore the story of God's mighty acts. In the Bible this story is limited to one single people—Israel. This does not mean that God acts only in Israel and nowhere else; it only means that in Israel he acts in a specific way and that he acts there on behalf of mankind. God does not speak in the void, impersonally, in terms of general "truths"; he does not speak privately to mystics; he speaks historically, i.e. to a living people, in a definite situation. It means that God does not reveal "mysteries" to satisfy our curiosity, but reveals himself as judge and pardoner. This is pre-eminently demonstrated in God's historic dealing with a definite people.

Naturally, he also deals with individuals; the Bible knows many such instances, but his dealing with them has always a wider purpose in view, otherwise it would not be revelation. For revelation, in all its aspects, points to the ultimate, to God's Kingdom, to the fellowship of the Saints in light; it points to the redemption of society.

Israel's history is therefore *special* history—an object-lesson of God's dealing with mankind.

(*a*) *Israel and Revelation*

Christian text-books usually describe ancient Hebrew history as "sacred history", as distinct from profane world history. But even the most prejudiced reader of the historical books of the O.T. will find it difficult to discover any "sacredness" in the political and national affairs of this people; unless the fact that these records are in the Canon of Scripture makes them "sacred". But in the pattern of the story of revelation these historical records are an integral part of what is called revelation in the Bible. For biblical revelation is always revelation in history, and history derives its meaning from it. Ancient Hebrew history is fore-history, an introduction to, or the background for, the Incarnation of the Son of God. In other words it is Church history. It is sacred with a view to its purpose, it is profane in every other respect. In this relatedness to the Messiah, Hebrew history is unique. For this reason it is part of the Canon, not an addition to the Canon but central to it. But in a sense the same applies to Jewish history *post Christum natum.*

Jewish history in the Christian era also bears upon messianic history in a twofold way: first, by reference back to the story of the Incarnation, Passion, and Resurrection almost two thousand years ago. It is the necessary background to the N.T. In the second place, Jewish post-Incarnation history has indirect eschatological significance; it is the history of the People of God in suspense—it points towards the End.

Jewish history, therefore, keeps the Canon open in one single respect, in respect of eschatology. It is a reminder that revelation is not only a reference to the past, but a pointer to the future. In the eternal Presence of God past and future coincide. In Israel God reveals himself as the God of history.

What, then, is the relationship between Jewish history and the Canon?

Jewish history is the visible, empirical aspect of revelation. It demonstrates to all who want to see that the God of Israel is not a philosophical concept, but the living God. He cannot be imprisoned in a book, no matter how sacred, and relegated to the past. He is still the enactor of history; he is still a Presence in human affairs and still acts against and on behalf of his people. It means that Jewish history overflows the Canon and has "revelational" significance. While the O.T. refers forward to the Advent of the Messiah, Jewish history refers backward to the same event. But herewith its significance is not yet exhausted.

Jewish history does not only refer backward to the story of the Incarnation; it has also *contemporary* significance. It relates somehow to the contemporaneity of the Word of God. In it God reenacts demonstrably and visibly that the God of Israel is and remains the God of the Covenant. It is for this reason that Barth does not hesitate to see in the Jewish people "the one natural proof of God's existence".[3] The same God who in times past spoke to the Fathers by the prophets speaks in these latter days to the Jewish people by his Son. This is a continuous confrontation between Israel and the Messiah till the end of time. While history lasts, God is and remains the speaking God. Israel's history remains continuous revelation of judgement and grace. This extends from the time of the calling of Abraham to the end of history. The story of the Church is caught up in the story of Israel; the two are inseparable. Here, too, the Canon is kept open with a view to eschatology, for history proper is the history of the people of God, from beginning to the End.

The Gentile Church is in constant danger of forgetting her connection with Israel. In her effort to avoid Jerusalem she finds herself anchored in strange places. Is it because she tries to avoid the offence of particularism, or does she want to cover up her own failure by dissociating herself from her origin? Or is it because the Church knows herself as a new beginning, a new creation which has succeeded where Israel has failed? This pretence of success is the Church's undoing, for it shuts her eyes to the crying facts and keeps her blind to her true position.

It is commonplace to hear the Church affirm her superiority over historic Israel: Israel has rejected the Messiah, the Church has received him; Israel has proved himself unworthy of his trust, the "new" Israel has complied with the Will of God and accepted his salvation. It is no coincidence that for the larger part of Christendom the centre of gravity has shifted from Jerusalem to Rome, from the City of Promise to the city of false gods. The recent German effort to establish the non-Jewish origin of Jesus is more than a passing phase; behind it is the subconscious desire to break loose from historic continuity into the boundless realm of myth. But whenever the Church is forced back upon the Bible she is faced with the fact of her origin: Abraham—the Prophets—Jesus of Nazareth—the Church in Jerusalem. Behind the geographical names of Bethlehem—Nazareth—Jerusalem—Golgotha—is the historic reality of a people and the historic particularism of the Son of God. The story of Jesus is thus not universal truth dressed in mythological imagery, but the Son of Man who is anchored in history: *passus sub Pontio Pilato*. . . . In this way Church history becomes linked to Israel's history and forms part of the history of the People of God. If it were otherwise, there could be no place for the Acts of the Apostles in the Canon of Scripture; only thus is it part of the story of revelation, which is a continuous story though the Canon itself is closed.

The history of the Church, like the history of the Jewish people, has "revelational" value. It is the story of God's dealing with humanity seen from the angle of the Cross. Here, too, failure and disobedience, faithlessness and sin, play their full part and mar the story of the People of God. Here, too, the verdict is the same: '*ammi* and *lo-'ammi* apply with equal force. The Church is the servant of God and the servant of sin, the people washed in the Blood of the Lamb and the people given to idols—exactly as in the story of historic Israel.

However, there is a difference. The difference between Jewish history and Church history lies in their relatedness to the Messiah. In the Synagogue the Messiah is the Unknown, he is the one without a name though constantly expected; in the Church he has a name: Jesus of Nazareth, the one who was, who is, and who is to come. The Church is Church and the Synagogue is Synagogue because of that knowledge. The story of the Church and that of the Synagogue is therefore not the *same* story, though it is the same community in which God reveals himself. This is the secret of the dichotomy of the People of God. Behind it is the hidden and innermost meaning of election.

That God is a righteous Judge is the supreme knowledge of the Synagogue. Jewry knows God supremely as the Law-giver. The Synagogue lays every stress upon human responsibility. Its entire effort is concentrated upon meeting the requirements of the Law. Judaism stands in history as the most consistent human attempt to *do* God's will.[4] But in this titanic effort lies revealed the Promethean character of human nature which turns man's gold to dross: man, chosen to be a son in loving dependence upon his Father, fights for his own autonomy *vis-à-vis* his Creator. This is the last secret of the Synagogue.

That God is the God of grace is the supreme knowledge of the Church. Not that she knows nothing about the Law. The Church knows of the condemnation of the Law and her need of pardon. But in the Church man capitulates before the Law and throws himself upon God's mercy. He knows himself inadequate to live up to the absolute demands of righteousness, and he pleads forgiveness and grace. Through faith in Jesus Christ he experiences at-one-ment with God and acceptance to sonship. In the Cross of the Messiah he discovers the token of God's favour. The Cross is thus the pledge of his adoption. His sonship is not a birthright, but an act of grace; he does not merit or deserve his position, it is conferred upon him as a special favour. This is a new experience of God, experienced in the context not of the Law, but of the Gospel. It is indissolubly connected with the Son of God who gave his life for the sins of the world. Here, too, the emphasis is upon righteousness, but it is a new kind of righteousness, it is the peculiar righteousness of God who graciously supplies what is lacking in the sinner to make him a saint.

We thus see that whether it be the Law as a challenge or the Gospel as pardon, revelation is here never a "truth" but an encounter with the living God. The Canon forms the pattern of God's invasion into the lives of men. Revelation is always commensurate with life; the Bible is not a record of a God who once spoke, but the irrefutable testimony to the speaking God. In the history of the Church, as in the history of the Jewish people, God stands revealed as the One who is a speaking God. Wherever he is heard as the God of the Law, there is Synagogue; wherever he is heard as the Father of Jesus Christ, there is the Church. Here Church and Synagogue overlap constantly, there is no rigid division between them. Outwardly, Church and Synagogue as institutions are completely separate; inwardly, Church and Synagogue as a relationship to God have no set frontier. The dichotomy of the People of God of which Barth speaks is not ethnic but existential. The Christian becomes a Jew whenever he lives by works and not by grace; the Jew becomes a Christian whenever he despairs of his own righteousness and throws himself upon the mercy of the righteous God. The Christ who is hidden to the Synagogue becomes visible to the Jewish man as he seeks for a token of God's forgiving grace.

Man in Israel therefore always stands in this double relationship of Law and Gospel; in other words he stands in the context of the Canon.

But what of the man outside Israel?

Is God the God of the Jews only, is he not also the God of the Gentiles? (Rom. 3. 29.)

We believe that all history is somehow connected with the will of God and his purpose for mankind. But this does not mean that there is a direct relationship between history and revelation; these are not synonyms. Man, whether Jew or Gentile, is not a marionette answering to the pulling of an invisible hand. If he were there would be no sense or value in history at all. Man too, both Jew and Gentile, has a will and a purpose, his own will and his self-chosen purpose, which he follows. These stand in opposition to the will and purpose of God. History and revelation thus do not coincide but clash and contradict one another. When we say that God reveals himself in history we do not mean that history reveals God, but that God stands over against history as Judge and King. The "historic proof" first suggested by Gamaliel (cf. Acts. 5. 34 ff.), and latterly raised to a historiosophical principle by some writers, rests upon a fallacy. God does not overrule to the extent of eliminating falsehood, but he uses it as a tool for his own ends. Even the devil serves his purpose. But right and wrong, truth and falsehood, good and evil, are not automatically decided by a decree from heaven; they are constant possibilities within the limits of history. If historic survival were the test of truth, then sun-worship has as great a claim as Christianity.[5]

History seen horizontally is a confused story without much rhyme or reason. Revelation is therefore not the same as history but the Voice spoken into history; history is the background and not the substance of revelation, not even the means or vehicle of revelation, but only the canvas. In the discussion about "natural revelation", theologians have been misled by the fact that the plane of history is vertically cut by the plane of moral values. This has led to the wrong conclusion that history itself is a means of revelation. Indeed it is, but only in the negative sense, in that it reveals man for what he is—a fallen and helpless creature.

Human history as the Bible presents it is the battle-field where two wills clash: the will of God and the will of man. The spark of this clash is revelation: revelation in terms of judgement. The nations of the world are never and at no time outside this expression of revelation. Nemesis is the goddess of history. But this is not God's only word.

The Word spoken in Israel is the Word of the Cross; here Israel is representative of mankind. It is of significance that the Crucifixion was enacted by Jews and Romans, representing Israel and the world. Gentile history is concentric to Jewish history; it surrounds it on every side. In Gentile history as in Jewish history the same forces operate. There is no difference between Jew and Gentile in their rebellion against God and in their need of grace. There is absolute equality in God's treatment of both—for he is no respecter of persons (Rom. 2. 11). The only difference between Jewish and Gentile history is in their relatedness to the centre on the plane of time. Here the Jew stands nearer to the story of revelation than does the Gentile. In this sense Israel's history is an introduction to world history. In the history of Israel the nations find reflected their own story. In the hope of Israel is included the hope of the world. God acts in Israel on behalf of mankind. Israel in separation is a theological fiction; it is Israel's destiny to exist for the sake of the world—a kingdom of priests and a holy people.

(*b*) *Israel and Jesus*

The subject of Israel and the Messiah, who according to the Church is Jesus of Nazareth, can be approached either historically or theologically. The author has dealt with the historical aspect elsewhere.[6] Here we shall limit ourselves to the theological implications.

Our starting-point is the fact that Jesus of Nazareth, whom the

Church regards as the Second Person of the Trinity, was born a Jew. Historically, therefore, Jesus belongs to the Jewish people, irrespective of their attitude towards him. But there is a further point: Jesus is tied to the Jews not only by the bonds of blood, but also by spiritual tradition. It has taken the Jews almost two thousand years to discover the fact. It is the merit of scholars like M. Buber and J. Klausner that they have rediscovered for the Jewish people the spiritual link between them and the Nazarene. The fact that much in the N.T. is genuinely Jewish is gradually bearing in upon the Jewish consciousness. Hitherto Jews have been accustomed to think that the Gospels represent an alien world entirely divorced from the O.T. It is now becoming evident to Jewish scholars that there are vital links between the Jewish and the Christian tradition and that rabbinic Judaism is not the only heir to the O.T. Furthermore, the fact that Jesus the Jew is still a mighty spiritual force among the nations after two thousand years, is a source of wonder to the thinking Jew. Jews have great respect for the "historical test", and the survival of the Church in history carries greater weight with them than is warranted. In the words of Gamaliel of old: "this counsel" has withstood the test. Martin Buber speaks out of the heart of many Jews when he says: "That Christianity has regarded and does regard him [i.e. Jesus] as God and Saviour has always appeared to me of the highest importance which for his sake and my own, I must endeavour to understand."[7]

It is no light matter to the Jew that while Israel's greatest hope is still in abeyance Jesus of Nazareth is swaying the hearts and wills of millions and bringing them into touch with the God of Israel.

There is yet one more factor which is slowly influencing Jewish opinion.

Traditionally, Jews deny sincerity to those of their own people who accept the claim of Jesus to Messiahship. In the past, they pointed to numbers of apostate Jews who accepted Christianity for worldly reasons. This was easy as long as Jewish conversions were rare, and as long as through social pressure Jews stood to gain from baptism. But the contemporary situation has completely changed. In modern secularized society there is no advantage in "conversion"; on the contrary, the converted Jew finds himself in a more difficult situation than his brother. Yet there has never been a greater influx of Jews into the Church than there is now. Secondly, the contemporary Jewish Christian seldom denies his origin but rather takes pride in the great spiritual tradition of his people. Lastly, the Church does not any more insist on the segregation of the Jewish "convert" from his people. The result is that there is a growing number of Christ-believing Jews exerting influence and gradually changing Jewish hostility.

In the face of these facts few Jews can maintain that Jewish Christians are all renegades and traitors, or just opportunists. In fact many acknowledge their sincerity and the fact that Jews are not entirely immune to the charm of Jesus' personality. The awareness of vulnerability is reflected by the defensive attitude of Jewish apologists.

The number of Jews who do not belong to any Church or even profess Christianity but who in daily life, in literary creation, in philosophical effort, in moral behaviour, reflect the influence of Jesus of Nazareth, is beyond counting. These by far outnumber the Jewish Christian element in the Church. Are they believers? No. But are they disciples? The Master said: "By their fruits ye shall know them. . . ." and: "Not everyone that saith Lord, Lord, shall enter into the kingdom of heaven, but he that doeth the will of my Father. . . ."

It is not our purpose to enter into details and to cover ground which has been explored many times over. Here we shall give only a few examples of the impact Jesus Christ makes upon the contemporary Jew.

The "synoptic" Jesus, i.e. the "historical" Jesus, is a source of fascination to many Jews. They know about him more from literature than from the N.T. But the social contact with believing Christians has the peculiar effect of turning mere historical knowledge into inspiration. This is not conscious faith but a stimulus to moral action. Jews know what it means to behave in a Christ-like manner. In fact Jews, having measured Christianity by the standards of the Master, have found it wanting. Jewish criticism of historic Christianity springs from a realization that the followers have betrayed the Master's ideals.

It is in this spirit of disappointment that Edmund Fleg (Flegenheimer) wrote the life of Jesus as told by the Wandering Jew.[8] The book is written in the interests of pacifism, and attempts to correct the false picture which Gentile Christianity has of Jesus Christ. Fleg is convinced that only the eye-witness, the Wandering Jew, who stood at the manger and the Cross, knows the truth about

Jesus. Traditional Christianity has only a counterfeit picture of the true Christ as he really was:

> The slender Christs on mosaics; golden-haired Christs with golden haloes; Christs in the guise of Jupiter and Adonis; Flemish, Italian, Spanish, Auvergnese and Bantu Christs; plaster, marble and margarine Christs—all goys!

But Fleg is not concerned with the outward appearance, but with moral values. Here Jesus Christ stands supreme, he has no peer and no equal.

The most remarkable thing about Fleg's attitude is that the Wandering Jew and Jesus Christ are inseparable; each waiting for the other. In Fleg's yearning for salvation we can hear echoed the yearning of the Jewish people:

> As I walk I wait for Messiah to come . . . and I also wait until Jesus returns! . . . But did he tell me that he would return, as my own eyes saw him, with his imperfections? Did he not tell me, as he told them, that on the contrary, he would reappear changed, glorious, transfigured? . . . If I see him thus, will he not be like another? . . . What other? . . . Israel's Prince of Peace? . . . If that were the same one . . . the one for whom I wait . . . let him return, or let him come!

Here we meet the doubts and the hopes of the Jewish people. Jesus of Nazareth is to them an enigma which awaits an answer. Indirectly such an answer is attempted by the greatest of contemporary Jewish writers, Sholem Asch.

Asch, who is the author of three famous books on the Christian theme, has expressed himself less circumstantially in a small book which appeared in 1944: *My Personal Faith.*

Here Asch sees Jesus as that unique person who has received from God the special mandate for the Gentile world. But Asch goes further than this; he accepts the fact that Jesus knows himself as a part of that mandate:

> He included himself as part of the substance of faith. He is a significant part of it by the "flesh and blood of the new Covenant".

In spite of this fact, Asch looks upon Jesus as a builder of the Law and not a rebel. In other words, Jesus to him does not stand in opposition to Judaism, but confirms it. The vindication of Jesus before history Asch sees in the fact that Christianity is still a moral and vital force in the world. This is not merely the result of the ethical teaching of Jesus or even his death upon the Cross; it is the result of the authority which God has delegated to him:

> The deeds of Jesus acquire their religious value and become factors of high importance in the new faith, through the proclamation, that he holds in his hands the authority of God—as the Messiah.

Viewed in this light, Asch accepts even the life and death of Jesus as "part of the cardinal principle in the creation of the Messiah".

Having gone so far, it is as well to ask: what is, according to Asch, the significance of Jesus for his own people?

The answer can be given only by inference. It would seem that to Asch, Jesus is the Messiah, but in suspense, in a hidden way. Here is his explanation: Jesus himself divided his mission in two separate stages, in two advents:

> In the first he was to prepare the world and man for the Kingdom of Heaven. . . . But it was only in the second advent, when he would appear on the clouds, would the Kingdom of Heaven begin, i.e. the rule of the Messiah.

To Asch, therefore, the first stage of the Messiah's function is to convert the Gentiles. The Jews are "already under the authority of God by way of Moses and the Prophets. . . . What they did need, what they did wait for—and are still waiting for—is the advent of the Messiah for the institution of the reign of the Kingdom of Heaven."

In a sense, therefore, Asch is a "Christian" and a Pauline Christian at that.[9]

As an example of the impact of the Christian *Weltanschauung* upon the Jewish mind we would quote the delightful legend by Stefan Zweig, *Die Augen des ewigen Bruders*.

The actors and the setting of the legend are Indian; but the values, ideals, and attitudes are straight from the Sermon on the Mount. Only a man brought up under the influence of a Christian outlook could have written such a story.

A similar case is that of Franz Werfel. An appraisal of his attitude to Jesus and Christianity would by far exceed the limits of this work. Here we are only able to hint at Werfel's lifelong struggle with the problem of faith in Jesus Christ.

In his play *Paul among the Jews* he dramatized the issue with remarkable skill.[10]

The two heroes of the play are Gamaliel and his pupil, Saul

of Tarsus. These two men represent the two opposing views which battle within the writer himself all his life:

GAMALIEL: Saul, say that he was a man. . . .
PAUL: How can I? From man new birth cometh not.
GAMALIEL: From man alone it cometh. . . .

After a moving scene between pupil and master, Gamaliel soliloquizes:

Who is Jesus whom they call Messiah . . .? Has the Messiah come? . . . Have we profaned Thy Light? . . .

By the time Werfel wrote his novel *Barbara* (1929), which is largely an autobiographical story against the background of the First World War, he had already reached a more positive answer to Gamaliel's question. Engländer, the hero of the novel, after a long inward struggle arrives at the conclusion that Jesus *is* the Messiah and that the Church is right in her affirmation of faith. Only because of lack of courage does he fail to acknowledge Christ in baptism. Public opinion, the fear of what others will say, keeps Engländer away from the Church.

In his book, *The Song of Bernadette*, written under the stress of a Jew in flight from Nazi persecution, Werfel reaches his ultimate goal. Had he ever joined the Church, he would have been a Roman Catholic. His posthumous book, *Zwischen Oben und Unten* (1946), reveals a wealth of positive Christian insight, in some respects of an orthodox nature.[11]

In novel, drama, verse, and even in visual art, Jews reveal remarkable attraction to Jesus. Primitive Christianity in its original Jewish setting has been dramatized by H. F. Rubenstein[12] and Nathan Bistrizki.[13] To these must be added A. A. Kabak's novel based on the life of Jesus and Max Brod's novel *The Master*.[14] Of equal significance are Sir Jacob Epstein's sculptures of Christ and Marc Chagall's paintings of Christian themes.[15] There are also a number of poems.[16]

Jewish interest in Jesus of Nazareth has its source in the yearning after deeper spiritual values and moral leadership. This is voiced in a passage by the once famous Hebrew writer Reuben Brainin:

I have wandered across oceans and continents, from east to west. I have searched after the mysterious, divine-human person who incarnates in himself our great past and our yet greater future. Where art thou, Saviour? Thou who hast power to attract everything that is still to be found of spiritual and moral value in our faith, of beautiful and good virtues? Who art able by a redemptive act to weld us together into a great nation?

Dr P. P. Levertoff, to whom we are indebted for the above quotation and who counted Brainin among his personal friends, remarks that though the name is omitted, "the face of Jesus is hidden in the person the writer is trying to find".[17]

It is true to say that Jewish appreciation of Jesus in the artistic field is frequently inspired by humanistic rather than religious motives. But in the field of philosophy Jewish writers seem to have combined the two concerns with sometimes startling results. John M. Oesterreicher, a Roman Catholic priest of Jewish descent, has surveyed the field of philosophy from the point of view of his particular church. Though the title of his book *The Walls are Crumbling* errs on the side of exuberance,[18] the book itself contains important evidence of the impact of Christianity upon the mind of the Westernized Jew in the field of philosophy. It is a fact that the most outstanding philosophers of our age, of Jewish birth, have tended towards a Christian point of view. Pride of place undoubtedly belongs to the great Jewish-French thinker, Henri Bergson. Bergson, though officially not a member of the Church, became convinced in the later years of his life of the truth of the Christian faith and died a believer.[19] Other philosophers whose thought Oesterreicher examines are Edmund Husserl, Adolf Reinach, Max Scheler, Paul Landsberg. Edith Stein, the deep-thinking Christian mystic and Jewish martyr, who together with thousands of her brethren found her end at Ausschwitz, occupies a special place of her own. Though there is justification in Dr Maybaum's contention that neither Bergson, Reinach, nor Landsberg had anything to do with Judaism,[20] yet the fact remains that these great men were born Jews and that they were led on the path of philosophy not to Judaism but to Christianity.

Even more impressive than the names of prominent men is the quiet influence which Jesus exercises upon the hearts and minds of ordinary Jewish people. The spokesman for these—the largest group of all—is the writer, publisher, and politician, Victor Gollancz.

Gollancz occupies an unusual position in British life. He is neither a Christian nor a Jew in the accepted sense of the words.

He is a deeply God-fearing man who has inherited from the Hebrew Prophets a burning zeal for social justice and divine mercy. His inspiration he draws from the N.T., but chiefly from the person of Jesus Christ. Here is the remarkable case of a man who is not a believer in the orthodox sense, yet is a faithful and humble disciple of the Master. Victor Gollancz, like thousands of other Jews, stands on the narrow line where the margin between faith and admiration is almost imperceptible.[21]

To Gollancz, as to many other Jews, Jesus is not a theological but a real and living figure whose presence impels to moral and courageous action. Such men and women are not captivated by the liturgical splendour of the historic Churches but by the humble service of sincere followers. Louis Golding has unintentionally spoken on their behalf while describing the emotions in the heart of a Jew in one of his novels:

> Mrs Travers was never clearly to realize that the young Jew had accepted no system of doctrine, was no Christian in any sense she and her friends and counsellors could consider valid. He had accepted solely a person; but all his body and soul were flooded with him.

Here Eli, the hero in this rather sad story, stands as a type for thousands of his brethren.[22]

This is the position of many Jews regarding Jesus of Nazareth, though they remain outside the visible Church. In fact, many of them do not even associate the real Jesus with the institution which is called after his name. What is their position in the Kingdom of God?

It is remarkable that Protestant theologians have never paid any attention to this question. There seems to be no evidence that they are even aware of such a problem on the Jewish side. There are of course non-orthodox or non-dogmatic Christians on the Gentile side, men like Albert Schweitzer, who have proved themselves remarkably true to the spirit of the Master but who are unable to subscribe to the orthodox creed. In the past they used to be burned; at present the Church tolerates them and refrains from passing judgement.

It is the Roman Catholic philosopher Jacques Maritain who discusses the case seriously and struggles for a positive answer. In his essay, *Who is my Neighbour?* he concerns himself with the position of non-Christians.[23] As an orthodox Roman Catholic he accepts the principle of *extra ecclesiam nulla salus*, but at the same time, and quite in accordance with the tradition of his Church, he makes the distinction between the soul of the *ecclesia* and its visible form.[24] In this way he is able to extend the border-line of the Church beyond the organized form to include every one who "invisibly and by the motion of his heart" becomes spiritually related to the body of believers. For, as Maritain explains, fellowship "is not fellowship of beliefs, but the fellowship of men who believe". Here we have a *rapprochement* to what in Protestantism is known as the invisibility of the Church, though Maritain insists that the Church is nothing if not a visible body. But his insistence upon the visibility of the Church is mitigated by the admission that "what each one is before God, neither the one nor the other knows", for "here the 'Judge not' of the Gospel applies with full force". It is worth remembering that Maritain's view is only an extension of Augustine's position, who refused to condemn the unorthodox out of hand:

> Just as in the Catholic Church there is much which is uncatholic, so there is also much that is catholic outside the Catholic Church.[25]

Augustine also admits that many who are outside the Church and are called heretics are better than some of those who are within the Church and call themselves Catholics.[26] Maritain has obviously gone beyond Augustine by including in the invisible fellowship of the Church "all men in good faith and good will, living by divine grace".[27] To Anglicans, at any rate, it seems to suggest a negation of Articles XIII and XXXIX of the Articles of Religion. But in spite of this it is not a view we can easily dismiss. The empirical Church cannot and must not claim the monopoly of God's mercy. The Grace of God is as unlimited as his love. In view of the facts we cannot but agree with Maritain that there are Jews "in whom grace dwells", and that with them also "the work of the Cross is present", though it is "veiled and unperceived and involuntarily experienced".[28]

The presence of Christ-believing Jews, to whatever degree, does not complete the picture of the relationship between Israel and the Messiah.

The Synagogue has created her own particular concept of the Messiah. This stands in direct contradiction to that of the Church. The Jewish Messiah and the Christian Christ are totally different both with regard to function and to position. It is enough to glance at Maimonides' statement and the Christian Creed to see the dissimilarity.[29] In fact, Jesus does not measure up to the Synagogue's messianic hope, he does not fit in; either the rabbis are wrong, or else Jesus is a false Messiah. Neither the Gospels, nor the rest of the N.T., nor the Creed of the Church, nor the experience of the Christian believer, correspond in any way to the messianic hope of Judaism. There is an interesting admission on the part of Maimonides which serves to emphasize the complete difference of outlook. He observes that Bar Cochba would have been acceptable as the Messiah of Israel had he succeeded in his struggle against Rome. Here the test of Messiahship is worldly success, whereas the Church's Messiah is the crucified Saviour. There canno be a greater difference of outlook. For the Synagogue, therefore, Jesus is on a par with all the other false Messiahs who have appeared in Jewish history from time to time. And yet even the most critically minded Jew has to admit that in view of world history Jesus stands in a place of his own. He is a unique phenomenon and does not fit into the pattern of messianic pretenders either Jewish or Gentile.[30] He stands not only before Israel but also before the world as the corrective of all false messianic idealism. As far as the Jews are concerned he is the great question-mark of his people's conscience. In the vicissitudes of Israel's pilgrimage through history as God's chosen people, the encounter with Jesus, his greatest Son, reopens the issue again and again. Jesus of Nazareth remains historic Israel's greatest challenge.

In this encounter between Israel and Jesus of Nazareth lies the secret of God's election of man. The word in Psalm 2: "Thou art my son; this day have I begotten thee", has exegetically a twofold application—to Israel and to Israel's Messiah. Has God chosen Israel because of the Messiah, or has he chosen the Messiah because of Israel?

Election is sonship. It is for every God-fearing Jew to decide personally who is in the truest sense the son of God: Jesus who died upon the Cross an outlaw's death, or he who scrupulously submits to the Law of rabbinic tradition?

Such a question can never be posed on a national scale. It is and remains a question of conscience. Here Israel must become a strictly personal noun; not *kelal Yisrael*, the community of Israel, can face such a question, but the individual Jew in his lonely responsibility before the God of the Covenant and the Judge of all flesh. The encounter here is personal, even private: Jesus of Nazareth and his brother, *the* Jew.

(*c*) *Israel and the Church*

On the plane of history, the Jewish people does not confront Jesus directly but indirectly, in retrospect. The relationship between Church and Israel is different. Here Jews and Christians meet in a direct and immediate relationship. The encounter between believing Jews and believing Christians results in a situation in which the question of election is of special significance. We shall illustrate the point by quoting a well-known parable:

> A man had two sons; and he came to the first, and said, Son, go work to-day in the vineyard. And he answered and said, I will not: but afterward he repented himself, and went. And he came to the second, and said likewise. And he answered and said, I go, sir: and went not. Whether of the twain did the will of his father? They say, The first. Jesus said unto them, Verily I say unto you, that the publicans and the harlots go into the kingdom of God before you (Matt. 21. 28–31 R.V.).

In this short parable we find enunciated a principle which is of first importance in our understanding of the relationship between Israel and Church. Behind it is the law of the privilege of the unprivileged which obtains in the Kingdom of God; the first shall be last and the last first. This principle is borne out by the Bible, by history, and by personal experience. Israel's prerogatives, the advantage of the Pharisees, the privilege of the Christian, can become a snare instead of a blessing. This is the peculiar danger of the Chosen People—that publicans and harlots can enter into the Kingdom of God before them.

It means that God is no man's debtor. The pious has no monopoly or sinecure of God's favour. No one, not even Israel, not even the Church, can claim him as private property. The God of Israel is not a national fetish, but sovereign and free; he is no respecter of persons. He looks upon the heart and searches the reins. In his presence no one stands in his own right. Here man's strength is his weakness and his weakness strength (cf. 2 Cor. 12. 9 f.). There is no "security" before him, unless he himself is the fortress. Let him that thinketh he standeth take heed lest he fall (1 Cor. 10. 12).

The pious Pharisee will for ever remain the classical example of the danger of false security before God: I thank thee, God, that I am not as the rest of men (Luke 18. 11). It is not accidental that in the Gospels the hardest words which fall from the mouth of

Jesus are against the Pharisees. They were not bad people; on the contrary, they were the most pious in Israel; but their piety became their undoing. Jewish apologists who fight so gallantly for the honour of the Pharisees quite misunderstand the whole situation. In the struggle between Jesus and the Pharisees is opened up the whole complexity of the spiritually privileged. We will quote a sentence from an article by H. L. Ellison, to show what we mean:

> For the Pharisee, man was dependent on the grace of God; the giving of the Law was an act of the grace of God; but this very grace made it possible for certain men to be autonomous. They were able to do the will of God apart from the grace of God, and were able to claim His grace as a right.[31]

It is this attitude of autonomy which is the downfall of the pious man. Count Leo Tolstoy has worked out the psychology of pious autonomy with great insight in his play *Father Serge*. The believer is destined to live in the peculiar tension between dependence and autonomy which keeps him at the brink of hell and the gates of heaven in every instant of time. "Pharisaism" is not peculiar to Judaism; from it no one is ever immune.

The danger of the Pharisee is the danger of the good, the pious, the "saved". Here a situation opens before us in which is combined something of the irony of the Greek tragedies with the paradox of life itself: the harlot and the publican embrace the Master, while the pious Pharisees shout, Crucify him! Or to put it differently: dissolute pagans of Corinth accept the Gospel of the Kingdom, while the Chosen People of God hardens its heart. This is not something which refers back to history, but is the constant and terrifying possibility for the People of God. Not only over historic Israel, but also over the Christian Church is the sentence written in flaming letters: He came unto his own, and his own received him not (John 1. 11). When we speak of Israel and the Church we can speak only in the context of this fact.

One son said: I will go; and went not. The other son said: I will not go; and went. Which of these two is Israel and which is the Church?

There can be no answer to this question from our level. But it may be that God has more than one answer. If the Church is not always the Church, as Israel is not always Israel, then may it not be that the obedient son is sometimes the Church and sometimes Israel? It all depends on the motives.

The Master said: "Whosoever would save his life shall lose it: and whosoever shall lose his life for my sake shall find it" (Matt. 16. 25). This is the only valid principle in the service of God's vineyard. When Caiaphas announced: It is more expedient that one man should die for the people, than that the whole nation perish (John 11. 50), he turned the principle of service into a principle of expediency. This is the principle which dominates history: survival at all costs. Here Caiaphas speaks for Israel *and* the Church: expediency takes precedence over right. The sins of the publican and harlot pale into insignificance before the arrogance of the pious man in his autonomy before God. The irony lies in the fact that Pilate made a similar choice; but Caiaphas did not even wash his hands. The High Priest of the God of Israel sends Jesus to the gallows for the sake of expediency!

The Son of God was not crucified in Rome but in Jerusalem, in the Holy City dedicated to the Holy One of Israel. On the human plane Caiaphas made the only possible choice; it is the kind of choice constantly made by religious and political leaders. History is made up of such choices. The same kind of decision is made daily, for compromise is essential to life. But on the other plane—on the plane of moral values—judicial murder is judicial murder, whatever the excuse. Here we look into the heart of human motives and discover the arrogance of autonomy which presumes to decide upon the life and death of a fellow-creature for the sake of expediency. Perhaps seen from above, it would be more "expedient" that the whole world perish rather than the priest of God become guilty of innocent blood.

Arrogance goes with faithlessness. It is a breach of faith in God to presume that God needs the aid of evil in order to protect his people. Is not right, right, irrespective of the consequences?

Caiaphas' dilemma is the dilemma of every age. It is the problem which the Church constantly faces: to lose her life for Christ's sake, or to save it and in doing so lose her soul?

A similar problem faced the Jewish people from the day of the dispersal. Israel's task, which was originally a priestly task, the task of service to humanity, became reduced to the task of self-preservation. National survival became Israel's chief and only concern. This took priority over everything else; it became the *religious* duty of every Jew to further the survival of the race. Not that Jews refused to suffer and die for God and Torah, but even God and Torah became *means* of national survival.[32]

This is also the problem of modern Hebrew Christianity. There are good reasons, tactical, missionary, and otherwise, why Hebrew Christians should not become assimilated to Gentile Christianity and lose their identity. The Hebrew Christian must remain a living witness to his own people. This is specially important in order to contradict the myth that Jews are wedded to rabbinic Judaism by reason of birth, and that Jesus belongs only to the *Goyyim* (Gentiles). But the motives against assimilation are not always so lofty; they are frequently mixed with national pride and primitive selfishness. The usual argument runs: the French, the English, the Germans do not lose their identity by becoming Christians, why should we?[33]

Hebrew Christians are specially sensitive on the question of national loyalty. They do not wish to give the appearance that their entry into the Church was for personal advantage. But behind their demonstration of national loyalty, there are frequently more primitive instincts which make for particularism and nationalism. The national instinct has struck deep roots into the Jewish consciousness and it is not easy for a Jew to eliminate feelings of superiority. Such feelings frequently result in spiritual pride—the most deadly of sins.

There is a marked over-emphasis in Hebrew Christian circles on the Jewishness of Jesus and the N.T.; this is sometimes an expression of self-justification and sometimes of crude chauvinism. On the other hand, the effort to demonstrate to Jewry that a Hebrew Christian can be a fervent nationalist, a faithful Israeli citizen, a good Zionist, may be a subtle way of trying to evade the scandal of the Cross. Does being a Christian imply nothing more than the private right to belong to a different "denomination"?

The question of Hebrew Christian survival is not a simple one, it is the motive which counts.[34] Hebrew Christians, too, may save their lives but lose their souls. Their greatest danger is to re-erect the middle wall of partition which Jesus came to remove; to re-establish the difference between Jew and Greek against which Paul so courageously fought; to deny the essential equality of believers by refusing to marry a Gentile.

The price of Hebrew Christian survival may be too great. Here the Hebrew Christian must be willing to follow the example of his Master by giving his life in order to win it. He must be ready to say: Let Hebrew Christianity perish for the sake of the Gospel.[35]

The historic Church is in a similar position in all her contacts with the world. Her relation to the State, the problem of survival by biological means,[36] her attitude to social questions, constantly place her before a similar choice: survival in history or death for the sake of the Gospel. She has to decide as Caiaphas did, whether ends sanctify means.

The Church wants to survive; the Jewish people wants to survive; Hebrew Christianity wants to survive; they all argue that their survival serves a higher end. But survival at what cost? As far as the Christian is concerned there can be only one loyalty, that to the Master. A Church protected by the State, safeguarded by institutions, secured by legacies, continued by the birth of babies, cannot be living by faith. But if she does not live by faith, is she still the Church?

This was the question which Dostoevsky raised in the vision of the Grand Inquisitor in his *Brothers Karamazoff*. But it was not possible for him to provide an answer. No answer is possible apart from historic Israel. Only in confronting Israel with the Church are we able to assess the situation.

Church and Israel face each other in their common humanity. There is only one solidarity among man, the solidarity of sin. Both Israel and Church are guilty of the same crime: the death of Christ. Both live by the same token of God's mercy. The Church can see herself only in Israel; and Israel can see himself only by looking at the Church. Seeing each other as they really are they discover the faithfulness of God:

> O the depth of the riches both of the wisdom and the knowledge of God! For God hath shut up all unto disobedience, that he might have mercy upon all (Rom. 11. 33, 32).

St Paul saw aright when he placed historic Israel and the Church side by side. Only in juxtaposition do they discover the fathomless love of God.

CHAPTER 2

THE CHURCH AND THE SYNAGOGUE

It is important that we proceed with a closer examination of terminology. At the outset it will be necessary to define what is meant by "Church". The term can be defined either theologically or historically. The two aspects do not coincide. When we speak of the Church theologically we always mean the ideal Church, the Bride of Christ, without spot or blemish. But in history there is no such Church, there is only an organization with many spots and many blemishes. An even more ambiguous term is "Christianity" or "the Christian religion". What is Christianity? What is the Christian religion?

A. THE CHURCH

It is inevitable that a movement which stretches over nearly two thousand years and covers many lands, climes, and civilizations should be impossible to describe by a single noun. "Christianity" may be viewed from many angles, such as the lives of the Saints, the intrigues of the Vatican, the Crusades against Islam, the superstitions of the Egyptian monks under the Byzantine Empire, the mistaken zeal of the Spanish Inquisition, or the lofty idealism of the Society of Friends. The same applies to the term "Church". The "Church" may mean the early Church in its various stages of development; the Roman Catholic or Greek Orthodox Church with their peculiar symbolism and ritual; or the Protestant churches of the Calvinist type. Further, it may mean the local church associated with a certain building and a certain group, or the "Church" in a vague and general way. It is, therefore, obvious that unless we are careful to state what we mean by "Church" we are bound to create misunderstanding.

There are two aspects from which to approach the subject: we can either look upon Christianity and the Church from without, i.e. from the perspective of history, and describe them as factors in the shaping of civilization; or else we can try to understand them from within as the spiritual ferment in human lives. Somewhere, the historical and the spiritual aspects meet, but the meeting-place is within the restricted sphere of personal decision.

It is the never-accomplished task of theology to try to define the meaning of "Church" and by doing so to grasp the Church's significance. The strain upon the theologians is derived from the discrepancy between the ideal Church of the text-book and the empirical church in history. Unlike the traditional approach to the subject, our starting-point is the discrepancy; what the Church claims to be, and what she is. For us the discrepancy is of special importance, for in it lies revealed the paradox of the human situation.

(*a*) *"Christianity" as "Religion"*

Seen from without, namely, from the point of view of comparative religion, Christianity is one of the many religions of the world. As such it has a common denominator with other religions and was shaped by the trends which pervade human history. It was influenced by rival movements and in turn influenced them. There is a certain relativity about all historical phenomena, the religious included. Here Christianity is no exception. As a religion it is bound up with the deep-seated human needs and fears which underly all religious phenomena. Basically, all religions cope with the same problems and suggest the same remedies.[1] To an outside observer there is nothing in the Christian faith to suggest a fundamental difference between it and any of the other great world-religions. But even those who stand within the confines of the Church have not hesitated to explain her in terms of religious life. If this is the right procedure, then the Church's claim to uniqueness is ill-founded and rests on a misunderstanding of her own position. In this case the difference between Christianity and other religions can only be explained as accidental. History, geography, culture, are the warp upon which the woof of religion is woven. The texture depends upon the background, but the pattern is always the same.[2] This is the attitude of the scholar who deals with the subject of comparative religion, but it is contradicted by the self-consciousness of the Church.

The Church knows herself unique not because of her theology, worship, moral insight, or great cultural achievement. Her uniqueness lies in what she calls the Gospel, which is inseparable from an historic person called Jesus of Nazareth. About that man she makes stupendous claims. If these claims are justified, then the Gospel is not "religion" in the usual sense of the word.

At this juncture we must attempt a definition of religion broad enough to cover most of the religious phenomena in history. Departing somewhat from the traditional approach to the subject, we would suggest that "religion is the Promethean attempt to name God".[3] But it differs from philosophy in so far as it is an emotional rather than an intellectual effort and is inseparable from the mystical experience. All religions are committed to mysticism and depend upon it. The mystical experience is the intuitive and inward vision of the Ineffable. Christianity, like Judaism, has its periods of mystical revival, but at no time is mysticism entirely absent. The measure of the religious element in Christianity is the strength of the mystical experience kept alive in the Church.

But mysticism is not homogeneous with the Christian message; in fact it contradicts it. In the centre of the Gospel is an historic person; experience of Jesus Christ is not by mysticism but by faith. The difference is of the greatest importance: the mystic meets God as a unitive experience and seeks annihilation of self; whereas, to the Christian believer, God is a real *vis-à-vis* who invades life from without and does not annihilate but establishes the human personality. He is and remains the opposite *Thou*, and the relationship discontinues to be an I–Thou relationship.[4] The Church has frequently realized the danger of the invasion of mysticism because it militates against the basic principle of the Christian faith: the mediatorship of Jesus Christ. Such opposition was shown by the medieval Church when she condemned as heretics the followers of Amalrich of Bena (in the second half of the twelfth century), namely the Beguines and the Beghards, and together with them the many followers of similar movements.

In essence both Judaism and Christianity are hostile to mysticism, for both depend upon the *verbum externum* as deposited in the Canon of Scripture and not upon mystical intuition. Their appeal is mainly to conscience, to reason, and to the moral sense. Though the emotional appeal is not entirely absent, it must not predominate.[5] The corrective is always in an appeal to history, whereas mysticism has no historical sense, it is a-historical, if not antihistorical. Biblical revelation is anchored in history. Synagogue and Church know God as the God of history, though they know him differently. It is this relation to history which differentiates biblical faith from the other religions.

The Christian faith is eminently rooted in history: Jesus of Nazareth, born of the Virgin Mary, crucified under Pontius Pilate. The Christian understands the coming of Jesus Christ as an historical event. To him God is not only the Creator of the world but the enactor of history. The story of the Birth, Death, and Resurrection of Jesus Christ is pre-eminently history of the highest order.

Seen in this light, the Christian Faith is not religion in the usual sense. On the contrary it militates against religion, and religion is its foe from beginning to end. For the Christian Faith, as the Church knows it, is not man's word *about* God, but God's Word *to* man. If our definition is right, then the Church is not an association of "religious" men, but the place where God's Word is pronounced and heard.[6] The pronouncing of the Word does not yet make it the Church; it is the hearing and obeying of the Word which creates the Church.

There is another important difference between religion and the Christian Faith. Religion desires to name, define, analyse God; in the Church God is not defined, but man is. The Word of God defines man as a sinner; this is the starting-point of the Christian Faith. Biblical "revelation" is first revelation of man before it is anything else. It is only to man who has discovered himself as a sinner in the eyes of the Holy One of Israel that God speaks the second Word—the word of forgiveness.

(*b*) *The Church as Society*

If it is true that the Church is not a religious association, it is equally true that she is not an association at all in the voluntary sense. She is not a club which can be joined like a conventicle of select members. It is unfortunate that the Church is frequently described as a "society". The best English rendering of *koinonia* would be "family"; the *ecclesia* is a family where God is Father, Christ Jesus the Elder Brother, and every member through Christ a brother and a sister.[7] Entry into this family relationship which transcends all physical ties is by the new birth, the birth of the Spirit.

There is an element of voluntary association in Church membership; it depends upon a personal decision. But such "joining" of the Church is rather a denominational affair. On the other hand anyone can join the local church and yet remain a stranger to the Church of Christ. The reason is obvious: the Church cannot be "joined"; as in a family, one is born into it. The fact that one has had Christian parents is not sufficient in itself; membership is by spiritual regeneration. Church membership is thus not a voluntary choice, but the inevitable result of spiritual quickening. Physical birth places man in a family, spiritual birth places man in the Church. There is no escape from this position, it is a *datum*. We do not join the Church, we are received into it. It is the birthright of the children of God to belong to his family.

In the family of God there is absolute equality; those who come first and those who come last are equals. Here distinctions of stature, acumen, or race, cease to be important. A church which adopts other than the rule of equality ceases to be the Church of Jesus Christ (cf. Matt. 23. 8).

In the Church of God there is unity. A divided Church stands under judgement. The Great High Priest of the Church prayed for the unity of all believers (John 17. 21–3). Where there is no unity there is lack of love, and a love-less church cannot be the Church of Christ.

The family of God is not exclusive but inclusive. It does not shut itself up in pride and self-sufficiency, but is always aware of its missionary task. The Christian family is an expanding family. The doors of the Church must always be open for the prodigal son. A church which has no concern for the other man is not the Church of Jesus Christ.

The Church of Christ has only one Head. Only where Jesus Christ is given the pre-eminence is there the Church. A church which has not him as the centre is not a Christian Church.

The family of God has only one concern: that God's will be done in earth as it is in Heaven. A church which deviates from this its central task has lost its *raison d'être*. It was the Master's meat to do the will of God (John 4. 34); it cannot be the disciples' choice to do otherwise.

The Church of Christ has only one task: the sanctification of God's holy Name. For this reason the family of God is told to pray: Hallowed be thy Name. It means that the Church of Christ presents herself a willing tool in the humble service of God's Kingdom. Like the Master, the disciples do not seek honour, but seek to serve (cf. Luke 22. 27). A church which does not serve is a contradiction in terms.

The Church of Jesus Christ lives by *koinonia*. Her life is that of fellowship with God and one another. A church which is a stranger to fellowship is not really the Christian Church. Here the analogy with the biological family unit gives out. In the biological unit members may become estranged, may abandon each other, may separate, yet they remain members of the same family by reason of the physical relationship. It is different in the case of the Church. No one can remain a member of the Church in separation, and no one can belong to Jesus Christ who does not belong to his brethren. The family of God lives by communion.

(*c*) *The Faith of the Church*

In the Gospels we frequently meet the sentence: Thy faith hath made thee whole. It is necessary to be reminded that here "faith" means *emunah* and not *doxa*. The difference is of fundamental importance: whereas *doxa* means opinion and is connected with intellect, *emunah* means unswerving trust and presupposes a personal positive relationship. It was left to the Reformers of the sixteenth century to rediscover the original meaning of *emunah*. The difference between *doxa* and *emunah* is the difference between the "Athanasian" Creed and the lively faith of the Psalter. The Athanasian Creed demands *ortho-doxy*—right opinion; the Psalms speak of a right relationship to God. To the philosophically trained Greek, faith is a matter of *doxa*, to the Hebrew it is always a matter of *faithfulness*. In the case of the former it is a venture in the realm of intellect, to the latter a venture in the realm of life.

It has been suggested that in the difference of emphasis between orthodoxy and orthopraxy lies the difference between Judaism and Christianity.[8] There may be some truth in such a view. But *ortho-doxa* is not homogeneous with the N.T.; here neither *ortho-doxa* nor *ortho-praxis* is the deciding factor, but only the grace of God (cf. Rom. 9. 16). In the context of the Bible, faith seems to have an entirely different connotation, and is connected with the promises of God. Faith here means faithful holding on to God's promises in spite of every contradiction. This is remarkably illustrated in the eleventh chapter of the Epistle to the Hebrews. The story of the Patriarchs and all the other heroes of the Bible serves as witness to this fact. St Augustine's conversion is another illustration. It was faith in the promises of God which made a Manichean philosopher into a Christian saint, for cleaving to

God means cleaving to his promise, and this means trust—*emunah.*[9]

This does not mean that there is no room for Christian doctrine or that dogma is of no importance. Augustine laboured hard to expound Christian dogma, for he knew that faith must of necessity express itself in a twofold way; by heart and tongue.[10] Dogma is the intellectual deposit of the faith; intellect is not to be despised, for it is God's special gift to man.[11] Christian faith is linked to reason, and is not afraid of intellectual inquiry. If faith is to have any meaning it must have an object, and the object of faith must be approached intellectually.[12] But the inquiry is secondary; faith in terms of dogma is of a different quality and in a different context to *emunah.* It is really *doxa* about God, objectivated and impersonal; as such it is only a pale reflection of what the Bible means by faith. Had Augustine, like Luther, been able to follow to the end his concept of grace as *gratia gratis data,* his teaching about faith would have probably taken on a more existential and less formal character. But it must be remembered that Augustine remains the great exponent of *justificari ex fide,*[13] and that in it is already implied a concept of faith which by far exceeds the scholastic concept of *doxa.*

The faith of the Church is thus primarily the common relationship to Jesus Christ which links all Christian believers. This is a personal relationship built on trust. The Church is not founded upon a common theory about God or a certain code of ethics, but upon Jesus Christ who is the corner stone (Eph. 2. 20).[14] It is the common faithfulness to the Master which is the faith of the Church in the primary sense. The Church, unlike the world, believes the Master, and because she believes in him she follows him as the Good Shepherd who loves the sheep. Her knowledge of God is inseparable from faith in Jesus Christ. In the light of this faith she reads the Bible and trusts in God.

(*d*) *The Church as Election*

In our effort to clarify the Church's position we have now come to the main question: How does the Church as described in the foregoing pages relate to the church of our experience, i.e. to the church in history? In other words, what is the connection between the ideal Church and the empirical church? To us the question is of supreme importance, for in it is hidden the secret of the connection between the Church and the Jewish people.

Be it then said at once that our definition of the ideal Church is inapplicable to the church in history. Here we meet an entirely different phenomenon: a church which is primarily an institution and not a family, where there is little equality, no unity, where not Christ but religion is the object, and which lives for herself rather than for the Kingdom of God. The historic church is primarily concerned with *doxa* and not *emunah*, and seeks to dominate rather than serve. The church in history is only a counterfeit of the Church in theological text-books. Her catholicity is belied by her divisions; her holiness is marred by her lust for power; her apostolic origin is vitiated by heresy; and her trust in God is frequently augmented by the arm of the State. In fact it is difficult to relate the historic church to the Church of Jesus Christ. Theologians of all ages have been aware of the discrepancy between the credal statement *credo . . . in sanctam ecclesiam catholicam* and the church of their own experience. It was with this inconsistency in mind that Christian thinkers have been led to the concept of the *invisible Church*. Again, it is Augustine who is the originator of the idea of the hidden-ness of the Church in the church. It was he who first expressed the possibility that it is possible to be inside the Church and yet not to belong to her: *multi tales sunt in sacramentorum communione cum ecclesia et tamen jam non sunt in ecclesia.*[15] He is able to speak of the *corpus domini* as a *corpus bipartitum*, split into two parts: *corpus verum atque permixtum* or *simulatum.*[16]

The logical conclusion of this fact was worked out by the Reformers in their doctrine of the hidden invisible Church behind the visible church in history. Luther perhaps went furthest in this view, when arguing against Rome he asserts that it cannot be the Church of our faith, for she is seen outwardly with the physical eye. In contradistinction to the Roman church he puts the true Church of God, which consists of the congregation of saints in faith which is not open to outward observation.[17] It is only to the eyes of faith that the true Church becomes visible. Yet even Luther is unable to keep the church of history and the Church of Faith entirely apart. He knows how to identify the Christian Church by outward signs such as Baptism, the Holy Communion, and the Gospel.[18] Such *notae externae* cause the invisible Church to become both visible and audible.

Just as at the time of the Donatist controversy in which Augustine was involved, so at the time of the Reformation and in our own days, theologians realize that there must be some connection between the ideal Church as confessed in the Creed and the empirical church of our experience, if the Christian faith is not to remain just a theoretical proposition. Luther, in spite of all the bitterness of the controversy with Rome, was unwilling to declare the pope outside the Christian Church: "Not everything that the pope says is wrong, for he still has the Sacrament of the Altar, Baptism, and the Ministry of the Word."[19] Herein he was right, for the existence of the Church cannot be made dependent upon the worthiness of its members; it lives by the promise that the gates of hell will not prevail against it (Matt. 16. 18). As long as the *viva vox evangelii* is heard, the Church exists, though visibly in the humiliated form. Luther, with remarkable insight, speaks of the *mirabilis profecto potentia verbi vocalis* and describes the Sacrament as *verbum visibile*,[20] which means that wherever the living Word of God is pronounced and received in whatever form, there the Church is a fact.[21] Human weakness cannot disrupt her existence, for she lives not by merit but by grace.[22] On this question hung the Donatist controversy. Although in the perspective of history Augustine may seem to appear in an unfavourable light with his "pharisaic assertion"[23] that only a Churchman can be saved, yet on the main issue he was right: only in *futuro saeculo* can there be a perfect Church. Here upon earth wheat and tares are always intermixed and have to grow together.[24] The Church by its very nature will always consist of the many who are called and the few who are chosen. For here upon earth she consists of sinners and not saints. The Calvinist position is therefore much more logical and true to fact than is usually admitted: "The Church so far as she takes outward form also includes hypocrites and dead members who do not belong to the community and covenant of grace. . . . The invisible [Church] is the community of the elect effectually called by the Word and by the Holy Spirit."[25] But because of this dual life of the Church we must not jump to John Hooper's conclusion that the visible church cannot be the Church of Christ for she contains the good and the bad.[26] It is an embarrassing position to be, and not to be, the Church at the same time. But this is the true position of the church in history.[27]

It is Hooker's great merit to have seen through this fact and to have taken full cognizance of it. He asks: "Is it then possible, that the selfsame men should belong to the Synagogue of Satan and to the Church of Jesus Christ?" His answer is that in the visible church this is the constant possibility, and he refers to the Master's parables about the Kingdom of God in the likeness of the net and the field where tares and wheat grow together. But above all he refers back to ancient Israel, who in spite of all their backsliding "continued even in the depth of their disobedience and rebellion to be God's people".[28]

This is the starting-point of our thesis regarding Israel's election.

B. THE SYNAGOGUE

Jewish scholars invariably speak of the Synagogue as the mother of Christianity.[29] Though the view finds frequent acceptance among Christians, it is inaccurate. By it is implied that rabbinic Judaism is the direct heir and exponent of biblical revelation. That Jews should hold such a view is natural, but that Christian scholars should accept it without challenge is strange. Gradually, however, as a result of more intensive study, the view is affirming itself that Pharisaic Judaism represents only one particular trend in the development of the O.T. faith. Though the disentanglement of the knots in the skein of sects and parties in pre-Destruction Jewry is no easy task, it is becoming obvious that rabbinic Judaism is only one of many movements. "Christianity" as it underlay the N.T. literature was another trend. We have put Christianity in quotation marks, because at that stage it was not an alien faith, but only a rival faith to rabbinic Judaism. The messianic movement which had Jesus of Nazareth at its centre had one major advantage over Pharisaism—it was more closely related to the O.T. religion. This is a point which for some curious reason seems to have escaped Christian scholars. The "Christian" faith in its early stages was thus also Judaism but was radically different from Pharisaism.[30] True enough, there is in Judaism and Christianity that which points to a common origin, but that similarity is derived from the influence of the O.T. upon the two faiths. Rabbinic Judaism and the Christian Church have a common legacy in the O.T. to which they owe their standards of morality, their common hope, and their eschatological outlook. Their differences are derived first from their attitude to Jesus and secondly from their attitude to the basic concepts of the O.T. religion. The best evidence that rabbinic Judaism is not the mother of the Christian Church comes from the N.T. itself. Here we find Pharisaism to be in bitter opposition to the rival messianic faith.[31] If our premiss is correct, rabbinic Judaism is only a second cousin to the Church and even so barely a blood-relation.

In order to establish our point we shall try to relate both faiths to the O.T. religion. The O.T. must remain our starting-point and the testing-ground because both Church and Synagogue appeal to it. But to avoid losing ourselves in detail we shall fasten our attention on the centre of O.T. worship, namely the Temple. The importance of the Temple cannot be too much emphasized in the development of Christianity. All its great concepts of propitiation, mediation, and redemption stem from this source. The whole Pauline system of theological thinking is inconceivable without the O.T. The O.T., and the O.T. only, is the source of the Pauline teaching about the Cross.[32] Without the sacrificial system as a background, the whole concept of vicarious suffering, which is the basis of N.T. theology, is inexplicable. On the other hand, the Synagogue too depends on the O.T. but in quite a different way. In this difference of relationship to the source, lies the difference between Church and Synagogue.

Scholars think that the origin of the Synagogue goes back to the Babylonian captivity[33] and that it grew out of the need dictated by the change of circumstances. In the Diaspora, if Jewish life was to continue, the Synagogue was the only answer.[34] The surprising fact is that in Palestine itself the Synagogue occupied an important part in the religious life of the nation. The Talmud purports to know as many as four hundred and eighty Synagogues in Jerusalem alone. Even the Temple had a Synagogue attached to it.[35] But while the Temple was in existence, these houses of study and prayer could only be regarded as auxiliary to the Temple. The Synagogue service was dependent upon the Temple and was, as it were, an extension of its worship. Jews unable to attend the worship of the Sanctuary by reason of distance or inconvenience forgathered at the liturgical hours of the sacrifices and united in prayer with their brethren in Jerusalem. This was an inevitable development, for the Temple area could hardly have accommodated the population of Jerusalem, let alone the rest of the country. The Synagogue served as an "overflow" of the Temple service. For this reason it was entirely orientated towards the Temple and made it the pattern of worship. The worshipper transferred himself in spirit to the Holy Place where propitiation was enacted and where God's blessing was sought on behalf of the whole of Israel. The times of the services in the Synagogue corresponded to the times of the sacrifices in the Temple. This has remained so to our own day. The daily Synagogue services are evening, morning, and afternoon. On Sabbaths, New Moons, and Festivals, there is an additional service (*musaf*) corresponding to the additional sacrifice offered in the Temple on such occasions. The afternoon service is still called *minḥa*, in reference to the daily meal-offering in the Temple.[36] Synagogues are usually built to face the direction of the Temple in Jerusalem; in the east they face west and in the west, east. To emphasize the interim character of the Synagogue in relation to the Temple the rabbis have ordained that the *shofar* shall not be blown on the Sabbath day, as this is a prerogative of Temple worship.[37] Prayer for the restoration of the Temple is a recurring feature in the liturgy of the Synagogue: "May it be Thy will, O Lord our God, and the God of our fathers, that the Temple be speedily rebuilt."[38]

The liturgical connection with the Temple cult becomes evident from the references to the sacrifices in the worship of the Synagogue. The *mishnaic* commentary which is inserted in the liturgy serves as "a reminder of those sacred rites for which prayers are now only a substitute".[39] The Synagogue's awareness of the need for atonement by sacrifice finds special expression in the liturgy of the Day of Atonement.[40] The importance the rabbis attached to the Temple can be gauged from the place they assigned to it in the order of creation: the *even shetiyyah* (foundation-stone) upon which the Temple was supposed to have been built is regarded as the centre of the earth and the basis for the rest of creation.[41]

From this it is obvious that the Synagogue knows herself as an interim institution. She lives in suspense, waiting and praying to be replaced by the rebuilt Temple. Her existence is inseparable from life in Exile and is looked upon as a sign of God's displeasure:

> On account of our sins we were exiled from our land and removed far from our country, and we are unable to fulfil our obligations in Thy chosen house, that great and holy Temple which was called by Thy name. . . . May it be Thy will, O Lord our God and the God of our fathers, merciful King, that Thou mayest again in thine abundant compassion have mercy upon us and upon Thy sanctuary and mayest speedily rebuild it and magnify Thy glory.[42]

Judaism is thus awaiting completion. The sacrificial system is in abeyance during the time of the Exile. The present position of replacing the sacrifices by prayer and fasting is only a temporary measure.[43] The Synagogue in its traditional setting looks back to the past and waits for the time when it can revert to its former status of serving as the handmaid of the Temple.

The vacuum created by the Temple was never really properly filled. Study of parts of the Law which refer to the sacrifices became in some measure a substitute for the sacrifices themselves. But this was only an emergency measure; without the Temple, Mosaic law became impossible to keep. The awareness of incompletion remains with the Synagogue to this day. The Sefardic and the larger "German" Prayer book bring this fact out more clearly than appears from Singer's edition.[44] The worshipper prays:

> May this recital [*amirah*] be acceptable unto Thee, O Lord, our God, and the God of our fathers, as if we had offered Thee continual burnt-offering in its due season.[45]

No one who has attended a Synagogue service and experienced the ceremony of the Reading of the Law can fail to appreciate the vital difference between rabbinic Judaism and the Temple cult. The two are entirely differently orientated: whereas in the Temple the focal point was the altar, in the Synagogue the central position is assigned to the Scroll of the Law. It is indeed a moving moment when the Reader turns to the Congregation while pressing the Scroll of the Law to his heart and calls: *gaddelu la-Adonai itti*—Magnify the Lord with me.[46] But behind this dramatic gesture is hidden the process which transformed the O.T. religion into rabbinic Judaism. The "Law" here is no longer the Law of the *kohanim* with its priestly code of sacred functions, but the *Torah* in the rabbinic sense as defined by *Mishnah* and *Shulḥan ʻArukh*. The change which is here revealed is more than a mere change in the centre of gravity, it is a transformation of concepts. Priest and rabbi present two entirely different worlds. In the difference of function between these two lies the difference between the O.T. and the Synagogue. This is the dividing-line between the O.T. and rabbinic Judaism.[47]

The Christian position is quite different. The great concepts of redemption which dominate the N.T. are unthinkable without the Temple cult as a background. For this very reason it is a mistake to try to fit primitive Christianity into the framework of Pharisaic Judaism. Valuable as is the work of men like Wünsche, Dalman, Strack and Billerbeck, and many others, in the field of

Judaica, the results have often led to false assumptions. The evidence of rabbinic literature has sometimes proved a hindrance rather than a help to a better understanding of the N.T. A case in point is the Johannine Gospel. Because of its seemingly un-Jewish nature when compared with rabbinic literature, scholars quickly jumped to the conclusion that the background of the Fourth Gospel is Greek. But there is enough evidence to prove the utter Jewishness of that Gospel once we are prepared to accept the fact that Pharisaic Judaism is not the only representative of the Jewish religion. In our essay *Die Juden im Johannesevangelium*,[48] we believe we have produced enough evidence to show an equally genuine Jewish tradition for the Johannine Gospel though it is bitterly opposed to Pharisaism. We venture to suggest that in many instances the N.T. is a better guide to the knowledge of the religious position in pre-Destruction Jewry than is the Talmud.

Admittedly, there are many features in the N.T. which are well illustrated and explained by rabbinic tradition. But this fact must not blind our eyes to the main truth that rabbinic Judaism as we know it to-day is not entirely the original background of the N.T. Pharisaism at the time of Jesus was fighting for supremacy, this is true enough, but it was only one of the trends in the religious life of Israel. It is a vain effort to try to bring into harmony rabbinic Judaism and Christianity, because the central premises of the one are entirely lacking in the other. The Christian faith is inseparably tied to the concepts of vicarious suffering and mediation; these two concepts are almost completely absent in the Synagogue, they are certainly of little consequence there. But they are deeply embedded in the O.T. Those who advocate a bridge theology[49] fail to recognize this basic fact. It is true that the further we go back into history the closer are the thought-forms of Judaism and Christianity because they point to a time when Pharisaic Judaism was closer to the O.T. as a result of the influence of the Temple.[50] But the Judaism the Church faces to-day lives in a different atmosphere and thinks in different categories.

The difference we are trying to elucidate is best illustrated by the Epistle to the Hebrews. In the writer we meet a man who stands upon the ground of pre-Destruction Judaism. The hypothesis that Hebrews represents typical gnostic theology is for this very reason utterly untenable. The importance of Hebrews is that we encounter here a genuine Jewish outlook at a time when the Temple[51] was still at the centre of Jewish life. To the writer the sacrificial system is at the heart of the O.T. religion. Before A.D. 70 such an outlook was natural to any Jew whether in Palestine or in the Diaspora. Hebrews' whole argument is based upon the premises of the Temple cult. Here the priesthood, the sacrifices, Levitical holiness, are all part of one central truth: the principle of mediation. A contemporary Jew reared in the tradition of Temple worship would understand immediately the author's point, but to rabbinic Judaism the argument appears far-fetched and out of context. The reason is that a Jew bred in rabbinic tradition has only historic knowledge of the Temple cult, the theological principles underlying it are missing. The same would apply to many of St Paul's arguments. The Apostle speaks from the midst of a religious context which has become foreign to later Judaism.

We shall give one more example. We have already referred to the difficulty of interpreting the Fourth Gospel in the context of rabbinic Judaism. Prompted by this fact, scholars felt justified in seeking an explanation in the non-Jewish world. But once a sincere effort has been made to place the Johannine Gospel against the sacrificial system of the Temple, a new situation arises. A case in point is John 6, where the Messiah is explained in typically sacrificial terms—the eating of his flesh and the drinking of his blood. Though the terminology is different, the Synoptic tradition presents a similar picture: the Son of Man gives his life a ransom for many. John the Baptist's reference to the Lamb of God which taketh away the sins of the world belongs to the same association of ideas.

The whole cycle of thought which revolves round the Cross is connected with Temple worship and most specifically with the Passover Service. At this juncture the importance of the Last Supper springs into prominence.

It is significant that the Fourth Gospel makes no mention of the Institution of the Holy Communion, though there is more than a hint that something approaching a Paschal Meal was celebrated by Jesus and his disciples. This is suggested by the reference to the supper (δεῖπνον), the washing of feet, the sop, the reclining position at the meal. But it is obvious that the writer of the Fourth Gospel is bent on correcting the mistaken idea that the Last Supper was a *real* Paschal Meal. It could not be, because the most important item which gives significance to that meal, namely the

Paschal Lamb, was lacking. To a Jew, prior to A.D. 70, it would have been unthinkable to celebrate the Passover without the Lamb. As in so many other instances, the Johannine Gospel reveals here typical Jewish sentiment. The writer of the Gospel has an obvious reason to emphasize the point, for to him Jesus himself is the true Paschal Lamb. He writes with a purpose in view: he wants to fix his readers' attention to the fact that on the very day[52] when Israel was sacrificing the Passover, Jesus the Messiah, the *true* Passover, died for the sins of mankind. The extension of salvation from Israel to the Gentiles is of great importance to the evangelist, for on it depends the fulfilment of the prophetic hope. Whereas the Paschal Lamb concerns Israel alone, the sacrifice on the Cross has world-significance.

In spite of the many attempts to synchronize the date of the Last Supper in the Johannine and the Synoptic traditions, no satisfactory solution has been found. But if our contention is correct, then Dr D. Chwolson's ingenious suggestion can in part be accepted: Jesus did in fact celebrate the Passover *before* the feast was due,[53] but it was an incomplete meal, for the Paschal Lamb was missing. Be it observed that in none of the other Gospels is the Paschal Lamb mentioned at that meal; the same applies to the Pauline account.[54] In fact there could be no Paschal Lamb, if, as most scholars are agreed, Passover night fell that year on the Friday.[55]

Thus it would appear that the Meal which Jesus celebrated with his disciples was in anticipation of the *real* Passover and adumbrated the Sacrifice upon the Cross. The reference in John 6 to eating of the flesh and drinking of the blood of the Messiah has sense only in the context of the Passover Meal. Let us remember that a sin-offering was never eaten by the worshipper himself, though it would sometimes be eaten by the officiating priest.[56] Even as a metaphor it would make little sense and appear outrageous to Jewish ears (cf. John 6. 60), apart from a reference to the Passover Meal where the blood of the Lamb was a recognized symbol of salvation. John 6 read in conjunction with the Last Supper completes the pattern of his message: just as the Israelites were saved by the blood of the Passover and participated in the first Exodus, so the believers in the Messiah are saved by the sacrifice on the Cross to participate in the second and greater Exodus—from the slavery of sin to the freedom of the children of God.

We meet in John 6 an assimilation of ideas between ἄρτος, σάρξ and αἷμα relating to Passover bread, the Paschal Lamb and the joy of Salvation. These are associated in Jewish tradition with the *se'udat ge'ulah*—the Feast of Redemption—which refers back to the Exodus and forward to the days of the Messiah.[57] The wine at the Paschal Meal has double significance: first, it symbolizes the blood of the Passover Lamb; secondly, it represents the joy of the redeemed. Here, then, we come upon the close connection between the Synoptic account of the Institution and the Johannine commentary of the same in John 6. The whole discourse is symbolic, as is explained in John 6. 63. The reference to the Vine and the branches in 15. 1 belongs to the same cycle of ideas.

We see thus how the Temple background, and more especially the Passover rite, is important for a better understanding of the Johannine Gospel. Without these it remains an enigma, unless we go for an explanation to the pagan mystery rites.

This may serve as an example of the close connection between the O.T. and the N.T.

The situation in the Synagogue is different. Rabbinic Judaism no longer operates with the basic concepts of the O.T. religion, such as propitiation by sacrifice, mediation by the priesthood, imputed holiness by the shedding of sacrificial blood. Judaism, by accepting the principle of *direct* approach to God, has by-passed the basic principles upon which O.T. faith was founded. This is the point of departure between Church and Synagogue.

In the course of history, Christianity has undergone many changes and has often deviated from the original pattern of ideas. But in one respect it remained true to its original nature, and this is in its interpretation of the Cross. Had the N.T. been treated by the Church as the O.T. is treated by the Synagogue, the result would have been different. But because the principle of dogma imposes upon the Church a constant reference back to its sources, it had to accept the classic interpretation as unalterable. In times of superficial idealism the Cross could have been interpreted as the symbol of heroic self-sacrifice had not the Christian faith been committed to the concept of vicarious suffering of the Son of God. But that this is so is largely due to the influence of the O.T. The Church without the O.T., if Marcion had had his way, would have become a Gentile edition of the Synagogue. The key to the N.T. is the O.T.; only together do they constitute an organic whole. Torn asunder they are not only incomplete but inexplicable. Only when O.T. and N.T. are kept together is it possible to discern a pattern in the story of revelation.[58]

But with all the difference between Church and Synagogue there is yet an essential connection which links them inescapably. It is this fact which places Judaism in a category of its own and makes it the only legitimate *vis-à-vis* of the Christian Church. That link lies in the Synagogue's unique self-consciousness.

(*a*) *Knowledge of Election*

That Israel is *'am segullah*[59] (Ex. 19. 5), i.e. God's special property, is the Synagogue's most precious knowledge. It is a phrase which recurs in the liturgy in connection with the re-affirmation of Israel's election: *attah veḥartanu mikkol ha-'ammim*—thou hast chosen us from all the nations.[60] The sense of election belongs to the peculiar self-consciousness of the Jewish people, though it has often been misunderstood by the Gentiles. Schoeps represents a true Jewish view when he describes Israel's election as the expression of the grace and love of God, though some rabbis have sometimes given the impression that it was self-merited.[61] But this was only under strain of controversy; the best Jewish piety always attributed to God's loving-kindness the choice of Israel as his special people. God's love for the Fathers is held by the Synagogue to be the ultimate reason for Israel's election (cf. Deut. 10. 15; but cf. Deut. 7. 7 f.). Before God, the Synagogue does not plead her own merits but the merits of the Fathers, chiefly the "binding of Isaac".[62] The pious Jew knows himself to belong to "an arrogant and stiff-necked people",[63] but he also knows that this people is God's people in a very special sense. As the People of God, Israel has both privileges and responsibilities which are unique; Israel's commitment to the Law[64] is connected with this special status. What the Torah means to the pious Jew can only faintly be grasped by an outsider. The restraint in the sentence, "Great is the Torah, for she giveth life to those who practise it",[65] reflects something of the sense of the privilege the pious Jew enjoys as a member of God's People. The word "Torah" itself is endowed with an emotional overtone which makes the pious Jewish heart rejoice. To study the Torah, to define it, to cogitate on it day and night, and to observe it in all its minutiae, is the special privilege of the Chosen People.[66] It is the Torah which makes the difference between Israel and the rest of the nations, and it is for its sake that Israel has to remain a separate people. In the Torah lies Israel's dignity and destiny. The Torah is Israel's mark of election.

(*b*) *Knowledge of God*

Torah is not an end in itself; its purpose is to lead God's People to the knowledge of the God of Israel. The Synagogue is rigidly and uncompromisingly committed to faith in the One, Incomparable, Invisible, Ineffable God, who is both the Creator of the Universe and the God of Israel. She knows him to be the God of the nations, but in a special sense the shaper of Israel's history. The Synagogue's knowledge of God has a definite historic aspect—he is the Initiator of Jewish history. God has revealed his will in the Torah but he remains the hidden God. For this reason the Synagogue refrains from pronouncing the Tetragrammaton (יהוה): first, because of the second Commandment; secondly, because of the infinite mystery of the Godhead.[67] This does not mean that the Synagogue's God remains nameless, it means only that his Name is too holy to be pronounced by human lips.[68] To Jewish sentiment the *nomen proprium* of the God of Israel appears to be co-equal with his Being; this shyness of coming too close to God is a vestige of the O.T. concept of God's holiness, which is connected with the need of mediation.

The Synagogue, though refraining from naming God,[69] has, however, defined him as One. The Unity of God she derives from the *shema*ʻ (Deut. 6. 4 f.). The absolute and incomparable Unity of God forms the core of Judaism. Every pious Jew begins and ends the day with the affirmation that God is One.[70] It is an old tradition in the Synagogue to write the last letters in *shema*ʻ and *eḥad* specially large: in case the ע be mistaken for an א, which would make it mean "perhaps", and the ד be mistaken for a ר, which would make it mean "another"—perhaps is Israel's God another one? The mere suggestion that there could be another god beside the God of Israel fills a Jew with horror. For this reason it is a rule in the Synagogue that the word *eḥad* (one) must never be uttered twice consecutively.[71] The last letters of *shema*ʻ and *eḥad* form the word עֵד—witness, so that every Israelite "by pronouncing the Shema becomes one of God's witnesses, testifying to His Unity before the world".[72]

Traditionally, Jews understand the text of Deut. 6. 4 to mean: Hear, O Israel: the Lord our God, the Lord is One.[73] But gradually it is being acknowledged by Jews that this is not an accurate translation.[74] The Revised Version of the English Bible suggests three possibilities in addition to the one in the text, of which the last seems to us the best: "Hear, O Israel, the Lord is our God, the Lord alone." Martin Buber, who uses ER to circumscribe the Tetragrammaton, translates: "*Hör Jisrael: ER unser Gott, ER Einer!*"[75] This is a compromise between "He Alone" and "He is One," but it seems to us that *eḥad*, like *yaḥid* in the Maimonidean Creed, intends to emphasize the *Einzigartigkeit*, that is, the uniqueness of God on the one hand and Israel's unswerving loyalty to him on the other. The undue emphasis upon the Unity on the part of the Synagogue is the result of the controversy with the Church. It is a deliberate effort to contradict the Christian doctrine of the Trinity. In this way the divine Unity became a fixed dogma of the Synagogue and was formulated in the second article of the Maimonidean Creed:

> I believe with perfect faith that the Creator, blessed be His Name, is a Unity (*yaḥid*), and that there is no unity (*yeḥidut*) in any manner like unto His. . . .[76]

The effect of the controversy with the Church was to shift the emphasis from an affirmation of loyalty to a philosophical concept of Unity, of which Maimonides is the chief exponent.[77] The concern with the Unity of God is now in the forefront of Jewish thinking. "The first affirmation of Judaism", says Dr Hertz, "is the Unity of God." This Unity is regarded as "the very cornerstone of Israel's Faith".[78]

In whatever manner the Synagogue may choose to interpret her deeply-ingrained Monotheism, she remains an unrelenting witness to the One and Only God of Israel. As a bastion against idolatry she has no equals. Her uncompromising attitude on this important point raises her to a position of a special witness in history.

(*c*) *Knowledge of God's Will*

Doing the will of God ranks next in importance to the Unity of God. Conformity to God's will is the sum-total of all Jewish piety. Judaism can be described as a system which concentrates every effort upon the supreme task of rendering obedience to the will of God. The many precepts which regulate the religious life of the Synagogue have only this aim in view. This intense concentration upon practice marks Judaism as an heir of the prophetic tradition: not words but deeds matter.

Martin Buber, the modern prophet, who preaches the this-worldliness of God's Kingdom here and now, never tires of stressing the human obligation to realize God's will in action:

> For the actuality of Biblical and post-Biblical Judaism, and also for the Jesus of the Sermon on the Mount, fulfilment of the Torah means to extend the hearing of the Word to the whole dimension of human existence.[79]

In these words Buber speaks not only for himself, but for the whole of Judaism. This is the *raison d'être* of the Synagogue—to do God's will and in this way to sanctify his Name. Buber, because he believes that this was also the driving force in the life of Jesus, does not hesitate to call him "the most eminent of Jews",[80] whose purpose it was to establish God's Kingdom in history. Israel's task, as Buber sees it, is to establish Truth in action rather than by an intellectual grasp of the faith.[81]

But once the question is asked: What is God's will? rabbinic Judaism has both a long and a short answer. The short answer: God wills that Israel should keep the Torah. The long answer: The written Law and the oral tradition come from the same source and are of equal sanctity; the written Torah cannot be understood without the oral Torah. Which means that the 613 Commandments which the rabbis have deduced from the written Law, plus the seven precepts which they have added without Scriptural warrant,[82] comprise God's holy and unalterable will. Many of these enactments seem to be so far-fetched from the original intention of the Law that any impartial observer would agree with St Paul that they have a zeal for God, but not according to knowledge. But though rabbinic casuistry has sometimes led to strange results and "the building of a fence round the Law" has often tended to become an end in itself, the intention remains with Judaism to this day: man's task is to do the will of God.

It is an awe-inspiring spectacle to watch the pious Jew busy himself day and night, at all times and under all circumstances, with the chief task of his life: the fulfilling of the *mizvot*.[83] This means for him translating Torah into action. To do this requires complete devotion of body and soul in joyful surrender to God. Every function of the body and every situation of life is covered and regulated by *torah*.

Judaism is monolithic throughout and hostile to any form of dualism. It refuses any suggestion of a division between holy and profane, religion and life. As religious monism it stands almost unique in history. It is an all-inclusive way of life: from food to dress, from the slaughter of animals to the procreation of children, from the keeping of the sabbath to the preparing of food—everything is covered by *torah*.

Every ceremony, every precept, every deed of kindness, every benediction has the same purpose: to sanctify the Name of the God of Israel. Israel is dedicated to this task: "Blessed art Thou, O Lord God, King of the universe, who hast sanctified us by Thy commandments."[84]

This awareness of being committed to the keeping of the Law is yet another feature of the Synagogue's peculiar self-consciousness.

(*d*) *Knowledge of the Messiah*

For centuries Judaism was upheld by a great hope: the coming of the Messiah. The modern idea of a messianic age without a personal Messiah introduced by the Liberal Synagogue, is utterly foreign to Jewish tradition. Although as a result of the controversy with the Church the messianic ideal tended to take a secondary place in Jewish thinking, it was never abandoned. Faith in the coming Messiah is deeply embedded in the Synagogue's liturgy. Expectancy of the Messiah's coming is expressed in the most central part of the Prayer Book, the *'amidah*. Already in the first benediction we read:

> Blessed art thou, O Lord our God, and God of our fathers . . . who rememberest the pious deeds of the patriarchs, and in love wilt bring a redeemer to their children's children for Thy Name's sake.[85]

In the fifteenth benediction the wording is even more explicit:

> Speedily cause the offspring of David Thy servant to flourish, and let his horn be exalted by Thy salvation, because we wait for Thy salvation all the day.

On New Moons, the Intermediate days of Passover, and on the Feast of Tabernacles the *'amidah* concludes with the following prayer:

> Our God and God of our fathers! May our remembrance rise, come and be accepted before Thee, with the remembrance of our fathers,

of Messiah the son of David thy servant, of Jerusalem thy holy city, and of all the people of the house of Israel. . . .[86]

There are many other occasions when faith and hope in the Messiah find expression in the Prayer Book. Notably so in the most popular hymn to usher in the sabbath day:

> Shake thyself from the dust, arise,
> Put on the garments of glory, O my people!
> Through the son of Jesse, the Bethlehemite,
> Draw Thou nigh to my soul, redeem it.[87]

The hymn is associated with the name of Solomon ha-Levi; this particular verse is almost Christian in its phraseology, specially in its expression of mediation.

Maimonides has defined the messianic hope in the following words, which form the twelfth article of his creed and which has won a place in the liturgy of the Synagogue:

> I believe with perfect faith in the coming of the Messiah, and, though he tarry, I will wait daily for his coming.[88]

Although Judaism is not committed to any particular creed, the Maimonidean creed has become a *minhag* (custom), and according to Jewish tradition *minhag* is as good as *halakah*.

Ignaz Maybaum tells of a moving episode which gives some indication how fervently the pious Jew waits for the Messiah. The well-known neo-Kantian philosopher and Jewish thinker, Hermann Cohen, at the very end of his life—and he lived to a great age—remarked to Franz Rosenzweig: "I hope I shall still live to see the days of the Messiah." Rosenzweig, somewhat startled by the old man's faith, ironically replied: "Yes, perhaps in a few hundred years' time." But Cohen, who was already slow of hearing, thought he had said: "In a hundred years' time", so he corrected him: "No, do not say a hundred years, say fifty years!"[89]

Here we see into the heart of the believing Jew. Even the Liberal Jew who has abandoned faith in a personal Messiah continues to yearn for the time of redemption and the realization of the prophetic hope. Judaism waits for fulfilment. We meet yet another sign of the Synagogue's interim position. The same element of suspense that we have observed in connection with the Temple, re-appears here in another form. The Synagogue, like the Church, is in a waiting position. The fulfilment of Israel's hopes is connected with the messianic advent. That hope Judaism has left ill-defined and has often given to it a narrow national aspect. Yet Church and Synagogue hold to a common ideal which places them both in a position of eschatological significance. Though they stand apart in history, they may yet meet at the end of time, at the feet of the coming King.

(*e*) *Knowledge of Revelation*

The Synagogue accepts the O.T. as its Canon. In it the Pentateuch occupies a position of its own. This is already indicated by the place of prominence it is assigned in the Synagogue and in the liturgy. The Scrolls of the Law are honoured as one would a monarch. They are covered with mantles of choicest brocade and ornamented with finery. The Scrolls are kissed and bowed to as if they were a living person. This is to show that Israel regards the Torah as God's greatest gift. The Order of the Reading of the Law on Sabbaths and Festivals is the most solemn act in the liturgy. The *hagbahah*—the lifting of the Scroll before the congregation—is the culminating-point of the ceremony.[90] On *simḥat torah*—the festival of Rejoicing of the Law—when the whole community literally rejoices "with boisterous mirth",[91] we meet Israel's corporate awareness of the miracle of revelation.

The Synagogue knows herself to be the custodian of the oracles of God. These oracles are contained in the whole of the O.T., but the Pentateuch is the core of it. The psalms occupy an important part of the liturgy and some portions of the prophetic books are read as the *haftarah*—the "closing" lesson.[92] But the main concern of Judaism is the "commandments", for they are the express revelation of the will of God and challenge man to action. Even when a "commandment" is obscure and does not seem to serve any obvious purpose, like the precept in respect of the mixing of species (*kil'ayim*), it is to be observed as an act of obedience to the will of God.[93] The whole purpose of rabbinic skill is to elucidate and relate *torah* in the widest sense to the exigencies of daily life. Rabbinic Law, though often far-fetched, and sometimes even contrary to the original intention of the Mosaic Code, is an expression of the Synagogue's desire to comply with the will of God. The inconvenience which accrues to the individual and the community from devotion to the Law is a measure of Jewish sincerity in this effort. The Jew submits to the "burden" of the Law in the conviction that behind it is the authority of God himself.

Revelation to the Synagogue is therefore chiefly commandment —*mizvah*. This postulates a threefold concept of the nature of God:

1. The God of Israel is a speaking God, in contradistinction to the idols (cf. Ps. 115). He addresses himself to man.

2. Israel's God invades human life. He is the Judge between right and wrong. He takes his stand on the side of justice. He requires holiness from his people.

3. He is the God of order. The Torah is not the caprice of a tyrant, but the will of the Heavenly Father. The Torah *aims* at a pattern of life which is for man's good: "He hath showed thee, O man, what is good; and what doth the Lord require of thee, but to do justly, and to love mercy, and to walk humbly with thy God?" (Micah 6. 8)—this is the most perfect definition of the Synagogue's concept of revelation.

(*f*) *Knowledge of Suffering*

It was Heinrich Heine who described Judaism as an affliction.[94] Though this was only a cynical remark, in one respect he was right. Viewed in the perspective of history, the Jewish devotion to the faith was a source of untold suffering. Anti-Semitism in its racial setting is a comparatively modern disease. In the past, Jews suffered not because of race but because of religion. From the days of Antiochus Epiphanes to the days of the Russian pogroms, Jewish suffering was mainly the result of loyalty to the ancestral faith. All the great national disasters in Jewish history, with one single exception,[95] had religion as the cause. The classical example is the Jewish-Roman war which led to the disaster of A.D. 70. The revolt against Imperial Rome would never have taken place but for the outraged religious sentiments of the Jews. To them the struggle against Rome was a holy war in which the honour of the God of Israel was at stake. The very fact that Israel had to submit to a pagan power was in itself an insult to Israel's God. Josephus tells us that to the last, John, the leader of the war in Jerusalem, refused to believe that the city could fall—"because it was God's own city".[96] During the later struggle under Bar Kochba, the religious motive was even more pronounced. It was often at pain of death that Jews practised the Law, and it was with reference to such times that the haggadic story about Pappos b. Judah and R. Akiba grew up. Pappos is supposed to have found the great Rabbi Akiba holding assemblies and expounding the Torah, a pursuit forbidden by the government. When he pointed out the danger, Akiba answered with the following parable: A fox was walking along a stream when he noticed a shoal of fishes in flight. He asked them why they were fleeing. They answered: From nets which men are bringing against us. The fox then suggested that they come out and dwell with him on the dry land. They replied: If we are afraid in a place which is our life-element, how much more (shall we be in danger) in a place which is our death-element. "So it is with us", said the Rabbi, "if now while we sit and study Torah, in which it is written 'For that is thy life, and the length of thy days' (Deut. 30. 20), we are in such danger, how much more so, if we neglect it?"[97] According to tradition, R. Akiba died a martyr's death with the words of the *shema'* upon his lips.[98] To die thus, "for the sanctification of the Name", is a glorious end to a pious Jew.

The *midrash* gives expression to the awareness of the Jewish destiny to suffer for God's sake when it puts into Moses' mouth the following complaint:

> Lord of the Universe, had we been uncircumcised or given to idolatry, or disobedient to the commandments, they would not have hated us, nor would they have persecuted us, but (now) it is only because of the law and the commandments, which thou hast given us (that we suffer).[99]

Naturally enough, the Exile was felt as a heavy burden and the rabbis have laboured hard to find an explanation for Israel's terrible lot. Many reasons were suggested for the catastrophe of A.D. 70. The classical passage is in *Shab.* 119 b, where a variety of reasons are advanced, such as: because Israel profaned the Sabbath, because the *shema'* was not said both morning and evening, because children were not sent to school, because of lack of decency, because the small and the great were treated as equals, because men did not reprove each other, because the rabbis were despised, because of corruption.[100] The need to explain the Exile was the more urgent, as the Church put upon it a completely different construction.[101] But even the Synagogue explained it as God's punishment for committed sins. She thus confesses to this day:

> On account of our sins we were exiled from our land, and removed far from our country.

And she prays:

> Lead us with exultation into Zion thy city, and unto Jerusalem the place of thy sanctuary with everlasting joy.[102]

There are many references to the Exile in the liturgy and the longing for its ending is ever alive before the praying community:

> Look upon our affliction, for many are our griefs and the sorrows of our heart. Have pity upon us, O Lord, in the land of our captivity, and pour not out thy wrath upon us, for we are thy people, the children of thy covenant.[103]

Judah Halevi, the great singer of the Holy Land, accepted the traditional explanation of the Exile in terms of punishment, but he also held to the conviction that his people could attain to freedom if it only had enough faith and will-power. Here is his reasoning:

> The divine power inspires man's power only in such a measure as the latter is prepared to receive it; if the readiness be small, little will be obtained, and much will be obtained if it be great. Had we been prepared to meet the God of our fathers with a pure mind, we would find the same salvation as our fathers did in Egypt.[104]

It was between these two sentiments of contrition and hope that Israel has borne the long years of the Exile, sighing for relief. The Synagogue has never accepted Exile as her ultimate destiny. The interpretation of Exile in positive terms, i.e. as a living witness to the Gentile world of the One God, is the specific discovery of Reform Judaism. Here a sincere effort is being made to give to the dispersion of Israel missionary and redemptive significance. "It is time that we should understand", says Ignaz Maybaum, "that *galut* is not a geographical conception, but means the life of Israel and of mankind in the time in which redemption is still far off and has to remain our dearest hope."[105] Reform Judaism is therefore trying to understand Israel's peculiar position among the nations as the God-given pattern for the Jewish community. The suffering which it entails is part of the price Israel has to pay for being the Servant of God. Exile is a privilege, for it provides the opportunity of witness to the special values for which Israel stands. It helps towards the "fulfilment of their function as the People of God".[106]

In whatever way the Synagogue may try to interpret her history, the fact of her suffering remains unaltered. Jews are supremely aware of their common destiny in suffering. In fact, it is the awareness of suffering which makes them a people.[107]

(g) *Knowledge of Continuity*

The Synagogue is singularly aware of her connection with the past. She knows of God not only as the Creator of the Universe, but most specially as the director of her history. Such knowledge is remarkably expressed in the ever-recurring formulae of the liturgy:

> Blessed art thou, O Lord our God, King of the universe . . .
> Blessed art thou, O Lord our God and God of our fathers . . .

Judaism is rooted in history. In all its feasts and holy days it relives its past. In this manner, every individual Jew, in whatever age he may be living, participates in the whole of his people's history. The rabbis felt Israel's unity so keenly that they refused to differentiate between one generation and another. Thus, at Sinai all future generations have become committed to the obedience of the Law.[108] To the Jew there can be no escape from the past. The Synagogue maintains that the whole of Israel, to the end of time, is under obligation to the Law, because of the Covenant. Israel's past and Israel's future are thus seen as one indivisible whole. Such an attitude may inconvenience the individual Jew, for it interferes with his personal freedom, but the rabbis were not concerned with the individual but with the community.

To the Synagogue the community of Israel is her chief concern; the individual has to fit into it. He enters the community at birth and is carried by it to the end of his life. He derives his significance from the life of the community. Community life is therefore a sacred thing, and its history is sacred history. To Judaism, there is no profane history, for Jewish history is the history of God's People. It covers the whole range of Israel's experience: freedom and slavery, prosperity and exile, joy and suffering, all these are aspects of God's reign over his People.

In spite of the fact that there is no such thing as a homogeneous Jewish race,[109] Jews of all continents are possessed of a remarkable awareness of a common destiny and of an unbroken continuity with the past. This is so deeply rooted in the Jewish consciousness that even non-believing Jews are seldom able to emancipate themselves from it.

This link with the past which every Jew carries within him is of special significance to the Church. Barth expresses true Christian sentiment when he regards the Jewish people as "the one natural proof of the existence of God". This "proof" must be linked not only to the fact of their survival, but also to the fact of revelation. It is the fact of Jewish history which prevents biblical revelation from becoming a myth and keeps it firmly rooted in history. Israel's physical presence provides the element of concreteness in the story of God's dealing with mankind. It is from the story of the Jews that we learn that God does not address himself to poets or philosophers to provide them with a subject for their special pursuits, but to man in the reality of his daily tasks. In Jewish history lies the guarantee that the same God who once spoke to the fathers . . . hath at the end of these days spoken to us by a Son. . . .

(*h*) *Knowledge of Moral Values*

Judaism has been defined as ethical monotheism. This is essentially true, though the philosophical terminology tends to obscure the fact that it is not merely a *Weltanschauung*, but eminently a religion. Judaism as a religion is rooted in moral values. It is concerned with the practice of righteousness in the sight of God. Ethics is its main theme. Rabbinic Judaism is not motivated by utilitarian considerations; it derives its ethical teaching from the character of God: Ye shall be holy, for I the Lord your God am holy, is its basis. The Synagogue understands God's holiness in moral terms, she has therefore made God himself the pattern of human behaviour. Judaism is as much *imitatio Dei* as Christianity is *imitatio Christi*.[110] *Shivviti Adonai lenegdi tamid* (Ps. 16. 8)—I have set the Lord constantly before me—is the highest aim of Jewish piety. Abba Shaul put it in the following words: The King has his family (*familya*), and what is their concern? To imitate the King.[111]

The rabbis asked in reference to Deut. 13. 4: "Ye shall walk after the Lord your God"—How can man walk after God, who is a devouring fire? They answered: Walk after his *middot* (attributes), clothe the naked, visit the sick, comfort the mourners, bury the dead, etc.[112] They speak of *shelosh 'esreh middot*—thirteen attributes—which they derive from Ex. 34. 6 f. and which they regard as the principles of mercy by which God rules the world. By means of a paronomasia upon the word *ve'anvehu*—and I will praise him (Ex. 15. 2)—Abba Shaul deduces the reading: *ani va-hu*—I like him—i.e. let me become like him: As he is merciful and gracious, so be ye merciful and gracious.[113] This shows how the Synagogue understands God's holiness. It is the duty of a pious Jew to reflect God's attributes in his daily life.

It is not accidental that the great work on Judaism in the German language produced by Jewish scholars begins with a chapter on ethics,[114] for ethics is at the heart of the Synagogue's faith: the promotion of personal morality is the main concern of Judaism. The aim is to secure social justice in all aspects of community life. *Ẓedaḳah* and *mishpat*—righteousness and justice (judgement)—are key-words in the social ethics of Judaism. Society must be just to be righteous; but to the rabbis *ẓedaḳah* is never far removed from *ḥesed* (mercy): for the God of Israel is both—he is righteous and merciful (Ex. 34. 6 f.). From Psalm 89. 2 the rabbis were able to deduce that the world itself is built upon mercy; and not only the world, for God's Throne has mercy as its foundation.[115]

Justice tempered with mercy is the Synagogue's ideal for society. These two attributes are complementary and must never be separated. God is concerned with both: righteousness and justice are dearer to him than the Temple.[116] In him are these two virtues, which are otherwise opposed to each other, united; for he, the Righteous One, is the pillar of the world.[117]

Intense moralism carries its dangers, but this must not blind us to the fact that Judaism is a great moral force in the world. In this respect it stands within the finest tradition of the O.T. prophets. In the voice of the Synagogue can still be heard the moral earnestness of the men of God who insisted that man is judged by his deeds and that God is incorruptible and cannot be bribed by pretended piety.[118]

It is only natural that in the fight for social justice Jews should have played so prominent a part. Personal integrity and social equity are the two pillars of Jewish ethics. The structure of Judaism is upheld by these two ideals.

CHAPTER 3

THE DIALOGUE BETWEEN CHURCH AND SYNAGOGUE

ALL human encounter results either in conflict or in dialogue. In the encounter between Jews and Christians both have played their part, but it was usually conflict which took precedence. Occasionally, however, the weaker side was allowed to speak, and dialogue took place. Yet even a dumb or silenced partner creates the necessary condition for a dialogue, though in fact only a monologue results. In the relationship between Church and Synagogue, the monologue on the part of the Church has been the rule till recently. The Church was too impatient and too narrow to allow the Synagogue to give voice to her scruples. Even Justin's *Dialogue* is only an imaginary one, as Harnack has pointed out. But whenever believers from both sides have really met in faith, dialogue has been the result. Such encounter creates an unusual situation, for both sides purport to speak on behalf of Israel. Herein lies the strange relationship between Church and Synagogue. In the Synagogue, the Church meets not another religion, but herself, yet in another edition, as it were. The same applies to the Synagogue. Church and Synagogue are like dissimilar twins, alike in some respects, different in others.

The characteristics of the Synagogue apply equally well to the Church: knowledge of election, knowledge of God, knowledge of revelation, knowledge of Messiah, knowledge of suffering, knowledge of historical continuity, knowledge of moral values, make up the self-consciousness of both. It is by these very marks that they are known and recognized. Yet this strange similarity must not deceive us, for the inner content of their respective self-consciousness is different. They know the same things, but they know them differently. The inner difference derives from the central fact: the Church draws her knowledge from Jesus Christ, the Synagogue by-passes him.

Whatever else the Synagogue may say about Jesus of Nazareth, one thing she says with undeviating consistency: he is *not* the Messiah. From the negation regarding the Messiahship of Jesus stems the difference of the Synagogue's self-knowledge in relation to the Church. That difference relates not only to content, but also to time: the Synagogue lives by constant reference to the past. The Church, on the other hand, lives in the present: this is the result of her faith in the presence of her risen Lord. A similar difference exists with regard to status: the Synagogue knows herself to be Israel by reason of her physical link with the Fathers; the Church knows herself to be Israel by reason of Grace mediated through Jesus Christ to all believers. We may thus say: the Church is not Church *without* Jesus Christ: the Synagogue is not Synagogue *with* Jesus Christ; here lies the difference. Apart from Jesus Christ, Church and Synagogue touch at many points and their demarcation lines are fluid. But without her Christology the Church is not any more the Church but a Gentile Synagogue, as is the case with Unitarianism. From this it is clear that both need the dialogue to clarify their positions and to reaffirm their faith. They need each other, to understand themselves. This in itself is remarkable and reveals something of the hidden connection between them.

The dialogue between Church and Synagogue is therefore not a pastime for theologians, but an act of faith on both sides. It is a tragedy that Jews and Christians so seldom meet each other on the level of faith. Here we can only briefly indicate the subjects which must form the basis of such a dialogue.

(*a*) *The Question of O.T. Exegesis*

Church and Synagogue accept the O.T.; both regard it as the Word of God. But in their exegesis they differ. The difference springs from the fact that their starting-points are different; the Synagogue starts from the Torah, the Church starts from the Incarnation.

It is obvious that exegesis can never become an objective science; it entirely depends on the position of the exegete. Yet when two speak about the same thing, their voices must be heard to mutual advantage. In this case the concern is the same: Church and Synagogue seek to hear the voice of God in Holy Writ, though the result is different. The Church, reading the O.T., finds in it the person of Jesus the Messiah; the Synagogue, reading the same book, finds no such person. Who is at fault?

The O.T. is an integral part of the Christian *kerygma*: καθὼς γέγραπται, ὅτι γέγραπται, ἵνα πληρωθῶσιν αἱ γραφαί are not just pious phrases, but important statements affirming the truth of the Gospel. That the O.T. Scriptures bear witness to Jesus Christ is the deepest conviction of the early Church (cf. John 5. 39). But how do the Scriptures bear witness to Jesus?

This was and still is the exegetical problem of the Church. It is not a question which can be answered once and for all. In every age and out of the context of her special situation, the Church has to answer that question again and again. The Synagogue has the right to reject the answer and to question the legitimacy of the exegetical method. She does so as the special guardian of the O.T.

In the controversy between Church and Synagogue, the exegetical question was a major issue. Whatever may have been the Christian approach to the Gentiles, as far as the Jews were concerned there was only one possible approach—by way of Holy Writ. But "Scriptural proof" was not only necessary for the missionary purpose, it was also important for the strengthening of Jewish believers. Herein the Church followed the example of the Master, who constantly fell back upon the Word of God: "Thus it is written. . . ."[1] The appeal to Scripture remains with the Church to this day, particularly in her dealing with Jews. This is the line the Church has followed from the beginning; the N.T., the Church Fathers, the medieval Disputations, modern missionary literature, all proceed from the same principle: it is possible to "prove" from the O.T. that Jesus is the Messiah. The Jewish missionary takes Saul of Tarsus as his example who "confounded the Jews who dwelt at Damascus, proving that this is the Christ" (Acts 9. 22)—from their own Scriptures.

The controversy between Church and Synagogue is not of a general nature: the point at issue is ὅτι οὗτος ἐστιν ὁ Χριστός—this very Jesus *is* the Messiah. It means that unless the Christian exegete identifies Jesus from the O.T., the argument is of no validity to the disbelieving Jew.

Though the principle remains the same, in procedure Christian exegesis has changed from age to age. We do not know in detail how St Paul made use of the O.T. as he argued in favour of Jesus. Naturally, his use of Holy Writ was peculiar to his own age and tradition. He uses the text as the rabbis have been wont to do before and after him. The Church Fathers have not only followed the example of the N.T., but have added to and elaborated exegetical procedure. We must, however, remember that at no time was the method of the Church far removed from that of the Synagogue.[2]

The far-fetched arguments of Christian exegetes sound strange to modern ears. But the Synagogue's rejection of Christian exegesis was not on scholarly grounds as we understand it to-day, but simply because her own tradition required a different exposition of the text. In other words, the text was used by both parties to support their *a priori* positions, and it could not be otherwise. The subjectivity of faith dictates such an attitude.

The Church did not believe in the Messiahship of Jesus *because* he was "foretold" in the O.T.; she believed *first,* and only with the eyes of faith could she see him in the Hebrew Scriptures. On the other hand, the Synagogue could not believe in Jesus because she could not find him in the O.T.; she disbelieved first, and therefore could not see him there. This is axiomatic; no argument is productive of faith, not even the scriptural argument.

Unfortunately, apologists seldom recognize the fact. It is perhaps Luther's greatest achievement in the sphere of Christian exegesis to have fixed the order of procedure: from Christ to Scriptures, and not the other way round. For the Christian, Jesus Christ remains "the central point of the circle",[3] for without him the Scriptures lose their meaning: *tolle Christum e scripturis, quid amplius in illis invenies?*[4] asks Luther. The Synagogue has no such knowledge; it would not be the Synagogue if it had. All the same, it can hardly be surprising that the exegetical acrobatics of a Barnabas, a Justin, a De Lyra, or even a Reuchlin,[5] failed to convince the Jews of the truth of Christianity.

On the Jewish side it is now recognized that the innermost motives of faith are inaccessible to the outsider, "for the secret of the other one is from within and cannot be comprehended from without".[6] This is true enough, but if it were accepted as a guiding principle in Jewish-Christian relationships the dialogue would come to an end. "I believe, therefore do I speak" is as much a Jewish as a Christian compulsion. Faith has to speak in faith that the outsider will become an insider, that the blind will see by the miracle of grace and the operation of the Holy Spirit. Exegesis must therefore take place on both sides with a view to the other partner.

The Church cannot but expound the Scriptures. This is an obligation she has as part of her task in preaching Christ; what Luther called "*Christus treiben*".[7] The fact that the Jew is unable to follow the inner logic of Christian evidence cannot deter the Church from doing her duty, though she knows full well, or ought to know, that there is no *direct* way from the O.T. to the N.T.—it leads by way of Jesus Christ. By this we mean that there is no compelling reason, apart from faith, for a person who accepts the authority of the O.T., *ipso facto* to accept the N.T. as well. The case is different, however, when the order is reversed: no one really accepts the N.T. unless he also accepts the O.T. For this reason Marcion had to rewrite the second half of the Canon before he could rid himself of the first. To the Church the approach to Scripture is by way of Jesus Christ, which means that faith comes first. A reversal of the order creates chaos, for it makes faith in Christ rest upon argument. Such faith is a contradiction in terms. When we read in John 1. 45: "We have found him, of whom Moses in the Law, and the Prophets, did write", we must understand it to mean that the discovery of Jesus as Messiah preceded the discovery that he is the one of whom Moses and the Prophets did write.

Let it be said once again: the principle of faith can in no way exonerate the Church from her exegetical task. The Synagogue asks and the Church must answer: How is Jesus of Nazareth the Christ in view of the Scriptures?

We have already said that the answer cannot be given once and for all. Every generation must face and answer the question for itself. The exegete will naturally take notice of the exegetical tradition, but this can be only his guide and not his rule, otherwise he runs the risk of doing violence to God's *living* Word. A reference to the past must never be a means of evading the issue, for our approach to Scripture must change with the times.

We will use an example to illustrate our point. De Lyra quite seriously attempted to prove the Virgin Birth from an orthographical mistake in one single word of Isa. 9. 6. Because, by some strange mistake, *lemarbeh* in the Massoretic text has a "closed" *mêm*(ם), he felt justified in concluding that the child will be born *ex matre clausa virginitate.*[8] No modern exegete, no matter how prejudiced, would adduce such a proof. Are we to conclude that because De Lyra was mistaken in his argument, he was also mistaken in his view as regards the Virgin Birth? The Virgin Birth still remains the doctrine of the Church, though this particular "proof" had to be abandoned.[9] Here is a task from which there is no escape and which demands constant attention.

The Synagogue's inquiry into Christian exegesis is insistent but sincere. She has not only a right but a sacred duty to ask how the Church, by all the rules of exegesis, is able to identify Jesus of Nazareth with O.T. messianic prophecy. The Church owes not only to her questioner, but to herself, an honest answer. Whether her answer appears valid to the Synagogue is another matter. The effort she makes is dictated by faith; even her exegetical embarrassment is part of her witness. The Church thus still confesses that she has found him of whom Moses in the Law and the Prophets did write. In reply the Synagogue asks: How does Moses in the Law and how do the Prophets write of Jesus of Nazareth?

1. This is a serious question, for the attitude of the Church to the O.T. canon depends on it. If Christ is not in the Law and the Prophets, then the Church has no interest and no part in the O.T.

2. The question is made more complex by the fact that the Synagogue's views on messianic prophecies have undergone a considerable change since the times of the N.T. We shall again use an example.

Trypho the Jew, replying to Justin's scriptural argumentation, makes the following admission: "Be assured that all our nation waits for Christ: and we admit that all the scriptures which you have quoted refer to him."[10] In these words we still hear the voice of the ancient Synagogue, whose views on messianic prophecies was not much different from that of the primitive Church. For the sake of contrast we quote Rabbi Dr Seligmann Pick, who expresses the view of contemporary orthodox Jewry. At the end of his small book dealing with the question of Christian exegesis on messianic texts, he concludes: "None of the O.T. texts here examined have any Christological significance."[11] Other Jewish writers hold a similar view.[12]

The exegetical situation as far as the Synagogue is concerned has undergone considerable change since the days of the N.T. The arguments valid then are invalid to-day. Here we meet yet another reason why Christian exegesis demands not a fixed but an ever-changing attitude. The Church in her dialogue with the Synagogue can make herself heard only when she speaks not only in her own context but in the context of her partner's position.

The exegetical issue between Church and Synagogue reduces itself to two problems: 1. Is Jesus of Nazareth the Messiah in the light of the O.T.? 2. Does the O.T. warrant a concept of the Messiah who is more than human?

That the O.T. envisages a Messiah is not really under discussion, though Jewish scholars are reluctant to accept as messianic many texts traditionally held to be so by the Church.

It must be admitted in all honesty that the Church's attempt to prove her point is not based upon compelling argument. In fact there is no "conclusive proof", nor can there be one, for reasons already stated. At best the Church must admit with Ed. Riehm that O.T. prophecy and N.T. fulfilment do not correspond in every detail.[13] Wilhelm Vischer's magnificent work, *Das Christuszeugnis des Alten Testaments*, has its legitimate place in Christian theology, but it is more the result of the believer's insight than objective statement of fact. Professor Vischer's approach is the only possible approach for the Christian: the O.T. as seen from the N.T. For the Christian believer there can be no other perspective. Only in this sense can we understand the O.T. references in the N.T. For the outsider this may look like *vaticinium ex eventu*—a subtle effort to mould the story to fit the prophecies. But for the Christian the picture looks different: those who told the story, in telling called to mind the prophecies.

It is thus obvious that Church and Synagogue are bound to speak at cross-purposes on this particular issue. The knot can untie itself only by faith. Basically it is the same problem whenever faith and disbelief meet: the believer *knows*, but the unbeliever *also* knows. Respect for each other's sincerity is the only answer.

If our premise is admitted, then it becomes obvious that Christian exegesis can never be pursued with an aim to "prove" but only to witness. The Church *does* see Jesus in the O.T., but she sees him there not obviously, directly, but with the eyes of faith. This vision she tries to convey to her sister, the Synagogue, whose sight is dimmed by the "veil", so that she cannot see (cf. 2 Cor. 3. 14). The Master himself is the only lifter of the veil and expounder of the Scriptures (cf. Luke 24. 27). Before the secret of the Synagogue's blindness the Church can only bow in awe, praying that she may see.

Unfortunately, Christian exegesis has mainly been exegesis of "proof" and not exegesis of witness. Expositors have lost themselves in the forest of exegetical casuistry to "prove" Christ from the O.T., instead of explaining the O.T. in the light of Christ.

The classical example of true Christian exegesis is the Epistle to the Hebrews, where the task is tackled quite differently.[14]

The Church, however, owes the Synagogue a great debt. It is thanks to the Synagogue's objections, questions, and doubts, that she is forced to re-relate herself to the centre and again and again make Jesus Christ her starting-point.[15]

(b) The Question regarding the Trinity

The implication of the rearrangement of sequence: Jesus Christ—O.T.; instead of the traditional: O.T.—Jesus Christ, becomes clearer when we come to discuss the doctrine of the Holy Trinity.

Though there is no explicit formulation of the Trinitarian doctrine in the N.T., it is implicit in it. The Pauline Epistles and the Johannine Gospel come so close to a Trinitarian concept that the Church Fathers could not but draw the obvious conclusion.[16] But to prove the doctrine they went to the O.T. It was from the Hebrew Bible that they determined to establish the divinity of Christ and the Trinity of the Godhead. We are here concerned with the exegetical aspect of the proof.

Can the Trinitarian concept of the Church be "proved" from the O.T. without violence to the text and without philological quibbling? Our fathers would have been shocked at the question. Much of the missionary literature for Jews purports to show from the O.T. the truth of that doctrine. But it is rather remarkable that the Synagogue has never taken cognisance of such a doctrine. In fact it directly contradicts her own reading of the O.T. Whereas the Church finds in the Hebrew Bible vestiges of the Trinitarian concept, the Synagogue finds there nothing but a fervent affirmation of the Unity of God. To the pious Jew the doctrine of the Trinity appears blasphemous, and he can understand it only as the survival of a pagan view. On this score there can be no compromise for the Synagogue; she stands and falls with her distinct monotheism. The *yigdal* Prayer which was fashioned after the pattern of the Maimonidean Creed stresses the point with obvious reference to the Christian idea of the Trinity:

> He is One, and there is no unity like unto his unity: inconceivable[17] is he and unending in his unity.

Even more explicit is the *adon 'olam*:

> And he is One, and there is no second to him to consort with him.[18]

There are numerous references in rabbinic literature to the absolute Unity of God. Whenever circumstances allowed, Jews took the opportunity to register their opposition to the doctrine of the Trinity, as in the case of Isaac ben Abraham of Troki.[19] The objections raised by R. Isaac have been stated before and after him: (1) the doctrine of the Trinity contradicts reason; (2) it finds no support in the O.T.; (3) Jesus himself never makes the claim to be co-equal with God.

Though Jewish controversialists have often based their argument on philosophical and logical grounds,[20] their main support they have found in the O.T.[21]

In fairness to the Church it must be admitted that much of the Jewish argument shows great confusion of thought as to the real meaning of the Christian doctrine of the Trinity. This is partly due to the obtuseness of the subject and partly to the ambiguity of the Christian presentation. "Trinity" in numerical terms has led Jews to emphasize the Unity to such an extent that God has become a mathematical concept: *eḥad*, *yaḥid*, *yeḥidut*, are now technical terms employed to "define" the Unity. Fear of the invasion of the Christian doctrine has given rise to an abstract and arid concept of the Godhead. An example is Maimonides: "Those who believe that God is One, and that he has many attributes, declare the Unity with their lips, and assume plurality in their thoughts." Maimonides adds: "This is like the doctrine of the Christians, who say that he is one and that he is three, and that the three are one."[22] Here God is a pure philosophical concept without attributes. That this has happened is partly the fault of the Church.

Luther was very much aware of the inadequacy of our vocabulary. The terms "Unity" and "Trinity" are most unsuitable, and bear witness to the limitation of human language.[23] Jews are seldom aware of the problem; it is therefore the greater merit of C. G. Montefiore to have seen through the difficulty. Montefiore complains that Jewish writers have never really tried to understand the Christian point of view. He says:

> I have not come across any passage which seriously tackles the Christian conception of the Trinity, or which attempts to show that a Unity, which is a simple and pure Unity, is a higher or truer conception of the divine nature than a Unity of a Trinity or than a Trinity of a Unity. Where the Rabbis reply to the *minim* . . . they always represent these *minim* as believing in many Gods.[24]

In his reasonableness regarding the Christian doctrine of the Trinity, Montefiore stands almost isolated among Jewish writers. His ability to distinguish Trinitarianism from tritheism has brought the wrath of the Chief Rabbi upon his head.[25] This is only natural. The Church cannot expect a sympathetic understanding on the part of the Synagogue on this question. At most, the Jew can try to understand the subject philosophically, as Montefiore does. Beyond this point he cannot go without surrendering his position. Lukyn Williams rightly says:

> It seems to me that it is unreasonable to expect a Jew to understand, in any satisfactory degree, the Christian doctrine of the Trinity in Unity. . . . For the doctrine of the Trinity is not a doctrine independent of others, but rather the final result and apex . . . of all Christian truths.[26]

The point we want to stress is that the doctrine of the Trinity is not primarily a philosophical question at all; it is essentially a theological question. It is inseparable from the Incarnation, Resurrection, and Ascension of Jesus Christ. The Trinity is the theological inference from the story as told in the Gospels. We therefore do not begin with the Trinity and come to the Gospels, but begin with the Gospels and arrive at the Trinity. For this reason the argument from the O.T. must remain invalid to the unbeliever. There is no "proof" of the Trinity in the O.T.; it is the Trinity who speaks there. But this we can know only from the empty grave, from Easter Day. Any other argument remains invalid, as long as men stand this side of the Cross.[27]

This discovery can be made only when the Church is faced with the Jewish question. In her effort to answer the Synagogue the Church learns afresh the danger of idolatry and the meaning of the "unity". She is forced to admit the fact that "Scripture is opposed to the belief in more than one God".[28] Then she has to face the question regarding Jesus of Nazareth. His position in the Church's faith she can never take for granted. She owes the answer to herself and to others: *cur deus homo?*

The question regarding the Trinity touches upon the nerve-centre of the Christian faith: Jesus the son of David, the Son of God. What does the Church mean by the Second Person of the Trinity? If God is One, whence his "Son"?

Here the Synagogue is in a unique position: she represents the only instance in history where the Second Commandment is taken seriously. She is thus the historic guardian of biblical monotheism. She has a right and an obligation to ask and she asks with true concern: How is Jesus of Nazareth God?

The Christian answer cannot be evasive. It must not fall back upon the authority of Church Councils. To refer a Jew back to the Council of Nicea is an admission of our own helplessness and lack of conviction. It is the task of theology to attempt a *contemporary* answer, but with a view to the past. The Jewish questioner to-day is not edified by the historical information what Christians in the fourth century thought about Jesus; he wants to know what we think about him in the intellectual context of our own time.

The Church in answering the question must remember that the answer she offers is to a Jew. It means that she must not lose herself in a maze of philosophical argument, but constantly retrace her steps back to the Scriptures. For though the Christological view of the Church cannot directly be proved from the O.T., the O.T. is important for reference back and for the historical perspective of revelation. Without it the N.T. remains suspended in the air and is without roots. The Church believes and believes rightly that there is indirect support in the O.T. for her view of the Messiah.

In the last resort the Church is not "proving" but witnessing; in the dialogue between herself and her partner she is giving expression to her faith. It cannot be otherwise. Although she is aware of Jewish scruples and of the long tradition of Jewish monotheism, she owes it to her Master and her conscience to confess her faith in the Triune God.

(*c*) *The Question regarding Israel*

In the discussion regarding the position of the Messiah in the Jewish and Christian view, the question of Israel is included. Many of the functions which the Church associates with the Messiah belong in the Jewish view to Israel as a whole. This is specially the case with regard to Isa. 53. But there is yet another issue of great importance. The Synagogue regards herself as Israel by tradition, by historical connection, by promise, and by the covenants, so much so that to her "Israel" and "Jew" are synonyms. The Church, though she does not deny the special position of the Jews in the economy of God, yet maintains that not all who are of Israel are Israel, and that she too has a claim to make to that position. Who, then, is Israel?

In the Jewish view, Israel has primarily an historic connotation. It describes the people which originated from Abraham, which has experienced a common history, which has a biological connection with past generations of Jews, and which stands under the obligation of the Covenant at Sinai. That Israel is not a collection of individuals, but a community, the *kelal Yisrael*, with an historic mission to fulfil. Israel's God-given task is to be a witness to the One and only true God, the God of Israel. The Jewish "commonwealth" is to the pious Jew not a political or social, but a particularly religious experience of a common destiny. Israel, to the Synagogue, is not a self-made people, but the Chosen People of God. God is the initiator of Israel's history, and for Israel to cease to be Israel is tantamount to a defeat of God's original purpose.

We come thus, once again, to the crucial problem of election. How does the Synagogue understand election? On the answer to this question largely depends the definition of Israel. Does the Synagogue understand election physically, spiritually, or both? Unfortunately, there is no straightforward answer.

Most Christian writers have maintained that the Synagogue understands her election biologically. Albrecht Oepke, who has re-discussed the subject in his learned book, *Das neue Gottesvolk*, does not hesitate to repeat the traditional Christian view. He thus says that the Synagogue interprets her election "*als ein dinglicher Besitz . . . der mit dem Blute vererbt wird*".[29] Some Jewish writers have certainly held such views. It would be difficult to deny that, for the ancient Synagogue as for many modern Jews, the expression "seed of Abraham" is no mere metaphor but a concrete biological fact. On the Jewish side the physiological concept of election has been worked out with remarkable consistency by the medieval philosopher and poet Judah Halevi. Some more recent writers like Ignaz Ziegler, Franz Rosenzweig, Hans Joachim Schoeps, etc., claim this to be the correct view.[30] But on the other hand, the fact that the Synagogue has always had her doors open for proselytes seems to contradict a straightforward biological concept.[31] Or does it suggest an inherent contradiction which Judah Halevi noticed and attempted to obviate by trying to work out the difference between the proselyte and born Jew?[32]

Judah Halevi's view is supported by an ancient tradition, but it is only a minority tradition. Most Jewish scholars contradict the view,[33] though they may err by giving a too definite answer. The

Ancient Synagogue was in a real difficulty about proselytes; for on the one hand she maintained the importance of Israel's blood-relationship, on the other hand she sought to encourage the entry of Gentiles. Some rabbis tried to solve the difficulty by the ingenious theory that the pre-existent souls of proselytes were already present at the giving of the Law at Mount Sinai and thus have a legitimate part in Israel's inheritance.[34] But this very expedient tends to discount the all-importance of physical descent by trying to introduce a spiritual and moral element into the picture. Blood-relationship is no light matter to the pious Jew; but in spite of this we shall misunderstand the Synagogue's position if we impute to her a racial concept of election. Judaism is worlds apart from the racial theories of men like Gobineau, Treitschke, or Houston Stewart Chamberlain. To accuse the rabbis of racialism is unjust.[35]

To the rabbis, Israel's election is an act of grace; they do not take it for granted. There is a delightful *midrash* by R. Ḥiyya which well illustrates the wonder of the Synagogue at God's grace: A king on a journey was passing a field in which a group of women were gleaning. Among them he recognized his own daughter. To everyone's astonishment he stopped the carriage, and took her with him. So it was also in the case of Israel. He was doing the work of a slave in Egypt, but God recognized his origin and made him free—to the astonishment not only of the Gentiles but of Israel himself.[36]

Israel is astonished at God's mercy; but there is the other side to it—God recognizes Israel's origin, his princely status. To the rabbis these two thoughts are complementary. On the one hand Israel is elected by the free grace of God: on the other, Israel by his obedience to the Torah approves himself worthy of God's choice.[37] Schoeps speaks in the best tradition of Judaism when he describes Israel's election as "an unconditional act of God's grace".[38] It is the grace of God which marks Israel out as a special People:

> Just as the lily is recognizable among other plants, so is Israel distinguishable among the nations, as it is said: All who see them shall acknowledge them that they are the seed which the Lord hath blessed.[39]

It is fair to say that the rabbis magnified Israel's election in order to magnify the grace of God. But for them the implications of God's electing grace were not to be sought in the domain of theology but concretely in the sphere of history. For them election was no mere concept but an incontrovertible fact: Israel was the living proof that God elects according to his grace. Israel must be preserved for a testimony of God's grace. Just because Israel is a special people he cannot mix with other nations, as oil cannot mix with water.[40] The physical survival of the Jewish people is to the rabbis a tenet of faith, for with it goes Israel's faithfulness to his trust. For Israel to disappear is as unthinkable as for God to suffer defeat. The rabbis do not think abstractly and in generalizations, but concretely in terms of life. To them Israel and Torah are the visible and physical expressions of God's revelation in history. The two are inseparable: without Torah, no Israel; without Israel, no Torah. In the connection between Israel and Torah lies the real meaning of election as the Synagogue understands it.

Traditionally, the Synagogue has always connected *mattan torah* (the giving of the Law) with Israel's election. Schoeps has shown how the experience at Sinai stands in the centre of Israel's vocation: by the giving of the Law original sin was washed away and a new people came into existence.[41] Commitment to the Law makes the difference between Israel and the nations: the Torah is Israel's distinctive mark. Thanks to the Torah, Israel has a special aptitude for God. This aptitude is transmitted by heredity and is almost a physical trait. Judah Halevi calls it the "prophetic" quality of the soul peculiar to the physical descendants of Abraham.[42] Proselytes may attain to the high status of sages and saints,[43] yet they lack this special gift, which is peculiar to the physical members of the Jewish people. We can now understand Ziegler's contention that a Jew is constitutionally a monotheist.[44]

Israel's special position puts him under special obligation: the keeping of the Torah is his peculiar duty. The nations are under no such obligation. A proselyte chooses to keep the Torah, a Jew has no choice. The Gentile need keep only the basic laws of morality[45] to comply with God's will. For this reason is a full proselyte called *ger ẓedeḳ*—proselyte of righteousness—because he does more than is required of him.

Here, then, is the real distinction between Israel and the nations. What divides Israel from the rest of humanity is not entirely physical, and is not entirely spiritual, but a combination of both. The physical and the spiritual are never separate entities in the Jewish view. They form an inseparable whole to make up the facts of history. Just because Israel's election is an historical fact, it must imply concrete physical existence.

Only against this background is it possible to appreciate the revolutionary implications of St Paul's pronouncement that in Christ Jesus there is *no* difference between Greek and Jew. The Synagogue cannot accept such a view without surrendering her position and annulling the Covenant. She therefore asks with concern and urgency: By whose authority is the difference removed?

This question the Church has answered in a number of ways. The traditional answer is: God has abandoned the old Israel, Israel according to the flesh, because of his rejection of the Messiah, and has substituted the *new* Israel, the Israel according to the Spirit, which is the Christian Church. In the new Israel there is no difference between Jew and Gentile, the "new" society consists of believers of all nations. For the principle of race, the principle of faith has been substituted. Unbelieving Israel is therefore not Israel any more.

This is the argument which runs through the whole history of Christian apologetics towards Judaism, from the time of the Epistle of Barnabas to this present day.[46] But this is not the only answer. There was always in the Church another school of thought, though it represents a minority view. In contemporary theology this other view has been formulated with fresh insight by Karl Barth in his *Dogmatik*.[47]

As is only right, Barth makes Rom. 9–11 the starting-point of his reconsideration regarding Israel's position in relation to the Church. To him both Church and Synagogue are Israel; it is the same congregation; but an inner dichotomy has taken place within it. Israel is therefore the people of Israel in all its historic extension both *ante* and *post Christum natum*, plus the Church which consists of Jews and Gentiles.[48] In this double existence of the People of God, Barth sees profound theological significance. We shall return to this subject at a later stage.[49] Here we can register only the important point: the Church is pressed for an answer regarding Israel. In her effort to answer the question she is forced to reconsider her origin and her destiny.

In this act of question and answer both Church and Synagogue find themselves under a question-mark. Israel is questioning Israel: Which is Israel, which is the People of God?

(*d*) *The Question regarding the Law*

In the dialogue between Church and Synagogue the question regarding the Law is a major issue. The centre of the controversy is not in respect to Torah in the wide rabbinical sense, but in relation to the Law of the Pentateuch. For it is the Pentateuch which stands in the centre of the Jewish concept of revelation. Here the question is not any more about the right exegesis but about the Law as such. To the Synagogue the *torat Mosheh* is immutable, unalterable, and permanent. There can never come a time when the Law will cease to be binding. There is no authority which can supersede the authority of the Law, for the Law is the Law of God.

The Synagogue has expressed the permanency of the Law in the following words:

> There hath never yet arisen in Israel a prophet like unto Moses, one who hath beheld his [i.e. God's] similitude. The Law of truth God gave unto his people by the hand of his prophet who was faithful in his house. God will never alter nor change his Law (*dato*) to everlasting for any other.[50]

Maimonides makes a similar statement in the ninth article of his Creed:

> I believe with perfect faith that this Law [i.e. the Law of Moses] will not be changed, and that there will never be any other law from the Creator, blessed be his Name.[51]

Modern exponents of Judaism combine the concept of immutability of the Law with that of progress. They hold that the changelessness of the Torah does not preclude development and growth.[52] But this makes sense only because in the Jewish view Torah comprises not only *torat Mosheh*, but rabbinic interpretation as well. Though the Torah itself is changeless, the interpretation grows and develops according to the needs of the hour.

We come here upon a fundamental difference of outlook between Church and Synagogue. To the Synagogue revelation is deposited in a Code, to the Church it is embodied in a Person. In the centre of the Synagogue is the Law, in the centre of the Church is Jesus Christ. But Jews ask with legitimate concern: If the Church regards the O.T. as part of the Canon, by what authority has she annulled the Mosaic Code?[53] This is a question which specially concerns Hebrew Christians, for Judaism has seldom held that Gentiles are under obligation to keep the Law.

The case with Jews is different. There is evidence in the N.T. that the early Jewish Church remained faithful to the Law and that Paul himself, though he fought for the freedom of the Gentiles, submitted to the Law.

The question regarding the Law cannot be answered lightly. The traditional Christian answer seems to us inadequate and based upon wrong premises.

To begin with, a distinction must be made between the moral and the amoral parts of the Law. About the moral side of the Law there can be no question. To the principles of morality both Church and Synagogue are equally pledged. Love of God and love of neighbour are to both the sum total of the Law and the Prophets.[54]

The case with the other Laws is different. These are Laws which relate to Levitical purity; to the Sacrifices; to ceremonial observances of one kind or another. Some of the Church Fathers were inclined to regard these Laws as signs of God's disfavour in order to punish the Jews for their obduracy and sinfulness.[55] Others tried to interpret them in an allegorical sense, so that they could be used typologically, prefiguring the Christian Gospel.[56] But both these methods are evasive. Luther's treatment of the Law as *coercere impios* does not answer our question, for the simple reason that the Law for him has mainly a moral connotation.[57] What concerns us here is not the moral or social aspect of the Law, but the Law in its totality as God's revelation to man.

The Synagogue's logic is here incontrovertible: the Covenant at Sinai was meant to be an everlasting Covenant, and the Torah was the basis and pledge of that Covenant—God cannot go back upon his word. It is a fundamental principle with Judaism that the Torah is Israel's inalienable gift from God—anyone who maintains that the Torah is not from heaven, shall have no share in the world to come.[58]

Historically, the attitude of the Synagogue to the Torah has undergone a considerable change as a result of her controversy with the Church. An older Jewish tradition counted with the possibility of a new Torah inaugurated by the Messiah[59]. It is admitted on the Jewish side that it is within God's power to change the Torah, but this is only an hypothetical possibility.[60] Rabbinic consensus is to the effect that the Torah shall not pass away, though the Prophets and the Hagiographa will—save Esther![61] It is felt, therefore, that had Jesus been a true prophet he would not have acted against the Torah, but would have enforced it.

What, then, is the Christian answer?

1. The most authoritative answer comes from Jesus himself. Whatever may be the interpretation of passages like Matt. 5. 18 and Luke 16. 17, there can be little doubt that for Jesus the Law had divine authority—it was God's Law. The purpose of his coming was to bring about the fulfilment of the Law. His quarrel was never with the Law but with the "lawyers". To no part of the Law—"neither to the statutory elements in it nor to the elements of promise, neither to its morality, nor to its hopes—was Jesus in any sense hostile".[62] Having said this, it must, however, be added that Jesus aims at a reinterpretation of the Law; he sees the Mosaic Law in a different light. This is exemplified by his attitude to the Sabbath, but specially by his attitude to divorce: "Moses for your hardness of heart suffered you to put away your wives: but from the beginning it hath not been so" (Matt. 19. 8).[63] We come here upon the problem of authority which characterizes Jesus' demeanour and which is the main source of offence to his opponents.[64] He knows of "the weightier matters of the Law" and takes it upon himself to make the distinctions. Jesus acts here in the prophetic tradition, for his attitude to the Law is similar to the Prophets' attitude to the Sacrifices. But he goes beyond the prophetic position by his Ἐγὼ δὲ λέγω ὑμῖν. "The Son of man[65] is lord of the sabbath" (Matt. 12. 8) can be extended to all his other sayings. This peculiar authority which Jesus assumes becomes most evident in his act of forgiving sins (Matt. 9. 6). In some cases he amends the Law, as in the question of *lex talionis*—the standards of the Kingdom of God exceed the standards of Mosaic legislation in respect to equity. But we should grossly misunderstand the situation if we looked upon Jesus as a reformer of the Law. He knew himself not as a reformer but as fulfiller: πληρῶσαι (Matt. 5. 17) is the key to the puzzle.

Klausner and other Jewish scholars interpret the meaning of πληρῶσαι to the effect that Jesus wanted to remain a Law-abiding Jew even to the extent of keeping the ceremonial part of the Law.[66] Against this Christian scholars hold that the word must be understood in the sense of πληρωθῇ, i.e. that Jesus came to fulfil the deeper intention of the Law.[67] There is, however, a suggestion made by Edersheim which seems to be more in keeping with other passages dealing with the same subject. Edersheim suggests that ἵνα πληρωθῇ should be read "till all be fulfilled".[68] In this case πληρῶσαι would be in reference to the appearance of the Messiah and to his destiny: the coming of the Messiah marks a new era; he introduces the Kingdom of God. The Mosaic Law was given with a view to this great event: the Law and the Prophets were until John, from that time the Kingdom of heaven is preached (Luke 16. 16; cf. Matt. 11. 12 f.). This is the sense in which Jesus came to "fulfil" the Law. Montefiore's rather arbitrary view that Jesus could not have reached a higher concept of "fulfilling the Law" is without foundation.[69] The idea that Paul is to be credited with the revolutionary concept is not borne out by the evidence, unless the Gospels mispresent the case. Paul's attitude to the Law stems from the conviction that the Messianic Era has broken in upon the world: the Messiah has come.

2. We thus come to the Apostle Paul. Here a straightforward statement is even more difficult. St Paul does not seem to proceed after a clearly defined pattern; he rather depends upon circumstances. He therefore copes with the problem of the Law in a variety of ways according to the need of the hour. This may give the impression of opportunism, of which Klausner[70] accuses the Apostle. But Klausner's view rests on the assumption that Paul is an innovator; that he was the first to introduce antinomianism into the Church.[71] If our description of the Master's attitude to the Law is justified, then Klausner's view is mistaken. For in that case Paul draws the last consequences only from the fact that Jesus *is* the Messiah, that the New Era was begun, that the Kingdom of God is at hand. It is reasonable to assume that there was already a tradition regarding the Law when Paul joined the Church, and that the tradition originated from Jesus himself.[72] We should have to remove a number of passages from the Gospels if we wanted to obliterate this fact. Yet Paul's contribution to the question of the Law was of great importance to the future of the Church. In this question not only the status of the Gentiles was involved, but the very meaning of the Gospel itself. If man was still dependent upon the Law for his salvation, then Christ died in vain. This either-or formulation is Paul's personal contribution to the solution of a vexed problem. The premise with which the Apostle operates is: Christ died for sinners—from henceforth therefore man is justified not by the keeping of the Law but by the blood of Christ. This basic principle extends to Jews and Greeks alike; in this respect there is no "difference" whatsoever. All have sinned and fallen

short of the glory of God (Rom. 3. 23; 5. 12), this the Law could not prevent. But Christ by his death has blotted out the bond written in ordinances that were against us . . . he has taken it out of the way, nailing it to the Cross (Col. 2. 14). The Messiah, by submitting to the Law, has become a "curse of the Law" in order that we should be free (Gal. 3. 13; 4. 4 f.; 2 Cor. 5. 21; Rom. 8. 3). From henceforth, the believer, be he Jew or Gentile, is not any more under the Law but under grace. This is the Apostle's main contention.

In this attitude there is nothing derogatory to the Law. St Paul would have been the first to admit the divine origin of the Law. He tells us himself: The law is holy, and the commandment holy, and righteous and good (Rom. 7. 12). But the function of the Law is negative; it reveals sin, but does not prevent it. Just because the Law is righteous and good it serves only to emphasize man's inability to comply with it. Man under the Law is under sentence of death, which only God can annul.[73] But God does not only annul the sentence of death, he justifies the guilty; but he does it through Christ—this is the Gospel according to St Paul. In Jesus Christ, the Law has therefore come to an end: Christ is the "end" of the Law (Rom. 10. 4), for he is its *telos*. The Messiah brings the Law to a positive conclusion; it "ends" in him because it is fulfilled in him, because its original purpose is accomplished in him.

We are in agreement with Lightfoot and Denney that παιδαγωγὸς εἰς Χριστόν does not mean that the Law acts as a tutor towards Christ, but rather that the Law is a tutor "until Christ came".[74] From henceforth it is faith—faith in the Messiah which justifies sinners, though before the Law they stand condemned.

Man is still under the Law, both Jew and Greek: the Jew under the Law of Moses, the Greek under the law of his own conscience. Both, therefore, Jew and Greek, are under condemnation. But if they accept God's "unspeakable gift" in Jesus Christ, they step out from under the Law into the realm of Grace. It is thus evident that to St Paul the Law is not a theological bugbear which he produces in order to frighten his audience, but a fact inherent to the human situation. Man is always under the Law, unless he is under Grace through faith in Jesus Christ. Under whatever aspect one may look upon the Law—Mosaic Law, the law of conscience, the law of sin—man stands guilty and can only plead for grace. Grace is offered by a merciful God in Jesus Christ: he is God's answer to man's deepest need. He is therefore God's answer to the condemnation of the Law. The Law accuses, but God justifies; in the Messiah the Law has therefore come to an end.

3. We must briefly refer to yet one more writer in the N.T. who deals with the problem of the Law, namely "Hebrews". J. Denney tries to work out the difference between the attitude of Hebrews and that of St Paul on this subject.[75] But it seems to us impossible to arrive at any conclusions from the few references which occur in Hebrews. The fact is that the subject does not require of the writer a detailed discussion of the Law. But on the main question both St Paul and Hebrews are agreed: since the Messiah has come—the new High Priest after the order of Melchizedek—a change has taken place. Priesthood and Law belong together: for, the priesthood being changed, καὶ νόμου μετάθεσις γίνεται (Hebr. 7. 12). This change is in accordance with God's original purpose as announced by the Prophet and is thus to be understood as the τελείωσις of God's promise (cf. Hebr. 7. 11, 28). Here we have exactly the same attitude as that of St Paul. The writer of Hebrews, like St Paul, knows of the insufficiency of the Law οὐδὲν γὰρ ἐτελείωσεν ὁ νόμος (Hebr. 7. 19); "What the Law could not do . . . God sending his own Son . . . that the ordinance of the Law might be fulfilled in us" (Rom. 8. 3 ff.). Although they use different language they both mean the same thing: for Hebrews the effect of Christ's death is ἁγιάζειν, for St Paul it is δικαιοῦν. But for both, the death of Christ is the beginning of the New Era and the fulfilment of man's highest hopes.[76]

4. When we come to the Church Fathers the atmosphere is different. Whereas in the N.T. there is reverence for the Law, although it is only a shadow of good things to come (Hebr. 10. 1), with later Christian writers there is noticeable a certain hostility to the Law. This is specially apparent in the Epistle of Barnabas. Here Christ is not the fulfiller of the Law but its abolisher: He has therefore abolished these things [i.e. the Jewish sacrifices], that the new law of our Lord Jesus Christ, which is without the yoke of necessity, might not have a man-made oblation.

In Barnabas we also meet the curious suggestion that the true Law was never received by the Jews but only a counterfeit, for the original Law which was intended for the Jews was broken by Moses. Irenaeus seems to go one step further when he suggests that the Law was given to the Jews in punishment for their obduracy in desiring to continue as slaves in Egypt.[77] Irenaeus distinguishes between the "laws of bondage" and the Decalogue, the latter being the only binding part of the Law for Christians.[78] Irenaeus justifies this by the discovery that there is a double law—one for slaves and one for the free.[79] The advancement from slavery to freedom he understands in a progressive sense, so that the lower Covenant gives place to a more perfect way of salvation. Here we have the embryo of the concept of progressive revelation. This concept of progressiveness is a new element in the interpretation of the connection between O.T. and N.T. It superimposes a foreign pattern into the story of revelation. Whereas for St Paul "the fulness of time" (Gal. 4. 4) in which Jesus came, is God's time, for all times are in God's hand (cf. Ps. 31. 15),[80] according to the concept of progressiveness it is man's time, who is on the march from a lower to a higher level of knowledge. Here man does not receive the Kingdom of God, he advances towards it.

Thus the Church seems to have several answers to the question regarding the Law. They can be summarized under two headings: 1. The Law was given to the Jews for their discipline. 2. The Law has been superseded by the Gospel, which according to Barnabas is the true Law reserved for the believers in Jesus Christ. Both answers already occur in Justin's *Dialogue* with Trypho.

Justin explains to his Jewish opponent that the Law was given to the Jews because of the hardness of their heart. Here we see an interesting development from the N.T. Whereas Jesus makes the same statement in respect of one law, Justin already puts the whole Mosaic code in the same category. To him Jesus is the *new* Lawgiver who gave a *new* Torah under a *new* Covenant to Christian believers. "New" here is new *ab initio*; a break with the past and a new beginning. This is a different "end" from the Pauline *telos*. Here there is a breach in the story of revelation. The new Lawgiver is dissociated from the old Law; he starts a new chapter in God's dealing with mankind. This is the argument that Cyprian follows with great consistency: the old Covenant is made void, the Law of Moses has ceased, the new Law is given, a new Covenant has been initiated.[81] Cyprian proceeds to use O.T. texts to prove his point. He argues that the Jews are unable to understand their own Scriptures because, as St Paul says, a veil is upon their hearts.

Origen draws the consequences of the Christian's better understanding by working out an elaborate system of allegory. He is quite convinced that the Scriptures while saying one thing mean another.[82] His tortuous twistings of meaning, his gross violations of the original intention of the biblical text,[83] made it possible for him to maintain a superficial unity of the Canon. In fact, he asserts that "there is no discrepancy between the God of the Gospel and the God of the Law",[84] but only after an artificial harmony has been introduced by his "right" interpretation. This system of allegorizing the O.T. goes back to an older tradition, and it has been suggested that Origen must have learned it from his master, Clement of Alexandria.[85] But this allegorical, esoteric method of playing with the text could hardly be taken seriously—Origen explains that the laws, as they are, are not good, but when interpreted spiritually, they are good[86]—and carried no conviction with the Jews. The fact is that while Paul had an answer to the Jewish question regarding the Law, the Church Fathers had no answer. All they did was to oppose the "old" Law by the "new" Law, thus turning the Gospel into "Law". Origen plainly speaks of "the difference between the constitution which was given to the Jews of old by Moses and the one which the Christians, under the direction of Christ's teaching",[87] seek to establish. In this way the Gospel became an "institution", a system, a set of doctrines, replacing the set of doctrines contained in the Pentateuch. Whereas St Paul puts against the Law the Gospel of Grace, the Church Fathers opposed the Law by another Law, the "Law" of Christ. The *kerygma* of the risen Christ is here transformed into an impersonal set of doctrines *about* Jesus. The Law which was replaced by grace is here Law again.[88]

(*e*) *The Question regarding the Messianic Age*

We have already seen that inherent in the attitude of the Synagogue is the messianic hope.[89] That hope has entered the Jewish outlook and has found manifold expression in legend and folklore. "The days of the Messiah" is a recurring theme in Jewish literature. In rabbinic writings it occupies a place of prominence and expresses the deep yearning of the Jewish soul. One glance at the Index of Strack and Billerbeck's *Commentary* is enough to reveal the importance of the subject to the ancient Synagogue.[90]

Here "the days of the Messiah" are frequently referred to as *he'atid lavo*—"the future to come"—and that future was anticipated as a time of return to Paradise. In those days Israel will be vindicated, the Land of Israel redeemed, the Scattered Nation gathered in, Jerusalem rebuilt, and the Temple restored to former glory. In this picture the prophetic vision plays an important part: the land is abundantly fruitful, the evil desire is vanquished, the Holy Spirit is poured out upon man, Israel becomes the nation of prophets and priests to the rest of humanity, all wars cease and there is everlasting peace and joy upon earth. Even nature takes part in the common bliss and women bring forth without pain.

This is the theme which runs through religious and even secular literature, and has been the subject of poets and mystics for centuries. The cry of the young lad Joselle as told by Martin Buber is but an echo of the Jewish cry of hope through the centuries: "Now, but now, the Messiah will come!"[91]

While the mass of the people was kept in suspense, waiting for Messiah's coming, mystics and visionaries were busying themselves with "calculating the end", as did Reb Yosi in Moses Smilanski's moving story.[92] The amazing and varied story of "false" Messiahs in Jewish history is enough evidence of the deep-seated longing for redemption. The question which the Synagogue poses is simple enough: How are Israel's messianic hopes fulfilled in Jesus of Nazareth?

In the controversy between Church and Synagogue this has always been a recurring theme. Rabbi Isaac of Troki has carefully enumerated the unfulfilled hopes as measured by the Jewish messianic vision, under the following eight headings: 1. In the days of King Messiah, he will be the only king, all other kings and kingdoms will cease. 2. In those days there will be one faith and one religion. 3. At that time all idols, false prophets, and unclean spirits will be destroyed. 4. All sin and trespasses will disappear, specially in Israel. 5. After the war of Gog and Magog, universal peace will reign and all weapons of war will disappear. 6. In those days the wild animals will live at peace with the tame ones in the land of Israel. 7. All suffering and sorrow will cease in the land of Israel, and its people will live long and happy lives. 8. In those days God will turn again to his people as in the days of old, and the Jews will abound in the wisdom and knowledge of God.[93]

R. Isaac's messianic idyll is typically Jewish, with Israel and the land of Israel in the centre. Even the truce among the animals is limited to the Holy Land. But R. Isaac is not content to ask the Church for the signs of messianic fulfilment, he also asks for additional evidence on a number of points before he can accept the Messiahship of Jesus. The text-book for his messianic vision is the

O.T., to which he makes copious reference. Canon Lukyn Williams has bravely tried to argue the points raised by the learned Rabbi so many years ago (died 1594) in his *Manual of Christian Evidences for Jewish People.* His answer is to the effect: 1. Some of the O.T. promises have been fulfilled; 2. The as yet unfulfilled promises are gradually being fulfilled in the course of history.[94] But this is really an evasion of the issue, for Christians claim that the Messiah has come and that Jesus was the Messiah.

The Church cannot but be honest on this important question; we do not live in a saved world. On the contrary, this is a world lost in death and sin. Though Jesus has died for the sins of the world, though the Gospel has been preached for nearly twenty centuries, though millions of believers have claimed to have been "saved", the world is where she was in the year A.D. 30. The prophetic vision is still a pious hope and belongs to the future. Not to admit this would be shutting our eyes to an obvious fact. If an answer is to be given it must be sought on different lines.

i. *Magic and Moral Values.* We have reached here the vexed problem of evil. The Jewish question about the completion of salvation implies the removal of evil automatically by the wave of a magic wand. Of course, God can remove evil in this mechanistic way, but he never does. There is an apposite remark by Maimonides which shows his great insight:

> Although in every one of the signs [related in Scripture] the natural property of some individual being is changed, the nature of man is never changed by God by way of miracle. It is in accordance with this important principle that God said: "O that there were such a heart in them that they would fear me" (Deut. 5. 29). . . . I do not say this because I believe that it is difficult for God to change the nature of every individual person; on the contrary, it is possible, and it is in his power, according to the principles taught in Scripture; but it has never been his will to do it, and never will be. If it were part of his will to change (at his desire) the nature of any person, the mission of prophet and the giving of the Law would have been altogether superfluous.[95]

The above statement is both logical and true to fact. God does not enforce his will, he leaves man to choose. If it were otherwise, moral values would have lost all meaning. This immediately raises the question of the Johannine concept of conversion: To what extent does being "born of the Spirit" mean a miracle performed without man's participation? It seems to us that palingenesis would lose all moral significance if there were no decision to make on the part of man. Man cannot save himself, but he can submit by ceasing to resist salvation. *Metanoia* is a moral miracle, but not a magical or mechanical experience. God gives his Holy Spirit, but only to those who ask for him (Luke 11. 13). The dialectic between freedom of will and grace cannot be dissolved this side of history. No one has seen it more clearly than Augustine: "Faith, good works, grace, come from God only—but he only gives them to those who want to receive them."[96] The paradox in the human position is undeniable; but it may be only a paradox within the limitation of human logic, and not within the sphere of spiritual values. In the domain of the Spirit other rules obtain. It was with a view to the higher order of things that Augustine uttered the memorable sentence: "God produces in man much that is good and what man himself cannot produce; no good, however, is produced by man which is not produced by God, so that man should produce it."[97]

In this contradictory position man remains: God chooses for him and it is he who chooses that God should choose. St Paul puts it the other way round, though it amounts to the same thing: "Work out your own salvation with fear and trembling; for it is God which worketh in you both to will and to do" (Phil. 2. 12 f.). Though man is meant to live by grace, he is not spared the moral effort. Any other solution to the human problem contradicts God's way with man as exemplified in the Bible. God does not save the world by the waving of a wand, but by giving his Son to die upon a Cross. The Kingdom of God is never man's achievement, but God's gracious gift; and yet man cannot cause his second birth, only by an act of God can he be born again.

This brings us to the second point.

ii. *History implies Suspense.* The Jewish question regarding the messianic age is legitimately asked. It is a question which concerns man vitally. But the validity of the question must in no way obscure the other fact, namely, that it is asked in the context of history. But all history means suspense. By the very fact that history *continues,* it cannot be complete. History would have no meaning if it were not relative. While the story of man's sojourn here upon earth is still unfolding, every demand for the final result is senseless. History knows of no absolutes; all man can do is to believe that "God is working his purpose out, as year succeeds to year". All over history is invisibly written "Not yet".

This the Apostle Paul recognized with great clarity when he spoke of the groaning and travailing of creation together with those who are "the firstfruits of the Spirit" while waiting in suspense for final and ultimate redemption (cf. Rom. 8. 22–4). There is a passage in Oscar Cullmann's book, *Christ and Time*, which deserves attention. It relates to the present as redemptive history with a view to the End of the end of history, or what he calls the "Christ-event":

> It is already the time of the end, and yet is not *the* end. This tension finds expression in the theology of Primitive Christianity. The present period of the Church is the time between the decisive battle, which has already occurred, and the "Victory Day". To anyone who does not take clear account of this tension, the entire New Testament is a book with seven seals, for this tension is the silent presupposition that lies behind all that it says. This is the only dialectic and the only dualism that is found in the New Testament. It is not the dialectic between this world and the Beyond; moreover, it is not that between time and eternity, it is rather *the dialectic of present and future*.[98]

It means that the Christian message spoken into history inevitably suffers from the strain of the ambiguity between "already" and "not yet". It is as much the task of the Gospel to open man for the future, as it is to bring him the assurance of forgiveness here and now. Christian preaching must therefore always have an eschatological bias: man is to live in suspense, waiting for God's last and ultimate Word. But while history still lasts, man is given the opportunity to turn and repent. History is therefore under a double sign: the sign of grace and the sign of judgement.

All this is implied in the concept of purpose in history. Because history has a goal it is in motion; it is moving towards its end. There is therefore an urgency in the N.T. which the Church must never lose: "The night is far spent, the day is at hand". The Christian motto is ἐξαγοραζόμενοι τὸν καιρόν, for the time is short!

There is yet one more point which must engage our attention. It concerns the question of personal and collective salvation. Within the confines of history the life of the individual and the life of the mass can never be fused if moral values are to mean anything at all. Here lies the difference between political and spiritual redemption. Spiritual redemption cannot be organized, legislated, or conferred. It is a strictly personal experience. We shall always be grateful to Kierkegaard for defining the individual as "the Christian category".[99] Indeed, "Christianity" begins and ends with every individual; in this respect it is utterly different from Judaism.[100] The Jewish question regarding the signs of the messianic age presupposes the possibility of collective salvation within history. Such "salvation" within history can be experienced only as institutionalized and legally ensured salvation, but as such it is a contradiction in terms. Whenever the Church offered such salvation, she fell from grace and prostituted her message. Unless the Church is a waiting Church, she is not the Church at all.

iii. *The Eschatological Answer.* On a superficial view it would appear that both Church and Synagogue share a common hope. But this is an illusion which arises from the fact that they speak the same language and derive from the same source. In fact, the Synagogue's eschatology is different from that of the Church on important points. Whereas the Synagogue's messianic hope is inseparably linked to history, the Christian hope exceeds history and goes beyond it. But there is also a difference about the Messiah himself. First, to Judaism the person of the Messiah is not as important as the benefits which accompany his coming; second, the vision of the "messianic age" frequently takes precedence over the Messiah's person; third, the Messiah the Synagogue expects is *not* Jesus.[101] The Synagogue rejects the man who though preaching the Kingdom of God, and teaching his disciples to pray: "Thy Kingdom come", yet said: "My kingdom is not of this world." Israel's messianic vision is utterly this-worldly. To him the messianic age is the continuation of history and not its end. In other words, to the rabbis the messianic age is history improved, a revised edition of what is now. "Let no one imagine", says Maimonides, "that in the days of the Messiah anything in the course of the world will be altered, or that there will be something new in creation. But the world will continue as always."[102] This, of course, is not eschatology in the Christian sense. Here the relativity of history and the absolute of the End are so reconciled as to remove all tension and to release man from the feeling of suspense. In the Jewish view the messianic age is an improved world but not a new heaven and a new earth.

In the Christian view history and eschatology never fuse, but stand in tension. Time and the End of Time are two different dimensions opposed to one another. Time is the "battlefield" where decisions are made and destinies decided. *Eschaton* is the end of time, the day of judgement—when he will come to judge the quick and the dead; the time when the sheep will be divided from the goats. The "new earth and the new heavens" are not a new edition of the old, but new *ab initio*: "The old things are passed away; behold, they are become new" (2 Cor. 5. 17). This is significant; to St Paul the End has already begun. Those who are in Christ have already a foretaste of that newness which is as yet to come. They are in the process of being translated into the dimension of eternity here and now. They already belong to the New Age, the *'atid lavo.* Thus "time of redemption", i.e. our time, and the Time of Judgement, i.e. the End, are not unconnected, they already overlap.

Thus, to the Christian believer the margin between time and the *eschaton* is imperceptibly narrow; he stands at the brink of the End. He knows himself already a participant of God's Kingdom and rejoices in the knowledge of salvation, though the Kingdom is not yet and salvation is incomplete. This is part of the paradox of faith.

The Jew looks on in amazement, for he cannot understand. He knows—and who could know better than he?—that the world is not redeemed. He knows this from his personal experience of evil; he knows it from the history of his people; and he knows it from world-history. All he can see is a world groaning under the weight of evil and sin; he therefore asks, and asks aright: How is the world saved?[103]

The question of the Synagogue goes beyond her personal experience of evil. She questions not only her own salvation and that of the world, but also the salvation of the professing Christian. How is he saved? Has evil no dominion over him? Has he vanquished the limitations of space and time and the frailty of the flesh? Do sin and the devil have no power over him?

These are embarrassing questions, specially for the Christian pietist who specializes in circumventing stark reality. But they are also wholesome questions, for they remind the Church of her true position, her eschatological position at the brink of time, poised between Now and the End. The Christian answer can only be that salvation in time is always salvation under a question-mark; that history, even Church history, can point only beyond itself to its *telos*—the Kingdom of God; that here in time, even the Christian walks by faith and not by sight; that the true task of the Church is to point away from herself towards her Lord—the Perfect Man who is the first fruit of the New Humanity; that in him is inaugurated the New World Order—and yet salvation begins here and now!

It begins here and now, for Jesus Christ died for the sins of the world.

In this position of "already" and "not yet" the Church stands, looking to the Cross for her salvation and praying: "Thy Kingdom come . . ."

CHAPTER 4

LAW AS REVELATION

We have seen that in the discussion between Church and Synagogue the problem of the Law is a major issue. But we should miss the deeper meaning of the whole question if we limited the discussion merely to an analysis of the content of the Torah. To the Jew, the issue hangs not on *what* the Law says, but on him who says it. Here we touch upon the central problem of the Church, namely the problem of revelation. The dialogue between Church and Synagogue revolves round this question: Revelation as Law, or revelation as Gospel?

This need not be an either-or. Gospel and Law may be complementary, or valid in their own particular sphere of operation. There are both Jewish and Christian scholars who contend that God uses a multiplicity of ways to reveal himself and that Gospel and Law are not exclusive: to the Jews God revealed himself upon Sinai, to the Gentile world the same God revealed himself upon Golgotha.[1] This would have been acceptable had both Law and Gospel said the same thing, but this is not the case. There are *two* voices spoken into history—the one by Moses and the second by Jesus Christ: the first is heard by the Synagogue, the second is heard by the Church. Yet the Church holds that there is one Bible; that it is the same God who speaks on Sinai and on Golgotha; that the intention of the Law and the intention of the Gospel is ultimately the same; that God who addresses himself to Jews addresses himself to Gentiles also, for he is no respecter of persons; that if revelation is valid it cannot be different, it must be the same if it is the same God who speaks.

In order to preserve the unity of the Canon the concept of progressive revelation was invented. It means that God reveals himself by degrees in accordance with man's capacity to receive. As man develops, so revelation grows. There is only one difficulty: why should it stop with the N.T.?

Progressive revelation is not a modern invention. It is already implied in early Christian apologetics. Its origin goes back to the Greek and Latin Fathers.[2] A passage in Justin's Second Apology may perhaps be regarded as the first attempt in the theory of progressive revelation. Justin is at pains to explain that the teaching of Plato is not very different from that of Christ, though they are not similar. He thinks that the same can be said with regard to "others, stoics, poets, and historians"; and he explains: "For each man spoke well in proportion to the share he had of the 'spermatic word' . . ." That Word, he holds, is fully revealed in Jesus Christ who embraces all that was ever rightly said among all men. For all that the others have well said is only an "imitation imparted according to capacity", whereas in Christ we have the thing itself.[3] Von Harnack points out that the early apologists from Aristides to Minucius Felix all proceeded on the principle that Christianity is both philosophy and revelation at the same time.[4] Thus Clement of Alexandria regards philosophy as "a preparation, a paving of the way for him who is perfected in Christ".[5] Augustine takes Cyprian, Lactantius, Victorinus, Optatus, and Hilary as examples of the usefulness of Greek learning to the Christian cause. He points out that Moses himself "was learned in all the wisdom of the Egyptians".[6] The implication is therefore that all forms of knowledge are stages of revelation, and that in Jesus Christ revelation has reached its highest point. Beyond this point, none of the Church Fathers, nor any of the medieval teachers, could possibly go. But logically, there can be no reason why revelation should stop at the N.T. once the principle of progressive revelation is accepted.

The question of the Law is for Christian theology closely linked to the question of revelation, and it is to this question that we shall have to devote our attention.

Professor Herbert H. Gowen in his *History of Religion* uses the geometrical figure of two triangles with their apexes touching to convey the concept of revelation as he understands it. This is the explanation: history is represented by the point where the two apexes touch. The base of each triangle represents eternity. The apex of the upper triangle is the point in history of God's full revelation in Christ; the apex of the lower triangle represents the beginning of the process of diffusion in the world. The latter is a process "by which the ideal realized in the firstfruits is reproduced in the mass". Professor Gowan explains:

> By a succession of expansions and inclusions, the effects of divine revelation are seen broadening out towards that ultimate baseline which represents—in contact with eternity—the purpose of creation realized, as a new heaven and a new earth, that is a new universe.[7]

This all-inclusive picture illustrated by a geometrical diagram purports to embrace the whole range of religious life from the "first dawn of consciousness" to the highest form of religious achievement. On analysis it becomes obvious that behind the illustration is a double line of evolution: first, progress of achievement, and second, progress of "diffusion". These lines run parallel: man grows in his knowledge of God; and as he grows, he affects others, until, gradually but inevitably, humanity evolves into the Kingdom of God. This is the modern concept of progressive revelation, but its roots go far back in history. It is somehow connected with the historiosophical view that history is the "unfolding" of a divine plan; some support for it can be found in the Bible. Augustine's perspective of history underlying *De civitate Dei* is based upon such a concept of progress.[8] Here history works itself inexorably towards a climax, ultimately to come to a successful conclusion in the *civitas Dei*. But here is the subtle difference: for Augustine it is God the Father *qui verissime se indicare animis cognituris et voluit et potuit, hoc ad se ipsum indicandum genuit, quod est ipse qui genuit*—the reference is to the Word.[9] In this way Jesus Christ and he alone is the only enabling factor in the event of revelation. But in the modern view progress is inherent in history itself—man is bound to grow. The latter view suggests that revelation is not really an event, but the sum total of human experience. This shows how remarkably "modern" the ancients were, for Lactantius expresses a similar view when he says: "If there had been somebody who took the trouble to collect the truths as dispersed among individuals and sects, he would have arrived at the same views as Christians hold."[10]

The concept of progressive revelation carries an inner contradiction when applied to the Christian faith: on the one hand it is held that revelation is progressive and therefore unlimited—an "unfolding" of divine knowledge by different stages "because the whole could not be apprehended at once"[11]; on the other hand it is asserted that revelation reached its zenith in the person of Jesus Christ.[12] Professor Gowan tried to overcome the difficulty by limiting the progress to the process of diffusion, but his inclusiveness in the concept of revelation robs it of its special significance as an Event in the biblical sense. It becomes once again the summary of man's religious experience through the ages as is the case with Lactantius. But if revelation is merely the sum total of experience, then revelation is not really revelation.

Augustine said rightly, that the Scriptures have a twofold function: *quomodo cum hominibus agant et ipsi deo serviant*; but *quomodo autem agant cum pecoribus suis, ipsi sciunt*[13]—what man can learn from experience requires no revelation!

It is our contention that on no other point have Church and Synagogue compromised to such an extent as on the question of revelation. That it should happen to the Synagogue is understandable, for she is committed to a rationalist view; but for the Church this is nothing less than a betrayal of her position. We hold that the question regarding the Law cannot be answered without a prior clarification of what is meant by revelation in the biblical sense.

(*a*) *The Traditional Concept of Revelation*

"Revelation" is usually understood to mean disclosure of the unknown—*revelatio*. In the religious sphere it is taken to indicate a process whereby God discloses himself to man. This postulates a God who uses various means and divers manners to make his character and purpose known to man. Revelation as a concept is peculiar to most religious systems. Thus those who have the gift of receiving "revelation" become the mouthpice of the speaking God.[14] For primitive man the hall-mark of genuine "revelation" was its irrational element, but as man advanced, "revelation" became more rational until it took on a moral character. All higher religions are in search of a formula whereby reason and revelation can be wedded. In the case of the Church this led to a change in the terms of reference as to what is meant by revelation. Plato and Philo came to the assistance of the Christian Church. By means of the Greek *logos*—a comprehensive term covering every aspect of "truth"—the Gospel became enlarged to mean the embodiment of "truth". By this fusion of "truth" and Gospel the rational element of revelation was saved. Revelation and truth are now different aspects of the same thing. Revelation is the religious way of expressing what humanity already possesses by a natural process of reasoning, only that by revelation such knowledge becomes linked to the divine.[15] This is the leading principle in Western theology dominated by Thomas Aquinas: "What is recognized as a truly divine word must be found to correspond to, and crown, the best intimation of human reason. . . ."[16] This confusion with regard to our terms of reference has been carried forward into neo-Reformation theology by the writings of Emil Brunner, who tells us that "even the perception of the simplest mathematical truth is possible only through a ray from the light of God", for all ideas of truth and good are a feeble echo of the Word of God.[17] Here the difference between revelation and reason is only a question of degree, though Brunner constantly reiterates that to him revelation is not "truth" but "encounter".[18] Brunner's view is really a compromise between revelation as "truth" and revelation as "encounter", but it is the conceptual element which usually wins. This is the traditional approach, and Buber is an exception,[19] not only among Jewish scholars but among Christian thinkers[20] as well, apart from the "Barthian" school.

(*b*) *Immediacy*

Revelation as traditionally conceived implies direct contact between man and God. This is understood to mean a natural relationship between mind and Mind, the finite mind of man with the infinite Mind of God. Such a relationship is possible only on the hypothesis that it is an inherent faculty of the human mind to break through the limitations of time and space in an effort to reach beyond them. This is the basis of all metaphysics and mysticism. The mystic believes that in moments of ecstasy or contemplation he can attain to knowledge which reaches beyond the ordinary course of reasoning. Dean Inge describes it as the "super-human faculty", which the Greeks called νοῦς in distinction to διάνοια.[21] The theory of *intuitive* knowledge is at the root of it. It means that man by proper adjustment to the divine sphere can "*recall*" the things which he has already known all the time deep down within himself. Maritain, who from his particular Christian point of view feels obliged to deny "natural intuition" as Plato understands it, still admits of the possibility of a "natural contemplation of God", though a "unitive experience of the depths of God" would require the gift of grace.[22] He apparently means that an authentic mystical experience of God is not possible in the natural order. But he himself admits that this is only a question of "degrees of knowledge" from physico-mathematical science to the height of mystical experience.[23] It is axiomatic for Thomistic philosophy that a "possession giving experience of the absolute" (so Maritain) can be obtained by *direct* communion with God. The same is true of much of Protestant theology.

The philosophical foundations for immediacy derive from

Platonic and neo-Platonic sources. Since Kant, the base of Platonic philosophy has been broadened by the categories of pure and *a priori* reason. Here lies the link between the two systems.[24] Rudolf Otto has clearly shown to what extent the principle of immediacy dominates the philosophy of Jacob Friedrich Fries and the theology of his disciple De Wette.[25] The same principle underlies Schleiermacher's system and recurs under various names in most theological works. Thus Troeltsch's description of what he calls "*Phantasie*" appears to be but another word for intuitive knowledge. Troeltsch describes it as an inherent gift to express the ineffable and to discover the things which remain hidden to science.[26] Söderblom subscribes to the same view: "Ultimately", he tells us, "all certainty of God and divine matters has its source in an intuitive sense of God."[27] For him mysticism is therefore "a point of contact" conveying "a real perception of the being of God".[28] This "inner light", a kind of predisposition for the reception of "truth", forms the bridge between time and eternity, both in liberal and in orthodox theology alike. It is therefore natural that "revelation" should come to be another word for "intuition".

The principle of immediacy is basic for the Synagogue. Judaism rejects every form of mediation.[29] The link between God and Israel is already established by way of the Torah.[30] The Torah is for Israel the bridge to God. Thanks to the Torah it is possible for Israel to establish and maintain a *direct* relationship with God. For the Synagogue the Torah corresponds to the Christian doctrine of the Incarnation: even its physical appearance is divine. Not only every single letter, but even every part of a letter is holy. According to an old *baraita*, he is a despiser of the word of God and shall be utterly cut off (Num. 15. 31), who maintains that the Torah is not from heaven, or if he asserts that the whole Torah is from heaven, except one single verse; or if he admits that the whole Torah is from heaven except, one single point, or even a certain *gezerah shavah* (i.e. hermeneutic analogy from the text).[31] There is a tradition that when R. Ḥanina b. Teradion was being burned together with the Scrolls of the Law, the parchment was consumed by fire but the letters were soaring upwards towards heaven.[32] This is a poetic way of asserting the supernatural origin of the Law. There is a holiness attached to the Scroll which is of a Levitical character equal to the objects in the Temple.

Another form of immediacy finds expression in the traditional *bat ḳol* frequently met in rabbinic writings. The *bat ḳol* is a direct voice from heaven—an echo of the voice of God which is uttered to decide on a question of Torah.[33] The *bat ḳol* takes the place of the Holy Spirit in the Christian Church, but its operation is quite different. Whereas the Holy Spirit works inside man, the *bat ḳol* is an audible voice. Behind the *bat ḳol* is the idea of a direct relationship between God and man: God speaks, man hears. In fact, the *bat ḳol* is a substitute for the Holy Spirit. According to an old tradition: "It has been taught, after the later prophets Haggai, Zechariah, and Malachi had died, the Holy Spirit departed from Israel, but they still avail themselves of the *bat ḳol*."[34] The passage is of special interest, for it describes a departure from a tradition of mediacy to that of immediacy: in old times Israel heard God through the mouth of the prophets, now he is heard directly by the "echo".

It must be admitted that some rabbis vigorously opposed the idea of a *bat ḳol*. R. Joshua bluntly declares that he refuses to pay any attention to the *bat ḳol*, and R. Jeremiah asserts that since the Torah was given on Mount Sinai, the majority decides and not the *bat ḳol*.[35] But the opposition had quite another motive than to assert the principle of mediacy; it opposed only the suggestion that the Torah is insufficient to decide on important issues. In the principle of immediacy the Synagogue speaks unitedly: there is a direct relationship between Israel and God and that relationship is warranted by the Torah.

(*c*) *Revelation as postulated by the Canon*

Traditionally, theologians divide revelation into two kinds: *revelatio specialis*, i.e. "special" truth as found in the Bible, and *revelatio generalis*, i.e. general truths which relate to the wider aspects of human life. But the division is only artificial, for it is held that the one complements the other. The "general" truths also convey knowledge of God, only the source of the knowledge is different; it is derived from nature, history, philosophy, and science. In this way God adds to and enriches our "special" knowledge which is derived from the Bible. This is an inevitable conclusion as long as revelation is conceived in terms of "truth". There are plenty of valid "truths" outside the Canon which add to our knowledge and enrich our lives and which reflect the glory of God. Here Clement is perfectly right when he says: "We shall not err in alleging that all things necessary and profitable for life come to us from God. . . ."[36] No believer dare deny the statement, though it be but a platitude. To the same category belongs Luther's statement: *Ratio est pars divinae naturae.*[37] No one in his senses would deny Brunner's affirmation: "The Logos of reason comes from God"—if God is the Creator of man, he is also the Creator of his reason. There are many things both "necessary and profitable" not contained in the Bible which man can comprehend by means of reason. What we deny, and deny emphatically, is that reason by itself can lead man to a personal relationship with God. On this, Luther, Brunner, Witte, and Barth are all agreed. All reason can achieve is the conclusion as to the *quod est* of God, but it cannot and it must not pronounce as to the *quid est* of God. But we are forced to go further than this. It seems to us that the issue is not merely between *theologia naturalis* on the one hand, and *theologia revelata* on the other; and not even about separation, supplementation, or synthesis of the two. The issue is posed by the question whether God reveals "himself" at all in terms of "truth" either inside or outside the Canon.

Revelation in the biblical context is a strictly narrow concept. It is not just revelation of "mysteries" for the enrichment of life and the satisfaction of human curiosity. Nor is it an appendix to what we already know of God through the works of his hands or the testimony of our souls.[38] In the Bible, revelation is always *opus proprium Dei*—acts of God—and not general "truths" of a theological or any other nature. But there is more to it than this: in the Bible the theophanies are peculiarly restrained and veiled. Here God never reveals "himself" without hiding himself at the same time. A case in point is Ex. 33. 23: Moses is to be "covered" with God's hand and even then he can only see his "back". It is probably true to say that in the Bible revelation is never revelation of God's "Self" but of his condescension towards man. This is what the Bible "discloses" about God. In himself he remains for ever the hidden God, not even Christ "discloses" him.[39] Here Luther saw remarkably well when he said: "*Man lasse viel lieber Gott seine dectreta et mysteria* . . ."; man is not meant to fathom the Godhead: *quae supra nos nihil ad nos.* There is only one way to know God and that is in Jesus Christ.[40] But in Jesus Christ we "discover" God, not what he is in himself, in his incomprehensible majesty, but what he is towards us, in his forgiving and saving grace.[41]

What, then, is revelation in the biblical sense?

We suggest a threefold answer:

i. *Revelation as an Act of God.* The story of creation, the story of man, particularly the story of Israel, reveal God in action. The Bible speaks of the mighty deeds of God. These deeds are in the direction of man; they are not deeds to display God, but deeds which manifest his power, his judgement, and his grace. In the Bible there is a synonymity between the speech and acts of God: he speaks and "it is so"; his word is his deed. God never speaks hypothetically, philosophically, theoretically: his word is a concrete, definite Word of interference. In this sense he is the God of history: his eyes behold the nations (Ps. 66. 7, A.V.) and he makes peace and creates evil (Isa. 45. 7). There is nothing man can do to restrain Almighty God in his eternal purpose.

What applies to the O.T. applies to the N.T. Here too, God is known as the Only Potentate, the King of kings and the Lord of lords (1 Tim. 6. 15), who is a consuming fire (Hebr. 12. 29; cf. Deut. 4. 24; 9. 3), and it is a fearful thing to fall into the hands of the living God (Hebr. 10. 31; cf. Isa. 33. 14). It would appear, therefore, that in the N.T., too, God is primarily revealed in action: he always takes the initiative. It is not that man is seeking him, but it is God who seeks and finds man; not that we loved God, but that he loved us, and sent his Son to be the propitiation for our sins (1 John 4. 10; cf. Rom. 5. 8, 10). He is the Good Shepherd who in Jesus Christ is stretching out saving hands (cf. Ps. 23). It is therefore obvious that Jesus Christ did not come merely to give us good advice, or to teach us "truths", but to save sinners. In Christ Jesus we meet God in action. This is illustrated by his whole life from cradle to Cross. His "mighty works" performed at Chorazin and Bethsaida, in Jerusalem and in Capernaum, in Judaea and Galilee, were "signs", veiled hints of the Presence of God who enters actively into the domain of human life. It is of some significance that already very early in the N.T. tradition Jesus is given the title of Κύριος—Christian faith began with the recognition that in the person of the Master man meets God in action, saving man from death and the devil. The Hebrew Bible has retained the noun *El* for God in spite of its heathen associations: power, motion, activity[42]; for like no other noun it expresses the very essence of revelation—the Acting One. To the Hebrew mind, as Thorleif Boman has clearly shown, Being and Acting are concomitant. All creative activity is rooted in God, who remains for ever the enactor of history. In John 5. 17 we meet a sentence which expresses genuine Hebrew conviction: "My Father worketh even until now, and I work." That God sent his Son to save the world is *actus Dei* of the highest order. This is quite different from the Aristotelean concept of *actus purus*, which has so strongly coloured Thomistic theology[43]. According to the Bible, God is personally involved in the act of salvation[44]; this is his will—to save man. Jesus Christ came to enact the will of God.[45] In Christ we meet God in the act of saving sinners. But that it is the passive, the humble, Christ, submitting to the indignity of the Cross, who saves the world, is the paradox of revelation. This is the power of God, that even through the Cross he attains victory; this indicates the veiling of the power of God who triumphs in weakness (cf. 1 Cor. 1. 25) and who makes the weak strong and the strong weak (2 Cor. 12. 9 f.).

ii. *Revelation as Encounter.* The second form revelation takes in the Bible is that of encounter: God meets man. Presupposition is that God is a real *vis-à-vis*: he confronts man in judgement and in the offer of forgiveness. This is the essence of the prophetic announcement. Martin Buber's insistence that revelation means primarily encounter, though a radical departure from the Synagogue's view, is in its nature prophetic. The insistence on the part of Judaism that revelation is primarily Torah, teaching, Law, has entirely obscured the prophetic concept of revelation.

In the Bible, revelation is experienced existentially: man quickens to the awareness of God's presence. A typical example of such awareness is Ps. 139. The psalmist discovers that there is no escape from God: 'Whither shall I go from thy spirit? Or whither shall I flee from thy Presence?" Neither in the heavens above, nor in the sea underneath, nor in the uttermost parts of the earth is there a hiding-place from the omnipresent God.

A similar example is that of Moses as he finds himself confronted with the burning bush: veiled in the flames is the Holy God. Moses hears the voice, obeys the command, takes off his shoes, and bows to the ground (cf. Ex. 3. 2 ff.). Here we must also notice the *indirectness* of the encounter: first, the encounter is not with God but with "an angel of the Lord"; second, Moses does not see even the angel but only the burning bush; third, the encounter is by audition. The medium of the Word is the most characteristic instrument in the encounter between God and man. This is the special peculiarity of the Bible: the God whom man meets here is a speaking God. In this light must be seen not only the prophetic utterance, but also the pronouncement of the "Law". By the Torah God addresses himself to man. The purpose of the Torah is to establish a *relationship*: to encounter God is to obey him. The "statutes", the "judgements", the "commandments", have their validity in relation to their purpose, they are means whereby man approaches God. The importance of faith is here as strongly emphasized as in the N.T.: the man who practises the Torah must believe that they are *God's* means of meeting him; in other words that God will graciously condescend to meet him. Torah is therefore a means of grace; it is a sacrament.

The Bible is infused with the total *otherness* of God: between sinful man and God there is a gulf. Man can approach only *conditionally*. Underlying the "Law" are two principles: moral purity and Levitical holiness, and they go together.[46] They are the two inseparable guardians of the otherness of the Holy One of Israel. They are reminders that God is Holy and that he is hidden, wrapped in mystery. The encounter is not on an equal level so that man can meet God whenever *he* wills, but only when *God* wills. Encounter is therefore the Great Event, an act of grace. The classical example is Isaiah's experience in the Temple (Isa. 6). That it takes place at all can be explained only in terms of the Gospel: God's gracious condescension to man: "For thus saith the High and Lofty One who inhabiteth eternity, whose Name is Holy: I dwell in the high and holy place, with him also that is of a contrite and humble spirit" (Isa. 57. 15).

The equivalent to this remarkable passage is John 1. 14: *verbum caro factum est, et habitavit in nobis*. That the thrice-holy God deigns to be present with and among his people is the miracle of revelation in the biblical sense.

This real and effectual Presence of God is symbolized by the Temple and pervades the "Law" and the Prophets. In fact, it is part of the peculiar Hebrew consciousness and is epitomized by the phrase: *Yahveh-yireh*—"the LORD seeth".[47] The God of Israel is the One who sees the affliction of his people (Ex. 3. 7); who arises in the defence of the needy (Ps. 12. 5). It is for this reason that the national, social, and political history of Israel is part of the Canon. It is in the truest sense the story of revelation, the revelation of the Presence of God. For Israel's history takes place *mippeney Elohim*—in *front* of God.[48] It means that all the thoughts and deeds of man in relation to himself and others, all his strivings individually and corporately, the whole range of both his hidden and his revealed life, are lived "in the face of God". Human life can be lived only in the Presence of the One who sees all and knows all. An interesting illustration of the Hebrew awareness of God is Ps. 51: here David's sin is committed "before" the Lord, and "in his eyes", although it was committed secretly, for the Lord seeth not as man seeth, the Lord looketh on the heart (1 Sam. 16. 7). The Presence of God is the overwhelming reality in biblical revelation: "The eyes of the Lord thy God are always upon it [i.e. the land of Israel], from the beginning of the year even unto the end of the year" (Deut. 11. 12).

It is in this context that the call to *teshuvah* must be placed: *shuv*—turn back, turn round, to face God is the never-tiring challenge of the biblical message. *Teshuvah*—"conversion"—is the decision to face God and to accept the verdict. This is the only thing man can do: turn! This turning to face God is revelation: "Turn, O Israel, unto the Lord thy God . . . take with you words and turn unto the Lord: say unto him . . ." (Hos. 14. 1 f.).[49]

This encounter, this coming face to face with the Holy One of Israel, this hearing and responding in contrition and faith, is revelation in the biblical sense.

iii. *Revelation as Torah.* In the wider perspective of the Bible, revelation is not only Event, and Encounter, but it is also Torah. It will be helpful to remember the root of the word. Torah is derived from *yarah*—to shoot, to direct, to aim at. Torah therefore serves the double purpose: (*a*) it defines the aim or goal; (*b*) it serves as a means to reach the goal; it is the way to it.

The aim of Torah (*a*) is plainly stated in the Mosaic text. Israel's holiness, the Covenant, the experience at Sinai, all serve the one purpose, to establish a positive relationship between God and his People. In the centre of the Torah stands the word: "I will take you to me for a people and I will be to you a God" (Ex. 6. 7). This is the theme which is specially pronounced in the last book of the Pentateuch (Deut. 4. 20; 7. 6; 14. 2; 26. 18). In fact this is the main theme of the O.T.: "I will be their God and they shall be my people" (Jer. 31. 33; Hos. 2. 23; Zech. 8. 8; 13. 9).[50] Thus, the aim of the Torah is to make Israel God's people.

But (*b*) the Torah is also the instrument which God uses to achieve his end. The festivals, the ritual, the sacrifices, the institutions, judgements, ordinances, the symbols and taboos, they are all meant to serve one purpose only, to bring Israel nearer to God. These are, as it were, prerequisites of an encounter between Israel and God. Here "Israel" is a collective noun and therefore misapplied. There was never a situation (except the one at Sinai, when the whole of Israel faced God. In the usual course it was the individual Israelite, as he "practised" the Law, who exposed himself to the possibility of the Great Event. There was no guarantee of its happening—from the formality of religion there is no escape—but it *did* happen to many a humble worshipper, as in the case of Isaiah.

In this connection the sacrifices are of signal importance. Israel could not take God's Presence for granted. The "tabernacling" of God in the midst of his people was a frightening and disturbing factor. The holiness of God and the sins of his people could never be reconciled. God cannot overlook sin, and man cannot endure God's holiness. Propitiation was therefore an ever-present and pressing need. It was the priests' task to seek at-one-ment and to "cover" Israel's sin from the burning Presence of God's holiness. Without the assurance of God's gracious acceptance of the sacrifices and of his forgiving grace Israel could not exist.

The aim of the Torah is therefore exactly the same as the aim of the Gospel. The theme is the same and the means are the same: atonement by vicarious sacrifice. There is, however, this difference: whereas in the Temple sacrifice is a continual necessity, the Great Sacrifice of the Son of God is once and for all (cf. Hebr. 10. 11–14). In this way the purpose of the Law is "completed", "fulfilled", "ended" in the Messiah. This is the point made not only by the letter to the Hebrews, but by the whole N.T.

In the Synagogue the Torah has become detached from its original background and is treated as an end in itself. The idolizing of the Torah is a warning that not even the Synagogue is immune from idolatry.[51] It is remarkable how this fact has escaped both Jewish and Christian writers.[52]

In the dialogue between Church and Synagogue an answer to the question regarding the Law is inevitably linked with the other and more central question regarding revelation. If our threefold definition in terms of Event, Encounter, and Torah is acceptable, then we have cleared the way for a better understanding of Israel's position in history.

CHAPTER 5

THE JEWISH PEOPLE AND THE CHRISTIAN CHURCH

So far we have worked on the assumption that in the dialogue between Judaism and Christianity the juxtaposition is: Church—Synagogue. But from both a biblical and a theological point of view this is incorrect. Particularly from the point of view of the Church such a premise is inadmissible, for it implies a tacit acceptance of the rabbinic claim to stand in direct relationship to the O.T. This the Church must deny for the sake of her own position. In the Christian view the direct link with the O.T. is by way of the N.T. and not by way of the Synagogue. The connection with Abraham, the Father of all believers, is not physical, but by promise; this is St Paul's contention.[1] But the promise is not to the Synagogue but to Israel at large.

According to the biblical record, God's Covenant was with Israel. The Covenant-relationship to God included the whole of the Hebrew people. The rabbis have always held that the Covenant extended to all future generations as well, as if they had been present at Sinai.[2] The story of revelation is therefore inseparable from the people of God. In our view that story extends from the calling of Abraham to this present day. In this story, which stretches over several thousand years, the appearance of the Synagogue as we know it in post-Destruction times is only an interlude. There was a time when the Synagogue was not, and there will be a time when she will disappear. Her existence marks a certain period in the long story of historic Israel. The people of Israel exceeds the limitations of the Synagogue and transcends it.

But also theologically the *vis-à-vis* is wrongly stated if our argument is valid. We have tried to show that the Synagogue is not directly but only indirectly related to the O.T. But if the relationship is to be stated in physical terms, then again it is not the Synagogue but the Jewish people which is the opposite of the Church. There was a time when Israel and the Synagogue were only two different names describing the same people, but this is no longer the case. The Church's opposite is therefore Israel κατὰ σάρκα and not the Synagogue.[3] In this juxtaposition, Church and the Jewish People, lies the crux of the problem for Christian theology. For in this case, and in this case only, the discussion turns from an academical to an existential nature and becomes a question regarding election.

Opposite the Israel κατὰ σάρκα, i.e. historic Israel, stands the other Israel, Israel κατὰ πνεῦμα. The question therefore is: What is the connection between the two Israels? This is the problem which will occupy us now.

(*a*) *O.T. Promises*

During a considerable time of Jewish history the Synagogue included the majority if not the totality of the people.[4] The equation, therefore, Jews = Synagogue, was a natural one. But since the time of Jewish emancipation a process set in with the result that the Synagogue is now only a minority. To-day, Jews and Synagogue are no longer coterminous. This does not mean that the Jewish people is devoid of spiritual life, it means only that new avenues have been found which by-pass orthodox Judaism. The spiritual situation in Jewry is clarifying itself since the creation of the Jewish State[5]; what ultimate form religious life will take cannot be predicted, but we doubt whether orthodox Judaism will ever recover from the present crisis. But though the Jewish people can break away from the Synagogue, it cannot break away from the O.T. It remains for ever the manifesto and the *raison d'être* of Jewish existence. In this Book are contained the deeds of the Covenant between Israel and God. According to these deeds Israel κατὰ σάρκα is called *'am segullah* (cf. Ex. 19. 5)—a special people—with a special vocation and destiny of its own.

From the beginning to this day the Church stands before the mystery of historic Israel in awe and wonder. She has never reconciled herself to Israel's fall and she continues to pray for his return: "Fetch them home, blessed Lord. . . ."[6]

Although the idea of the "new" Israel has obscured her vision of historic Israel, the Church has never given up the *other* Israel. By clinging to historic Israel she clings to the promises of God. These promises the Church rediscovers each time she reads the O.T. It is true that she has often tried to spiritualize and re-apply these promises, but she has always done so with a bad conscience. She cannot and dare not circumvent the main fact: the faithfulness of God. Unless the Church knows God as a Covenant-keeping

God, i.e. the God of Israel, she does not know him at all. The faithfulness of God does not depend upon the fickleness of man; though man may become faithless, he never changes. And because the God of Israel is a God who never changes—the sons of Jacob are not consumed (Mal. 3. 6).

There are some promises in the O.T. which even Origen would find difficult to spiritualize. One of these is Jer. 31. 35 ff.:

> Thus saith the Lord which giveth the sun for a light by day and the ordinances of the moon and of the stars for a light by night. . . . If these ordinances depart from before me, saith the Lord, then the seed of Israel also shall cease from being a nation before me for ever.

The Prophet continues to assert that as it is impossible to measure the heavens above and to search out the foundations of the earth beneath, so it is impossible for God to cast off his people—in spite of Israel's misdeeds. It would be a gross misunderstanding of the case to explain the Prophet's attitude in terms of nationalistic prejudice. Jeremiah is in no way blind to his people's unworthiness, and does not hesitate to throw their sins in their teeth. The reason why he holds on to Israel is not because of an exaggerated conception of his people's importance, but because of his knowledge of God's faithfulness and sovereignty. That God is both faithful and sovereign is the deepest knowledge of the O.T. Because he is faithful he will not let Israel go (cf. Hosea); and because he is sovereign he will have his way with his people (cf. Deutero-Isaiah). It means that God has a purpose with his people and that there is no escape from his hand. A people's fall cannot alter its destiny, and human ingratitude cannot divert God's mercy:

> As I have sworn that the waters of Noah should no more go over the earth, so have I sworn that I would not be wroth with thee nor rebuke thee. For the mountains shall depart, and the hills be removed; but my kindness shall not depart from thee, neither shall my covenant of peace be removed, saith the Lord that hath mercy on thee (Isa. 54. 9 f.).

This is the kind of God we meet in the Bible.

There is an aspect of Jewish history which remarkably corroborates the faithfulness of God. No theologian can seriously write about this people without paying attention to the miracle of its survival. If we really believe that there is some purpose in history, then the fact of Jewish survival must be interpreted in consonance with that belief. Traditionally the Church is inclined to tear Jewish history into two parts, and to give positive meaning to the time *ante Christum natum* and negative meaning to the time *post Christum natum.* Thus Jewish survival is sometimes seen as an anachronism and more frequently as judgement. It is held that since the appearance of the "new" Israel, there is no *raison d'être* for historic Israel. For the medieval Church, the only reason for the survival of the Jews was to endure punishment for the Crucifixion. As deicides they were to serve as a lesson for the nations of the world of the frightful vengeance of God. This is the moral of the legend about the Wandering Jew.[7]

It is our conviction that Jewish history requires a more positive interpretation and that such an interpretation must be more closely linked to Holy Writ.

Jewish history is inseparable from the story of revelation. But though we hold strongly to the importance of the written Canon, it seems to us that in one particular instance Jewish history exceeds the Canon; it is, as it were, a continuation of biblical history with a view to the End. In other words, Jewish history has an eschatological bias, and because of this special feature it carries on where the Bible left off—pointing to the Messiah.

Such a view is possible only by a revision of the concept of revelation. Traditionally, revelation is interpreted to mean revelation of "truth". Such a definition implies *direct* speech on the part of God; consequently the Roman Church admits the possibility of "private revelations".[8] The Protestant position is less consistent: on the one hand it interprets revelation as "truth" and on the other hand it limits it to a definite period in history, namely biblical history.[9] But once a more biblical definition of revelation is accepted not with "truth" but with God in the centre, then Jewish history has still "revelational" significance *post Christum natum.* For in the story of the Jewish people, as in no other people's story, God *continues* to reveal one particular aspect of his character: his faithfulness. Written over the story of the Jews are the words: *semper fidelis*; not Israel's fidelity, but God's is here made visible. He keeps his promises: this is the lesson for the Gentiles. By revealing his faithfulness to Israel, he reveals it to the world; by dealing with Israel, he deals with the world; by acting on behalf of Israel, he acts on behalf of the world; for Israel and the world are never separate.

(b) Israel and the World

The Synagogue is in constant danger of forgetting her responsibility towards the world. But the world looms large in the biblical outlook. From the day of creation to the last page of the N.T. the "world" is included in the story of redemption. God's redeeming love goes out to the nations of the world—this is the message of the Bible. The part the world plays in the purpose of God is specially indicated in the calling of Abraham: "In thee shall all the families of the earth be blessed" (Gen. 12. 3).

In the case of the Prophets, God's concern with the nations is even more pronounced. The great Prophets of Israel have a message and a responsibility for the surrounding nations and for the world at large. The Psalmists never tire of singing of the God of Israel who is the God of all the nations. Isaiah looks to the day when there will be a highway out of Egypt to Assyria and both Egypt and Assyria shall worship the Holy One of Israel: "In that day shall Israel be the *third* with Egypt and with Assyria" and God will say: "Blessed be Egypt *my* people and Assyria the work of my hands, and Israel mine inheritance" (Isa. 19. 23 ff.). It must be noted that Israel is here the "third" and that Egypt, the very land of Israel's humiliation, becomes God's people.

The vision of the Gentile need of the God of Israel the Synagogue has never entirely lost. There is an interesting *midrash* to the effect that every word which went forth from God split up into seventy languages—the traditional number of the nations of the world.[10] In reference to Canticles 5. 13 the rabbis said: "With every single word that went forth from the mouth of the Holy One, blessed be he, the whole world was filled with spices [i.e. fragrance]." There is a moving passage in the Talmud in which the Gentiles are represented as asking God to give them another chance and they will obey the Torah—the implication being that in the days of the Messiah even the heathen will observe the Law of God.[11] The rabbis decreed that there was nothing permitted to an Israelite which was forbidden to a Gentile,[12] though there were many things which were an obligation to a Jew but not to a non-Jew. It means that the Jews carry a greater burden of responsibility without corresponding privileges; the God of Israel is also the God of the nations.

Concern for the Gentile world goes right through the biblical tradition. The book of Ruth, the story of Jonah, the episode of Naaman, the incident about the widow of Zareptha—they all point in the same direction. Even Moses' wife was an alien. The presence of the two non-Jewish women in the genealogy of Jesus is by no means fortuitous.[13] The N.T. is insistent that the Gentiles have a share in Israel's heritage. This is in alignment with the O.T. attitude.

We know from Josephus and Philo that a daily sacrifice was offered in Jerusalem on behalf of the Roman Emperor. This in itself is significant and remains so in spite of the uncertainty at whose expense this was done: according to Josephus the Jews paid, according to Philo the Emperor paid. It is quite likely that this said sacrifice has some connection with the rabbinic tradition that on the Feast of Tabernacles seventy oxen used to be offered for the nations of the world.[14] The sacrifice on behalf of the Emperor will have been justified, no doubt, in the eyes of Jewry, as Israel's duty towards the Gentile world.[15]

The rabbis have also discussed and defined the kind of sacrifices Gentiles are allowed to bring to the Temple in Jerusalem.[16] This goes to show that the nations are not entirely excluded from Israel's worship, though they are allowed only as far as the outer court, and like the Jewish women are excluded from the Holy Place. The "wall of partition" which warned the Gentile against trespass will have been dictated by fear of defilement rather than mere exclusiveness.[17]

The legend connected with the Septuagint and also the name are still wrapped in mystery. Scholars have suggested that the number seventy is connected with the seventy elders in Ex. 24. 1, 9; or else with the number of members in the Sanhedrin, or other such bodies.[18] But this is complicated by the fact that Aristeas raises the number of translators to seventy-two.[19] Paul E. Kahle, the greatest living expert on the Septuagint, does not seem to offer a satisfactory explanation for its name[20]; also his thesis that the LXX was the Bible of the Greek-speaking Jewish community in Egypt seems to contradict the psychological and religious facts in Jewish history. Except in modern times, Jews have been wary of translating the sacred text for their religious use. Every Jew was expected to know the sacred text in the holy tongue, though Hebrew may not have been his daily language. The Targumim are an interesting example of a compromise: they are a paraphrase rather than a translation; and then, they are an oral tradition which was written down much later, as was also the case with the Mishnah. It seems to us that a translation of the Bible in a Gentile tongue must have had other motives than the edification of the Synagogue in the Diaspora. It rather points towards a missionary effort on the part of Judaism. The Matthean reference to the missionary zeal of the Pharisees (Matt. 23. 15), though described as "exaggerated and unhistorical",[21] may yet prove a true description of fact. It points in the same direction as the LXX—the Synagogue's consciousness of an obligation towards the nations of the world. That she was not entirely unsuccessful is amply borne out by the N.T.

But the Synagogue's success was only sporadic; her universalism was hampered by her particularism; the two do not combine. In essence Judaism is the religion of the Jews. Even the proselyte is only a stranger who has been admitted into the fellowship of the Synagogue not as an equal but as an act of grace. He is instructed to pray: "O God of the fathers of Israel" and to say: "O God of your fathers".[22] The Mishnah lays down that a woman who is the offspring of a proselyte may not marry into priestly stock even to the tenth generation.[23] This is not to deny universalistic tendencies to Judaism but only to emphasize its limitations.[24]

Judaism is separated by the severe restrictions of rabbinic law from the nations of the world. Whereas in the Torah a "separate" people means a holy people, in the Synagogue it means a "separated" people. The Synagogue feels little responsibility for the nations and has no message for them. It does not even aspire to become a world religion.

The nations found their way to the God of Israel not by way of the Synagogue but by way of the N.T.; they entered into the promises of God through faith in Jesus Christ. Thus a different Israel came into existence, an Israel which has no pedigree, no claim, and no privileges; it exists by faith in the mercy of God. Its symbol is not the tables of the Law, but the Cross upon which Jesus Christ died. The question we have now to answer is: Have the Christ-believing Gentiles entered the commonwealth of Israel stealthily, by the back door, or are they there by the will of God and in accordance with the promises of the O.T.?

It is frequently held, specially by Jews, that it was Saul of Tarsus who treacherously opened the door to let the Gentiles in. Indeed, no one can deny that the Apostle to the Gentiles proved himself the greatest champion of the equality of believers. He refused to differentiate between Jews and Gentiles, once they became believers in Jesus the Messiah. But did he act on his own authority or did he draw the consequences of an older tradition?

(*c*) *Israel and the Church*

It is an injustice both to the O.T. Prophets and to Jesus of Nazareth to make Saul of Tarsus solely responsible for the admission of Gentiles. "Universalism" is deeply ingrained in the message of the whole Bible. The biblical record, be it noted, does not begin with the story of the Hebrew people but with the creation of man. Significantly enough, the Bible ends with the magnificent vision of the Tree of Life with its leaves for the healing of the nations (Rev. 22. 2). This vision of the Seer of Patmos is in substance hardly different from the Isaianic vision of God's triumph over evil: "He hath swallowed up death for ever; and the Lord God will wipe away tears from off all faces . . ." (Isa. 25. 8). Isaiah's God makes a feast for the nations of the world!

It is incredible that on so important a matter as the admission of Gentiles, Paul should be held to have decided on his own authority. Be it remembered that on questions of lesser importance the Apostle knew how to distinguish between his own opinion and that of the Master (cf. 1 Cor. 7. 10). The authority for the decision Paul found in the O.T., but chiefly in the Master himself.

The Gospels contain many references, hints, and allusions to the Gentile world. These cannot easily be eliminated as spurious glosses without violence to the whole structure of the record. The universalistic tendencies in the Fourth Gospel are only too obvious, but the Synoptic Gospels, too, contain enough material to warrant a genuine tradition which undoubtedly goes back to Jesus of Nazareth. The rule he laid down—the first shall be last and the last first—extends far beyond his own people. The story about the Centurion is very revealing in this connection; even the Master himself "marvelled" at the faith of this Gentile. It is in connection with this story that we first meet the revolutionary pronouncement which indicates a complete reversal of privileges in the Kingdom of God: Many shall come from the east and the west and shall sit down with Abraham, and Isaac, and Jacob, but the sons of the Kingdom shall be cast forth into the outer darkness (Matt. 8. 11, 12). It has been suggested that the Lucan context appears to be more original (cf. Luke 13. 28 ff.); but to whatever context these words may have originally belonged, the main fact that they go back to the oldest tradition of the Gospels remains unaltered, so much so that Harnack did not hesitate to assign them to Q.[25] It is difficult to see why Montefiore should doubt their authenticity, except that they do not fit in with his preconceived picture of Jesus.[26] We believe that by the time Paul appeared on the scene, the early Church had already a small adherence of Gentile converts mainly recruited from proselytes. This was only natural, as it reflected the situation in the Synagogue itself; and the Church was only a Synagogue which consisted of people who believed that the Messiah had already come and that Jesus *was* the Messiah. The issue was not whether to admit Gentiles, but on what condition they were to be admitted. The principle for which Paul fought was concerned with the all-sufficiency of Jesus Christ: did the death of the Messiah introduce the new era of grace, or was the law still the only path which leads to God? But even on this central issue Paul was no innovator. In the fluid situation of the early Church the two opinions regarding the Law seem to have coexisted side by side. This can be seen from the undecided behaviour of Peter (cf. Gal. 2. 11 ff.). Peter's difficulty may well have been to decide the extent of intercourse between law-abiding Jewish-Christians and Gentile believers, rather than whether Gentiles were under obligation to keep the Law.[27] It is on the question of *koinonia* that the problem broke out. On this question hung the decision regarding the Gentiles' place in the commonwealth of Israel.

Paul was quick enough to realize that unless the fellowship were complete, the "middle wall" was still in existence, which meant that the Messianic Age was not yet. This is an important point in the controversy: the realization of the promises was inseparable from the entry of the Gentile world upon Israel's heritage. If there was still a difference between Jewish and Gentile believers in Christ, Paul reasoned, then the Gospel was not the Good News and Jesus was not the Saviour. To this the Judaistic party would have answered: The Gentiles are admitted into the commonwealth of Israel but by way of the Law. This Paul could not accept, for an obvious reason: if entry into the commonwealth of Israel was still by way of the Law, then the Death of Christ is not central but only incidental, salvation is not complete. It means that man must save himself and depend upon his own merits. This vitiated the main Pauline supposition that man is saved by grace. Out of this supreme fact grew his conclusion that "there is no distinction; for all have sinned" (Rom. 3. 22 f.). This led the Apostle to a redefinition of the meaning of Israel.

i. *The Root.* If there is no distinction between Jew and Gentile—for all have sinned—the conclusion would have been that there is no advantage in being a Jew. This the Apostle denies. To the question: τί οὖν τὸ περισσὸν τοῦ Ἰουδαίου; ἢ τίς ἡ ὠφέλεια τῆς περιτομῆς; he answers: πολὺ κατὰ πάντα τρόπον! This unexpected turn in St Paul's reasoning does away with any suggestion that the Apostle is merely a cosmopolitan egalitarian. Scholars are embarrassed by the supposed inconsistency in his attitude and try to find an explanation for it.[28] It will remain an inconsistency unless we try to penetrate beyond his apparent "nationalism" to a Christological view of Israel.

This brings us to the problem of the "root". N. P. Williams is greatly puzzled, as most commentators are, by the simile of the olive tree in Rom. 11. 16–24: "It is remarkable", he says, "that St Paul should, even momentarily, write as though the Jewish Fathers were the sole source of the spiritual vitality of the *Ecclesia*, with no mention of Christ or of the Holy Spirit. . . ."[29] It is therefore the practice of commentators to introduce at this point a more or less learned dissertation on the "merits of the Fathers" as conceived by the ancient Synagogue.[30] But this is a poor expedient, for it contradicts the very principle Paul labours to establish, namely that both Jews and Gentiles are saved by grace. We venture to question whether there is any direct connection between ἀγαπητοὶ διὰ τοὺς πατέρας of v. 28 and ῥίζα in v. 16. The latter is a typical prophetic concept, the former refers to an ancient rabbinic view. The connection between the two is by an association of ideas and by a synthesis of thought. The point the Apostle is making is about the holiness of the "root" and not the merits of the Fathers.

Sanday and Headlam explain the meaning of ῥίζα as "that stock from which Jews and Christians both alike receive their nourishment and strength, viz. the Patriarchs, for whose faith originally Israel was chosen".[31] They thus point to verses 28 and 29 for an explanation of verse 16 and speak of the "national qualities which Israel inherits and which caused it to be selected as the Chosen People".[32] To us this is a misguided view; it not only contradicts St Paul's main purpose but their own explanation regarding the sovereignty of the choosing God.[33] We would rather suggest that the connecting link between Israel and the Fathers is the "root", i.e. the Messiah. It means that Israel's election has nothing to do with "national qualities" or with the "merits of the

Fathers", but that God himself in his sovereign grace chooses and that his choice is of the Messiah. He is the Chosen One; he is Israel *par excellence*. He is the Holy Root, as Origen already held long ago. Alford's argument that such a view is inconsistent with Isa. 11. 1 falls to the ground when it is realized that for St Paul the Messiah exists before the Patriarchs.[34]

In the explanation of the "root" the question of the pre-existence of the Messiah is of special importance. In this connection it is worth remembering that one of the many names given to the Messiah by the rabbis was *rishon*—the First One (or the Beginning).[35] There can be no doubt that in St Paul's mind the Messiah took precedence over the Patriarchs not only in position but also in time (cf. Col. 1. 17). Here again St Paul represents an early tradition which is as Jewish as it is Christian; and it is borne out by the Synoptic Gospels. In Mark 12. 35–7 the question is raised: How do the Scribes say that the Messiah is the Son of David—when David himself called him Lord?—the implication being that the Messiah precedes David. John 8. 58 is therefore genuinely Jewish sentiment, when the Master is reputed to have said: Before Abraham was, I am. We would suggest that the expression ῥίζα τοῦ Ἰεσσαί (Isa. 11. 10) meant to St Paul, at any rate, that the Root was carrying Jesse and not Jesse the root. This is consonant with the main principle of Pauline thought: the central position of the Messiah.

In the definition of Israel ἁγία ῥίζα is a key-expression. That historic Israel has his roots in the Patriarchs was a truism to a Jew. But to the Apostle, God's dealing with the Patriarchs was with a view to the Messiah. He is the fruition of Israel's election. It therefore looks as if διὰ τοὺς πατέρας rather stresses the faithfulness of God than the merits of the Fathers. It is, as it were, a reference back to the Promises made to the Fathers and fulfilled in the Messiah.

In support of our view regarding the Root we would also quote Isa. 53. 2—a text which was given a messianic construction long before St Paul. Here *shoresh* (LXX: ῥίζα) is in direct reference to the Messiah; related expressions are *ẓemaḥ* and *neẓer*, both of which are used by the rabbis as names for the Messiah and have a long prophetic tradition.[36] If Delitzsch's suggestion is accepted, and there is no good reason not to accept it, then the name "Nazarene" itself is only another appellation for Messiah, signifying Branch.[37] The point we want to make is that to St Paul the Messiah was both "root" and "branch"—Root in that he is the ground of God's election of Israel: and Branch in that historically he stems from Jesse.

Such a view is possible only on the basis that the Messiah is a pre-existent figure as well as an historic person. It is of interest to note that though in the Pauline letters there is no mention of the Logos, the concept is near at hand. W. R. Inge rightly observes that St Paul's Epistles "give us almost the whole of the Logos-doctrine which we read in the Prologue of the Fourth Gospel".[38] There can be little doubt of the accuracy of this statement.

We now come to the equation of Israel and the Messiah. This is something which occurs frequently in Deutero-Isaiah and has its parallels in the N.T. The fates of Israel and of the Messiah seem to coincide to such a degree that it is often impossible to distinguish the one from the other.[39] Matthew reveals the same outlook when he identifies the fate of the whole of Israel with that of the child-Messiah.[40] Edersheim is specially emphatic on the question of identification, and speaks of the Messiah as the Representative Israelite; in other words, Messiah is Israel *par excellence*. In the life and experience of the Messiah is Israel's history re-enacted, but with a difference. Where Israel failed, the Messiah succeeds; what Israel was meant to be, the Messiah is—the perfect Servant of God.

Something of the symbolic equation of Israel and Messiah is conveyed in the story of the transfiguration. Like Israel, the Messiah stands between Moses and Elijah, the Law and the Prophets. The mount itself is the New Sinai and the radiance of the Messiah exceeds the radiance of Moses (cf. Ex. 34. 29 f.), for he is the New Moses. In the life of the Messiah is the whole experience of Israel rehearsed.

We note here an association of ideas: in one sense the Messiah is Israel personified, the perfect Son; in another sense he is the New Lawgiver, the harbinger of God's Kingdom, the perfect Servant. He therefore acts on behalf of Israel and represents Israel at the same time. This close association between Israel and the Messiah is perpetuated by St Paul: he is both the Root and the Branch—Israel's Root and a branch of Israel.[41]

This is Israel's greatest advantage. The Jewish people is closest to the "root" in time, in history, in experience, and by reason of the Promise.

ii. *The Physical Aspect of Election.* We have now reached the most difficult stage in our discussion: we have to decide whether election in history has or has not a concrete physical meaning. Here we are on precarious ground and we shall have to proceed with the greatest caution. What is said in the following is an effort to look at a particular angle of the problem which is usually neglected.

We have had occasion to see that, for the Synagogue, election, however spiritually construed, ultimately amounts to a concrete blood-relationship which is automatically transmitted from father to son. The cruder physical theory, formulated by Halevi and expounded by Rosenzweig and Schoeps, may appear startling to some Jews, but has the irresistible logic of history behind it. Indeed, there is an historical and concrete aspect of election which corresponds to the historical and concrete aspect of revelation. Seen theologically, the two are different aspects of the same fact. Revelation and election are concomitant and lose meaning when kept apart: God reveals a purpose, and for that purpose he elects. But on the plane of history God's purpose is not accomplished mechanically but by moral decision. In time, everything that happens, happens by degrees. Election is therefore tied to history. If this is the case, then election has a corporate and physical aspect, it is vested in a people. Does it then depend on physical descent?

The Jewish view, which ties election to biology, violates the moral laws; it throws a shadow upon the nature of God and gives to election an accidental meaning. The God of the Bible is no respecter of persons and no one's debtor. He can awaken sons unto Abraham from the stones of the desert. He depends upon no race, not even the Jewish race; and yet there is "advantage" in being a Jew.

The answer lies in the biblical view of history. For the Bible, history is not a succession of fortuitous happenings but consists of a planned purpose, however difficult it may be to discern the mosaic of a meaningful pattern. In that pattern the election of Israel is an act of God. As such it is unalterable, irrevocable, and inexplicable to human reason. To explain Israel's election otherwise than as an act of grace is a supreme form of arrogance. There is only one answer: He chooses as he wills. But we must remember that election in the Bible is never privilege but responsibility: God does not elect for pleasure but for the chosen to be instruments of his will. Israel's history is the supreme proof that there is no escape from a God-given task; even when Israel is rebellious, he still fulfils the purpose of God. Even Israel's rejection of the Messiah serves the purpose of bringing him to the Gentiles (cf. Rom. 11. 15).

There is thus no escape from the will of God; and yet personal responsibility is not annulled thereby but enhanced. It is for man to recognize and accept the will of God. But if he does not, even his disobedience serves God's purpose. Israel cannot step aside and spoil the God-willed pattern of salvation. What Israel fails to do, his greatest Son accomplishes on Israel's behalf. However puzzling it may be to us to understand the contradiction between God's sovereignty and human freedom, one thing is certain: if God is God, his will triumphs over the failure of man.

From this fact we may conclude about the past that man cannot annul the past or escape from it. He cannot start again without reference to what was. Only God in his sovereignty can wipe out the past, but he never does. He forgives the past but does not annul it: the present is always rooted in the past. Such is the order of things on the level of time. In the Christian perspective Jesus Christ stands in the middle of history, not only of world history but of Israel's history. In him history is divided and united at the same time. He is the link between the Old and the New, the past and the future. Israel's election and Israel's re-election are anchored in him. It means that the Word of God spoken in the past: "Ye shall be unto me a kingdom of priests and a holy nation", also holds good for the future. If it is God's Word it must remain eternally valid; this is what St Paul means when he says that the gifts and calling of God are without repentance (Rom. 11. 29). N. P. Williams paraphrases aright: "The Jews can never lose their *status* of the Chosen People: for God never takes back a vocation and dignity which he has once bestowed."[42]

The same God who called Israel to holiness some thousands of years ago, still desires Israel's holiness to-day. If it were otherwise there would be no meaning in reading the Bible, except as an historical record. There is an inherent contemporaneousness in the Word of God with regard both to human need and to God's answer. Otherwise salvation would have to be varied according to the fashion of every age.

Lastly, in history there is an indissoluble connection between spirit and matter, between form and content, between ὕλη and νοῦς. Only in the philosopher's mind can these be kept separate as abstractions. In life, νοῦς and ὕλη are inextricably interwoven: matter is the vehicle of the spirit. In history, therefore, the People of God is not a concept, a universal truth, an ideal to be aimed at, but an historical fact. The People of God is here among us, in history. If it were otherwise, revelation and history would remain two different entities on two different planes, and would never coincide. Revelation in history is anchored in Israel, in Israel κατὰ σάρκα, a living people.

iii. *The Remnant.* Does it mean, then, that every individual biologically connected with historic Israel participates in election? It is at this point that we come upon the doctrine of the Remnant.

Professor W. Zimmerli, faced with the difficulty of an either-or decision, tries to circumvent the problem by making Israel's election conditional on Israel's acceptance of the free grace of God.[43] This is a worthy view and it deserves our sympathy, but it still fails to do justice to the main premise of the Pauline Gospel, namely, that God chooses the unworthy, that Christ died for sinners. Any conditional concept of election ultimately places salvation in the hands of man, thus playing havoc with the doctrine of the sovereignty of God. If Israel were able to elude his destiny and to turn his back upon God once and for all, it would mean that man had the last word and that God was defeated. If this were the case there would be little hope for humanity, for in Israel's destiny is involved the destiny of mankind. This is an important point and lies behind St Paul's reasoning in Romans. St Paul, like the Prophets, is carried by the conviction that at no point in history is Israel an end in himself. In Israel's election God chooses mankind. If God, then, were to leave Israel to himself until he is ready to accept free grace, there is no hope for the rest of humanity. The answer is that we must take God's calling more seriously than Israel's refusal. Here we stand on the side of Barth: only God can be taken seriously—there is no such thing as ontological godlessness.

Yet from history and experience we know that man does turn his back upon God and refuse salvation. How does he do it? We answer: He never does it *en masse*, as a people; he can do it only as an individual. Here lies one of the most tragic mistakes in the reasoning of the Church. That the Church has let herself be deceived into mass-thinking in spite of biblical evidence is one of the major proofs for the subtlety of the devil. The whole N.T. proceeds on the principle that decisions about God can only be made personally. On this issue the democratic principle based on a majority vote breaks down. About God we do not vote—we decide personally. In the Presence of God man becomes isolated from the group and finds himself an individual. To illustrate our point we would take as an example the sin against the Holy Spirit. It is obvious that a whole people corporately cannot commit such a sin, only the individual can. Another example is responsibility for the Crucifixion. Jews have carried the stigma of deicides[44] for nearly twenty centuries, because a crowd in Jerusalem, instigated by a few demagogues, shouted: Crucify, crucify him![45] But can a crowd be held responsible for and representative of a whole people? Why a Jewish mob two thousand years ago should be an exception, no one has ever explained.

Responsibility is a strictly personal quality. On this matter the O.T. prophets had already decided the issue[46] (cf. Jer. 31. 29; Ez. 18). Mosaic Law itself is built on the basis of personal responsibility. This is amply demonstrated by the ritual of the sin-offering. In the act of seeking forgiveness we meet man in his true significance: a person responsible *before* God.

It is in the context of personal responsibility before God that we must discuss the doctrine of the Remnant. Its origin goes back to the O.T. Prophets, but in St Paul's treatment it has a significance of its own. It seems to us that in the O.T. "remnant" is not yet a *terminus technicus*. This can be seen from the way the Prophets treat the subject: *she'ar yashuv*—"a remainder will return"—means return to the land, but not necessarily to God (cf. Isa. 7. 3). "Except the Lord of hosts had left unto us a very small remnant we should have been as Sodom . . ." (Isa. 1. 9). The context implies national survival; except perhaps in 1 Kings 19. 18, where God leaves unto himself (*hish'arti*) seven thousand faithful who have not bowed their knees to Baal. An unusual combination between national survival and spiritual blessing we meet in Joel 2. 32, where *peletah* are the "escaped" who receive the Holy Spirit. This text anticipates the Pauline concept of the Remnant.

It is profitable to make a comparison between Rom. 9. 27 and 11. 5. In the first instance the Apostle uses "remnant" in the typical O.T. sense of national survival; in the second instance the faithful are meant κατ' ἐκλογὴν χάριτος—"according to the election of grace". The "election of grace" vested in the Remnant is a new and specifically Pauline development. Unlike the O.T. concept it is no longer morally but theologically defined: "So then it is not of him that willeth, nor of him that runneth, but of God that hath mercy" (Rom. 9. 16). The "election of grace" expresses here the last secret of God's inscrutable judgement. Such *ultimate* judgement God applies to every individual. It is a mistake to apply the concept of the Remnant to a whole nation, specially in the Pauline context. This becomes obvious when we remember how St Paul uses the story about Elijah and the seven thousand, and how he applies it to the faithful who like himself are of the house of Israel. It simply means that "no Church or nation is saved *en masse*. . . ."[47] No, not even the Jews!

We contend that St Paul uses election in a twofold manner: sometimes he speaks of election in personal terms and sometimes in collective. The two are not the same. Israel's election is in respect of revelation; individual election is in respect of salvation. Sometimes the two aspects coincide; and it must be granted that St Paul did not manage to keep them entirely segregated. In fact this is not quite possible, because in the Pauline view both the individual and the community stem from the Holy Root and are therefore holy seed (cf. Isa. 6. 13), if not by nature then at least by Promise. But Rom. 9–11 cannot be properly understood unless the two aspects of election are kept separate. Once we substitute "salvation" for the word "election", this becomes quite clear: Israel's salvation belongs to the future—"all Israel shall be saved" —the "remnant", however, is saved here and now. Here, then, is the difference: Israel's salvation is eschatologically conceived; the individual's salvation is personally experienced.

iv. *The "Wild" Branches.* We have already had occasion to observe the deep-seated awareness of the world outside Israel, as manifested in the Bible. It is best summed up in the prophetic hope that "many peoples shall go and say: Come ye, and let us go up to the mountain of the Lord, to the house of the God of Jacob; and he will teach us of his ways, and we will walk in his paths: for out of Zion shall go forth the Law, and the word of the Lord from Jerusalem" (Isa. 2. 3; cf. Zech. 8. 20–3). That hope has never entirely left the Synagogue, for she knows the God of Israel to be the God of all flesh. There is a talmudic passage which beautifully expresses the Synagogue's vision:

> Four times does it say: "I adjure you, daughters of Jerusalem" (Cant. 2. 7; 3. 5; 5. 8; 8. 4). God calls the Gentiles "Jerusalem's daughters". R. Johanan said: In time to come God will make Jerusalem a mother-city for the whole world, as it is said: "And I

will give them to thee as daughters, though they be not of thy covenant" (Ez. 16. 61).[48]

In the N.T. we meet with the same vision in the process of realization. Concern for the outsider runs parallel with concern for Israel's sons. We categorically reject Harnack's view that Jesus showed little interest in the Gentile world and that the missionary zeal of the early Church was due more to the influence of the spirit of Jesus than to his example.[49] Harnack arrived at his conclusion by eliminating the other texts which prove the contrary and putting them in footnotes.[50] Harnack's mistake is that of most scholars who leave out of account the powerful influence of the O.T., and specially that of the Prophets.[51] Be it then said with all emphasis that for Jesus to by-pass the Gentile world would have been equivalent to a denial of Messiahship. If Jesus' vision was less than that of the Prophet who called the whole world to turn unto God and to be saved (Isa. 45. 22), then he was a false Messiah. Whatever one may say about Jesus, he knew the messianic rôle well enough to include the Gentiles in his message. Here the Fourth Gospel only corroborates the Synoptic tradition. One thing Harnack completely overlooks, and that is that the message of the Kingdom of God in itself already carries universalism by implication. Another example is the Lord's Prayer, specially the clause: Thy will be done in earth as it is in heaven. To leave out the clause on the hypothetical assumption that it was not in Q is a daring conclusion.[52] Another example is Matt. 21. 43: "Therefore say I unto you, The Kingdom of God shall be taken away from you and shall be given to a nation bringing forth the fruits thereof." Harnack understands "nation" to mean the ordinary Jew as against "official" Jewry.[53] But when we read the parallel version in Mark it is difficult to see why our Lord's reference to ἄλλοις should meet with such violent opposition, unless it was understood to be a reference to the Gentiles. It is equally difficult to see why in Mark 11. 17: "My house shall be called a house of prayer πᾶσι τοῖς ἔθνεσιν" should be eliminated as a gloss, considering that it is a literal quotation from the O.T. (Isa. 56. 7).[54] But there is one text which even Harnack has to admit: "And I say unto you that many shall come from the east and the west and shall sit down with Abraham, and Isaac, and Jacob, in the Kingdom of Heaven: but the sons of the Kingdom shall be cast forth into the outer darkness" (Matt. 8.

11 f.). Harnack naïvely asks: "Why should Jesus not have said it?"— Exactly! There can be no other reason except the prejudice of scholars.[55]

About the universalistic tendencies in Luke we will say nothing, as these are generally acknowledged by scholars. But it is noteworthy that Harnack himself, who regards Matthew as the most Jewish of the Gospels, is surprised that of all the Evangelists it is Matthew who opens his story with the visit of "the wise men of the east".[56] It is our considered opinion that behind the universalistic appeal of the early Church is Jesus himself. It cannot be too often reiterated that Paul was not the founder of "foreign" missions, he found one already in existence. Scholars who attribute the commission, to preach the Gospel to the whole world, to "the historical development of later times", overlook the evidence from the N.T., the influence of Deutero-Isaiah, and the fact that the presence of proselytes was already a commonplace in the Synagogue.[57] Though we are unable to give a satisfactory explanation to the opposite tradition—"Go not into any way of the Gentiles, and enter not into any city of the Samaritans" (Matt. 10. 5); "I was not sent but unto the lost sheep of the house of Israel" (Matt. 15. 24)—the other evidence by far outweighs the nationalistic attitude. Be it noted that according to the Synoptic tradition Jesus undertook a double mission: the twelve for the twelve tribes of Israel; the seventy for the seventy nations of the world. Though the double mission is peculiar to Luke it may well represent a genuine tradition, specially as Luke 10. 1 ff. is counted in Q.[58]

As already pointed out, St Paul's struggle with the Judaistic party was not on the question of admitting Gentiles, but on the question of Law observance. On the other question there could be no doubt for a Jew.

It is important to revert to St Paul's attitude once more. We are now concerned with the "wild" branches which are grafted into the good olive-tree. If our view, that for St. Paul the "root" stands for the Messiah himself, is correct, then the effort of "grafting" should not be understood as a new beginning, but rather as an extension from Israel to the world. It is not a new development, but something which has always been within the purposes of God. The sequence of the biblical story of salvation is therefore: The Messiah—Israel—the nations of the world. The Messiah is the root, the olive-tree is Israel, the branches are the Gentiles: the root carries the tree, the tree carries the branches.

These branches, though "contrary to nature", are the fruit of the holy seed. Commentators have taken exception to St Paul's faulty horticultural knowledge, but the reversal of the usual order is part of the picture. Herein lies the miracle that the "wild" branches, by being grafted into the good olive-tree, become the holy seed of Israel, children to Abraham and heirs of the Promises. This grafting unites the branches with the tree: from henceforth there is no difference between believing Jews and Gentiles; their difference is only in function but not in quality. Before God they are all saved by grace and grace alone. Israel from henceforth includes both Jews and Gentiles. Israel separated from the Gentile world is Israel in suspense; the true Israel is Israel completed with Jews *and* Gentiles. This is so important to the Apostle that he defines the messianic community as the new humanity in which the twain are made "one new man" (Eph. 2. 15).

From this it would appear that to the Apostle Paul, Israel is a much more comprehensive term than was traditionally accepted. Represented in the figure of a tree with root, trunk, and branches, Israel includes the Messiah, the faithful remnant, and the believing Gentiles.

v. *The "New" Covenant.* It is customary to divide the Bible into two parts, O.T. and N.T. The division indicates that the event of the Messiah's birth broke history into two parts: *ante et post Christum natum.* But does such a division also mean that the story of revelation is a broken story and begins anew with Jesus Christ? This is a question of considerable importance to our thesis.

In what relation, then, stands the adjective "new" on the title-page of the N.T. to the adjective "old" of the O.T.?

On the basis of cause and effect, "old" and "new" are always connected; there is nothing "new" which has not assimilated or derived something of the "old". But our question is not meant to be understood in this causative sense. "New" here we mean in the sense of a *new* beginning; for it is the supreme fact of the Incarnation which is the *novum* in the messianic age. Seen horizontally it would indeed appear that the coming of Christ into history is a *novum* of the first order. No one dare contradict Oepke's statement: *Gott kann einen neuen Anfang machen.*[59] But the theologian is also meant to look vertically, beyond the line of history, and unless the two lines of vision focus, his perspective is at fault. Seen vertically, a "new beginning" makes nonsense either of history or of God.

It suggests by implication that God has been defeated in his purpose and has to start all over again. If the "new" Covenant means a new beginning in God's dealing with man, then there was no sense in all that went before. Such a view is inadmissible. Scholars have to admit that there was never any intention on the part of the early Church to augment or enlarge the canon of the O.T., it was her only holy Book; the N.T. is a much later development. Marcion's effort to eliminate the O.T. may have greatly speeded the process. Streeter points out that the spurious Epistle of Clement to Rome still treats the O.T. as the only valid Scriptures with a claim to inspiration, although the writer knows of the Epistle to the Hebrews and 1 Corinthians.[60] For quite a while, especially on Jewish soil, there could be no question of supplanting or even adding to the Hebrew Bible. But though there was no N.T. in the technical sense, there was the idea of a "new" Covenant which played an important part in the *kerygma* of the Church.

The "new Covenant" goes back to the O.T. itself. Though the reference in Jer. 31. 31 is unique, there are enough hints that the idea of renewal is a feature common to the great Prophets: "I will do a new thing" (Isa. 43. 19; 48. 6); "I will put a new spirit within you" (Ez. 11. 19); "I will make you a new heart" (ibid., 18. 31; 36. 26); "I will create new heavens and a new earth" (Isa. 65. 17; 66. 22); "Sing unto the Lord a new song" (Isa. 42. 10; Ps. 33. 3; 96. 1). We maintain that the idea of a "new" Covenant belongs to exactly the same cycle of ideas. It can be seen already from the context that the "new" Covenant of which Jeremiah speaks related to the everlasting Covenant between God and Israel. This is Hosea's special message; in fact Hosea can be treated as a commentary on Jer. 31. 31. Though Israel, like the adulterous wife, breaks faith, God, like the faithful husband, remains true. In this light we must read the text in Jer. 31. 32: "Which my covenant they brake, although I was a husband unto them . . ."—the breach occurred on the part of Israel, God still remains faithful to his people. There is no suggestion whatsoever that the "new" Covenant is with another people. If this is the case, it means that the "new" Covenant is a renewal of the old, only on a more permanent basis: "I will write my Law in their heart . . ." As far as God is concerned the Covenant with

Israel stands: the emphasis upon the lasting value of the Covenant recurs in Jeremiah (cf. Jer. 32. 40; 50. 5) and in the other Prophets (cf. Ez. 37. 26; Isa. 55. 3). So far, then, as the O.T. is concerned, the "new" Covenant is not new *ab initio*, but only a renewal of the old.

We now turn to the N.T. We will first pay attention to the words of the Institution: ἡ καινὴ διαθήκη,[61] which is a literal reference to Jer. 31. 31 and was meant to be understood as such. But if this is the case would not the "new" covenant mean the same here as it means in Jeremiah? In view of the messianic meaning of the text and the circumstances of the Last Supper, there can be little doubt that its meaning is exactly the same: "Renewal of the Covenant." Behm, who discusses the meaning of καινός in the same connection, is not to be taken too seriously, first because he is guided by the usage of the Greek language, and second because he proceeds philologically with a theological concept.[62] The same would apply to the meaning of διαθήκη. Behm maintains that in the Greek Bible διαθήκη does not mean "pact" (*Bund*), nor does it mean "testament", but rather "disposition" or "revelation" of God's sovereign will in history.[63] If Behm's view is correct, then by his own definition καινὴ διαθήκη would mean a radical change in God's sovereign will—an absurd proposition. We find much more agreeable the more conservative view as formulated by T. C. Edwards, which gives to διαθήκη the meaning of "pledge".[64] "Pledge" has a comprehensive meaning and includes "pact" and "covenant", but it also has the advantage in that it conveys exactly the prime intention of the N.T.—that in Jesus Christ God reaffirms his promises to his people. This T. C. Edwards has clearly shown in connexion with the difficult text of Hebr. 9. 16 f. For this reason Behm's rabbinic quotation: one testament abolishes the other—*diyyatiḳi mebaṭṭelet diyyatiḳi*[65]—is quite inapplicable: for the "old" is not annulled but reaffirmed by the "new". This is also evident from the circumstances: the contracting parties are the same: Israel (= Messiah) and God. The purpose is the same: I will be their God and they shall be my people. The only difference is in the form of the Covenant: the death of the Messiah instead of the sacrifice of an animal; the Blood of the Messiah seals the "new" Covenant. In this special sense, in the sense of finality, it is a New Covenant; it accomplishes the inwardness of spiritual growth: "I will put my law in their inward parts and in their heart will I write it" (Jer. 31. 33).

This is something the Old Covenant could not do. St Paul alludes to this promise in Jeremiah when he speaks of the tables which are not any more of stone (i.e. the tables of the Law) but of the believer's heart (2 Cor. 3. 3). This transition from the outward to inwardness is to the Apostle a sign of the messianic age—the result of the outpouring of the Holy Spirit of God.

The situation, then, as the early Church conceived it, can be thus described: Israel has broken his pledge. The Prophets already accuse God's people of apostasy. The Covenant at Sinai is therefore inoperative *de facto*, though *de jure* it is still in existence. A rift has been created between God and his people, and estrangement has taken place. The Messiah came to bridge the gulf, and to make at-one-ment by his own Sacrifice upon the Cross between God and his people. But because the Messiah is not just a human being whose sacrifices (like those of the Priests in the Temple) need constant repetition, this Sacrifice is final. In the Messiah, therefore, all the Promises are fulfilled. He is God's pledge to Israel and through Israel to mankind. This is the Good News—εὐαγγέλιον. In it is included the discovery of God's eternal faithfulness; he remains a covenant-keeping God, though Israel became faithless—he cannot deny himself (2 Tim. 2. 13).

The "new" Covenant is therefore *not* a different covenant,[66] but the original Covenant established once and for all.

Confirmation for our view we also find in Professor Dalman's equation of *berit* with *ḳeyam*. If this is correct, then the new pledge in the Blood of the Messiah carries the idea of re-establishing of what has fallen into desuetude.[67] Here the Messiah acts on behalf of Israel. What the Priesthood could not accomplish, Jesus does. The Sacrifice of his own Self thus brings to an end the old order of the sacrificial system. Not in the sense that Jesus "did away with the Old Testament dispensation, and put something new in its place" (Dalman), but only in the sense that the "old" has found its ultimate and deepest fulfilment in the "new".

In our view the emphasis upon the unity of the Covenant preserves the unity of revelation and frees theology from the rigid dispensationalism which militates against the free and sovereign Grace of God.[68] Law and Gospel are expressions of the same Grace of God and stand in relation to each other as promise to fulfilment. The shadow of the Cross falls not only forward but backward; it means that God's dealing with Israel was already with a view to ultimate salvation.

Here we must touch upon the question: How did the Master himself view his connection with the past?

This is a difficult question, chiefly because there seem to exist two contradictory trends within the N.T. tradition. On the one hand we are told that Jesus upheld the sanctity of the Law, so that "not one jot or tittle shall pass away"; on the other hand he implies that the old bottles cannot contain the new wine and that it is of little use to patch up an old garment with a new piece. But it is very probable that we are misreading the text by applying these sayings to the "Old Covenant" instead of to the outworn forms of Judaism. This does not mean that all in Pharisaic Judaism was unworthy—a scribe who becomes a disciple of the Kingdom of God is like a wise householder, who brings forth out of his treasure things new and old (Matt. 13. 52)—but that the system itself was unsuitable for the new era. To Jesus, the elaborate system of Pharisaic Judaism was nothing more than the "tradition of men" (cf. Mark 7. 5–13).[69] Behind this expression of criticism is a history which goes back to the Prophets where the charge is repeated in almost the same words: "Their fear of me is *mizvat anashim*—a precept of men" (Isa. 29. 13). The charge that the Pharisaic system consists of ἐντάλματα καὶ διδασκαλίας τῶν ἀνθρώπων is in the forefront of our Lord's controversy with contemporary Judaism. In the later controversy between Church and Synagogue, the accusation that Pharisaism misapplied the Law is the strongest criticism on the part of Christianity and was already used by St Paul (cf. Col. 2. 20–3). As in so many other cases, it goes back to the Master himself. Jesus categorically rejected the "tradition of the Elders" whenever this clashed with the original intention of the will of God. In this light we must read the Sermon on the Mount. It was not the Messiah's task to abolish the Law or to substitute another Law, but to recover the Law's original intention.

When we turn to St Paul we find a similar situation. At first sight it would appear that the Apostle makes a definite break with the past: before Christ "we were kept in ward under the Law", but *now*, since Christ has come "we are no longer under a tutor" (Gal. 3. 23, 25).[70] But at closer examination the position is different; it all depends how we translate: ἐλθούσης δὲ τῆς πίστεως. . . . The R.V. translates: "but now that faith is come"; the A.V. reads: "but after that Faith is come". Never in the history of exegesis was the use of a capital letter more striking as in this case. There is a remarkable difference between "faith" and "Faith". In the first case faith refers to time, in the second it refers to doctrine. St Paul intends to emphasize the time factor only. Lightfoot therefore paraphrases aright although he uses the dispensational concept too rigidly:

> Before the dispensation of faith came, we were carefully guarded, that we might be ready for it, when at length it was revealed. Thus we see that the law was our tutor, who watched over us as children till we should attain our manhood in Christ and be justified by faith. But when this new dispensation came, we were liberated from the restraints of the law.[71]

Let us look at the context of the above text more closely. The Apostle writes to believing Gentiles. The whole tenor of Galatians is to show Gentile Christians that through faith in the Messiah they become equals with Christ-believing Jews. Faith is therefore the only condition of entry into the commonwealth of Israel. This was different before the Messiah came, when Gentiles who wanted to join Israel had to submit to the rigours of the Law. But since Jesus came, things are different, the new order prevails. From now on it is not the Law but faith which is the deciding factor: ὥστε οἱ ἐκ πίστεως εὐλογοῦνται σὺν τῷ πιστῷ Ἀβραάμ (Gal. 3. 9). In the centre of St Paul's argument is Jesus Christ. "Faith" here, as throughout, means faith in Jesus the Messiah, i.e. a personal relationship between believer and the risen Christ.[72] In this way man's relationship to God is decided not by obedience to the Law but by a personal, positive attitude to Jesus Christ. Gal. 3. 25 ought therefore to read: "Christ having come, faith in him frees us from the tutorship of the Law." Christ's coming is therefore not a new dispensation but the beginning of the End. There is no warrant for a dispensational doctrine in this text. The fact of Messiah's coming does not break the story of revelation but completes it. From henceforth there is only one way for Jews and Gentiles, the way of faith in Jesus the Christ.

It therefore appears that in the Pauline view Christ is not inaugurating a new beginning, but is the final fruition of the prophetic hope. In him are all God's promises fulfilled. He is the climax of history and the End of the ages (1 Cor. 10. 11).

The *novum* in God's dealing with mankind is called εὐαγγέλιον because it is a manifesto of God's grace, a declaration that God has kept his Word and fulfilled his promises. This "new thing" in Israel was foretold by the Prophets[73] and has now come true; the

Apostle therefore cries: "The old things are passed away; behold they are become new" (2 Cor. 5. 17). This is the renewal of the Kingdom of God; not another dispensation, but that in Jesus of Nazareth the End has become visible.

It is significant that the expression ἡ παλαιὰ διαθήκη occurs only once in the whole N.T. (2 Cor. 3. 14). But the meaning is not "Old Covenant" as distinct from the "New", only "ancient covenant"—another name for the *torat Mosheh,* i.e. the Pentateuch.[74]

vi. *The "New" Israel.* Even less warranted than the concept of a "new" Covenant, is the idea of a "new" Israel. There is no such expression in the whole Bible. Not only do we never hear of a "new" Israel, but even the idea of an Israel κατὰ πνεῦμα is only by inference; it is deduced from the expression Israel κατὰ σάρκα which occurs once (1 Cor. 10. 18). It is still a question whether the "spiritual Israel" is a legitimate counterpart to the Israel according to the flesh. It is doubtful whether the Apostle ever visualized *two* separate and distinct Israels. He knew how to distinguish between a Jew who is one "outwardly" and a Jew who is one "inwardly". He also knew that not all of Israel are Israel; but this can in no way warrant the assumption that he counted with two Israels.

There can be no plural to Israel. The idea of another Israel is utterly alien to the N.T., as alien as the idea that beside the God of Israel there can be another God. That this is so can be seen from St Paul's argument in Rom. 9–11. Here we have the complete Pauline statement concerning Israel: υἱοθεσία (a *terminus technicus* in the Apostle's vocabulary) he uses primarily in relation to his "kinsmen according to the flesh" (Rom. 9. 3).[75] They still hold a position *sui generis,* by reason of Promise. His thesis can be stated in one sentence: God hath not cast off his people (Rom. 11. 1). The Apostle labours hard to establish his point and he builds his argument not upon Israel but upon the trustworthiness of God.

That the Church could have ever conceived the idea of Israel's rejection shows how little she understood St Paul's point of view. Jewish rejection would have become a dogma with the Church but for the fact that it is contradicted by St Paul. Hand in hand with the rejection of Israel goes the idea of a "new Israel".

The expression "new" people occurs twice in Barnabas: ὁ λαός ὁ καινός (5. 7; 7. 5). In Justin's *Dialogue* the idea of *another*

Israel is already carefully developed (cf. ch. 23). Here the theory of complete separation makes its appearance: there are *two* seeds of Judah, and *two* races, as there are two houses of Jacob: the one begotten by blood and flesh, the other by faith and the Spirit (ch. 135). The Christians are the true descendants of Judah, Jacob, Isaac, and Abraham—"the true spiritual Israel" (ch. 11); the Jews are strangers and foreigners. We meet here an echo of St Paul's argument in Gal. 4. 21 ff. about Abraham's two sons, the one of a bond-woman and the other of a freewoman. But the application is quite different. Paul still knows himself a member of "the children of promise" and only equates those who cleave to the Law with Hagar's descendants; Justin feels himself emancipated from historic Israel and knows himself a member of the "true spiritual Israel". This is the difference: Paul never breaks away from the past and never leaves historic Israel behind him. This apparent inconsistency Oepke can understand only on "psychological" grounds.[76] He regards it as a flaw in the Apostle's thinking which prevented him from drawing the final conclusions from his new insight. We, however, see in his attitude deeper theological motives.

Oepke has rightly recognized the importance of the concept of the People of God for the early Church. He also sees clearly how the N.T. insists on the continuity of the People of God from the time of Abraham to the Church of Christ.[77] But he fails to find a place for Israel κατὰ σάρκα, though he grapples with the problem and occasionally comes within sight of a positive solution.[78]

The fact is that our modern racial ideas are foreign to the Bible. Neither for Jesus nor for Paul was Israel a purely physical concept. Israel is only Israel by reason of revelation and not by reason of physical descent from Abraham. The People of God is the canvas upon which the pattern of revelation is woven. To displace the canvas means to displace the pattern itself.

St Paul never reckoned with a situation when whole Gentile nations would become "converted" by order of the reigning prince, as happened later in Church history. In his days, the Gentiles entered the Commonwealth of Israel by personal conversion and individually. These converts were grafted on to the living body of historic Israel. They were thus "proselytes" in the strict sense of the word. Though once upon a time foreigners and strangers, and without God in the world, the believing Gentiles, through faith in Christ, have become by the Grace of God fellow-heirs of God's own People (Eph. 3. 6).[79] This was St Paul's main difference from the more conservative party in the Church. He regarded it as his special "stewardship of the mystery", namely, the preaching to the Gentiles "the unsearchable riches of Christ" (Eph. 3. 8 f.).

But though the Gentiles were freed from the obligation of the Law, they were not free from historic Israel. Being joined to the People of God was the privilege of the believing Gentile. But the way to Israel was from henceforth by way of the Messiah and not by way of the Law: "He [i.e. the Messiah] is our peace" (Eph. 2. 14).

Christ thus fulfils a double function: he is the guarantee of Israel's continuity—as long as he is, Israel is; and he is the bridge to the Gentile world. This is the πλήρωμα of the Messiah (Col. 1. 20) in that he has made peace through the blood of his Cross "of all things in heaven and earth". From this it would appear that the Gentile believers are not a substitute for Israel, a kind of "new" Israel, but, having been grafted into the Messiah, they become part of Israel.[80]

vii. *The "New" Man.* We have already had occasion to show that in the view of the early Church the Messiah inaugurated the new era. From henceforth, history moves precariously on the very brink of the Kingdom of God. The End has now begun: God's reign has broken in upon humanity, time is running short. God's intention has become revealed not only among his own people but throughout the world. For believers in Christ, eschatology was not something belonging to the dim future, but a present experience: they knew themselves already translated into the Kingdom of the Messiah (cf. Col. 1. 13). The final and ultimate triumph of the King-Messiah was only a question of time. Evidence that the End had begun they found in the remarkable success of the mission field: the Gentiles turned to the God of Israel, thanks to the preaching of the Gospel. The Holy Spirit of God was the experience of believers, irrespective of whether they were Jews or Gentiles. The fact that Gentiles also received the Holy Spirit created a new situation: it served to emphasize the eschatological character of the new age. Here was prophecy being fulfilled before their eyes. Something of the glow and the wonder of the experience we find reflected in the Epistles of St Paul and the Acts of the Apostles.

The new age was inaugurated by the New Man, the Second

Adam (Rom. 5. 12–19; 1 Cor. 15. 21 f.). He, the Messiah, is the first fruit of the New Humanity. The Church, the body of Christ, is the link between the present and the End. The *ecclesia* is "God's gathering in Christ",[81] in time for the realization of the Day of the Lord.

To grasp something of the meaning of eschatology as it was felt in the early days of the Church, we shall have to rid ourselves of our modern concepts of evolutionary progress conceived as a single line of development. In the N.T., "progress" and cataclysm stand in an unresolved relationship and run parallel. In one sense, the Kingdom of God spreads and develops like leaven inside dough (Matt. 13. 33); like mustard seed which grows up to become a big tree (Matt. 13. 31); like the good seed in the ground which grows together with the tares (Matt. 13. 24 ff.). But on the other hand, the Kingdom of God comes suddenly, unexpectedly, like the floods in the days of Noah (Luke 17. 20 ff.). With the coming of Christ Jesus the Kingdom of God has already broken in—"is come upon you" (Matt. 12. 28); but at the same time the disciple is under obligation to pray: "Thy Kingdom come".[82] In this dialectic between the presence of the Kingdom and the coming of the Kingdom moves the life of every believer. Through faith in Christ he enters the Kingdom, but at the same time he waits for the consummation of the Kingdom, the Day of the Lord, which is also a day of judgement, when the sheep will be separated from the goats (cf. Matt. 25. 31 ff.).

Expectancy of the imminent End is the feature of the eschatological attitude. Preparedness to receive him who comes as a thief in the night (1 Thess. 5. 2) marks the believer from the unbeliever. *Maranatha!*[83] is therefore the slogan of the faithful Church (1 Cor. 16. 22). It is a source of comfort to the little flock that the Lord is at hand (Phil. 4. 5).

Meanwhile the process of transition has already begun, the new humanity is being born, the Body of Christ is replacing the body of dying men. The presence of the Church is of profound significance to the believer. Whereas before the advent of the Messiah the world was divided by religion, culture, and social standing, now, in Jesus Christ, a new unity has taken place. Out of the old body of humanity a new σῶμα is being fashioned, of which the Messiah is Head (Col. 2. 19). In the new order of the Kingdom there is no difference between Jew and Greek, slave and free, male and female (Gal. 3. 28).

Corresponding to the New Adam, the καινὸς ἄνθρωπος stands as the symbol of the New Humanity (Eph. 2. 15). It does not seem to us sufficient to dispose of the text by merely relegating the concept to the Gnostic cycle of ideas.[84] We doubt whether there is a parallel in any ancient literature, be it gnostic or otherwise, to the "Ephesian" concept of the "new man": a combination of Gentile and Jew. This is the very point of the *novum* of the messianic age: the new man is Jew and Gentile united. It apparently means to the writer of Ephesians that without the Gentile the Jew is incomplete and has failed in his historic mission. To bring the nations to God is Israel's messianic task. What Israel as a people failed to accomplish, Israel in the person of the Messiah has brought about. Jesus Christ has abolished the enmity and has reconciled "both in one body unto God through the Cross". The *ecclesia* therefore stands in a special relationship to the Kingdom of God, it is the *kenesset Yisrael* of the messianic age, its messianic feature is the unity of Gentiles and Jews in one single body. "He is our peace", for he has brought Israel to the nations and the nations to Israel. From henceforth both have the same "access in one spirit unto the Father", and are thus brothers; the age-old enmity is done away with.

Eph. 2. 19–22 is of immense importance to our thesis. The passage is unique and reveals how the early Church saw the connection between Israel and the Gentiles in relation to the Messiah.

The Gentiles who by birth were ξένοι have now by faith in the Messiah become συμπολῖται with the saints; in other words, they have been joined to the people of God and have received a share of Israel's heritage. This miracle of grace did not come about by a natural progress of history but by a new act of God. This creative act was accomplished by the Messiah when he died upon the Cross to remove the enmity between Israel and the nations. The Gentiles are thus built into the edifice of which Christ is the chief corner stone and the apostles and prophets the foundation.[85] The edifice of the new Temple is thus a mosaic of Jews and Gentiles "fitly framed together . . . for a habitation of God in the Spirit" (Eph. 2. 20–2).

The simile of the Temple is a most apt figure to depict the new situation. Messianic humanity is a magnificent sanctuary of the Holy Spirit, of which the corner stone is the Messiah. He supports and upholds the edifice of the New Temple of God (cf. 1 Pet.

2. 4 ff.), which is built up of Jewish and Gentile believers. It is possible that the writer of Ephesians had in mind the ancient Jewish legend that the Temple in Jerusalem was built upon the stone on which Abraham was preparing to sacrifice Isaac. Like the old Temple, the new Temple has its corner stone—the risen Christ, corresponding to the living stones of the edifice. The point to be remembered is the monolithic character of the building—it is Israel, the holy nation, the people of God, reconstituted of Jews and Gentiles.

The messianic man is, according to Ephesians, a "composite" creature, partly Jewish, partly Gentile, standing as a symbolic figure of the ultimate ingathering of God's elect. Messianic humanity is thus the concrete sign of the "age to come" when all distinction will be abolished and when God will be all in all.

The Christian believer is not a mere onlooker in this great drama of redemption, but an active participant in the unfolding of God's purpose with mankind. He is on the way, hastening unto the day of the Lord (2 Pet. 3. 12). This is the meaning of Christian eschatology.

viii. *The Israel of God.* The "Israel of God" in Gal. 6. 16 is a much-discussed theme. Professor Gottlob Schrenk sees in the phrase an exclusive reference to Christ-believing Jews who accept the Pauline point of view. This would exclude not only Gentile Christians, but also "Judaizers" on the one hand, and non-believing Jews on the other.[86] Against this narrow interpretation, Professor N. A. Dahl places his own, which identifies the Israel of God with the Christian Church consisting of Jews *and* Gentiles.[87] Although we greatly appreciate Professor Schrenk's gallant effort to prove his case,[88] our sympathies are with the latter. Our reason is connected with the Apostle's attitude to the Gentile world. If what we have said before is trustworthy, then St Paul's interpretation of Israel is not far removed from that of Ephesians. It reflects the view of the Hebrew Prophets: Israel is not complete without the Gentiles. It is the hall-mark of the true Israel that the Gentiles have a legitimate claim upon him. Without them Israel has not fulfilled his mission and remains barren. The strange self-sufficiency and exclusiveness of the Synagogue during the centuries of Exile serve only to emphasize this important point. Here we meet with the difference between Paul and the Synagogue's definition of Israel. Separation is the motto of Pharisaic Judaism, integration is the motto of St Paul. These are two diametrically opposed views. For the Apostle, Israel is the suffering servant of God who, like the Messiah, spends himself in the service of the nations to bring them "under the wings of the Shekinah". Israel is the tool in Messiah's hand for bringing into the Kingdom of God the sheep of the *other* fold (cf. John 10. 16). The true Israelite carries upon his body the marks of Jesus, the Suffering Servant (Gal. 6. 17), and makes up in his own flesh what is lacking in the affliction of his Master (Col. 1. 24). This is not suffering self-imposed for its own sake, but vicarious suffering on behalf of others. Only thus is the true Israelite spiritually related to the Messiah who came to serve and to give his life a ransom for many (Mark 10. 45). The Gentile is his neighbour in need, as the Jew was to the Samaritan in the parable. Thus serving the outsider with the Gospel of God's love, the Israelite has true fellowship with the Messiah. Relationship to the Messiah leads by way of the other man. The Apostle's suffering results in the comfort of salvation for the Gentiles (2 Cor. 1. 6).

The Jewish people is a people acquainted with sorrow. There is no people which has suffered as intensely. The Synagogue knows and practises suffering *'al-ḳiddushat ha-Shem*—for the sanctification of God's holy Name. But it knows nothing of suffering for the sake of the Gentiles: vicarious suffering plays no part in Jewish thinking. Here we come upon the great division which separates the Ἰουδαίοι from the Israel of God.[89]

The Israel of God is therefore the Israel who is inspired by the spirit of the Master, and a Jew is ἐν τῷ κρυπτῷ (Rom. 2. 28 f.); and yet a Gentile cannot become a Jew. There is only one difference between them: whereas a Gentile to become an Israelite has to renounce his religious past, the Jew only reaffirms it. The difference derives from the concreteness of biblical revelation, which is not spoken into a vacuum, but enacted in the life of a people. This is the meaning of "Church"—Church is the place where God manifests himself in redemptive action. There is therefore an indissoluble bond between the Church and the Jewish people.[90]

CHAPTER 6

A DEFINITION OF ISRAEL

IT is a mistake to suppose that the term "Israel" carries the same signification right through the N.T. Walter Gutbrod in his learned article in Kittel's theological dictionary has shown how the meaning varies from book to book and writer to writer.[1] To try to give the term a unified meaning is to do violence to the text. We suggest at least four different connotations which cover the term Israel, either by implication or by context:

(*a*) Israel as applied to the historic people of the Covenant.

(*b*) "The Israel of God", which we take to mean the Church consisting of Christ-believing Jews and Gentiles.

(*c*) The individual Israelite in his dignity and responsibility as a member of the People of God.

(*d*) Eschatological Israel, that is, Israel in his completion at the End of time.

In order to gain a balanced picture of the meaning of Israel it is, however, necessary to emphasize that there is a vital connection between all these shades of meaning. The interrelation is the implied principle of election. Neither historic Israel, nor the "Israel of God", nor Eschatological Israel, nor the individual Israelite, can be explained in any other way than by the fact that the God of Israel is the One who elects. Israel is unthinkable apart from the concept of election.

(*a*) *Israel: the Historic People of the Covenant*

In the context of history, and specifically in the context of the story of revelation, Israel here means the historic people of the Covenant. This covers not only a common experience but also a common ancestry and a common destiny. But it is important to stress that in no sense is historic Israel a people in its own right: the initiator of the history of Israel is the God of Israel. He, God, the God of the Fathers, calls Israel into being by calling Abraham from his father's house into the Land of Promise.

Israel is here a strictly collective term with a definite ancestry. But it is noteworthy that the *nomen proprium* does not refer back to

Abraham but to Jacob. Gutbrod points out that there is no direct reference to the Patriarch as Israel in the N.T., but he admits that in several passages he is referred to by implication.[2]

We believe there is reason to see special importance in the noun as it is used in the N.T. Underlying the description of the Jewish people as Israel is the desire (*a*) to emphasize the coherent unity in its totality as a people: Jacob was the ancestor of the twelve tribes; (*b*) to emphasize Israel's spiritual dignity: Israel was Jacob re-born. He was the one who fought with God and men and "prevailed" (Gen. 32. 28). In this name is thus reflected the spiritual task and dignity of the chosen people: to be a kingdom of priests (Ex. 19. 6).

In Israel collectively we meet the community as chosen by God. Israel here indicates the community in its awareness of the task, responsibility, duty, and vocation as set by God before the people in its totality. But the Bible in its realism never overlooks the other side of the fact, namely that Israel is not only the Chosen People of God, but also the people fallen from God. Israel means also the struggling, rebellious, murmuring people of God, with all its sins and failures. It is the people in history which is both *'ammi* and *lo-'ammi* at the same time.

It is at this point of contradiction that we are forced from a purely exegetical to a theological interpretation of historic Israel.

Israel in history poses the question: What is the ultimate meaning of a people's togetherness? Whenever and wherever we meet historic Israel we face this question. Why? Because in the life of Israel we find depicted as nowhere else the community on its way to the Promised Land, always wandering but never reaching the goal. Between Israel and the Promised Land are always the deep waters of the Jordan.

In historic Israel we find mirrored the problem of society in all ages. The goal of Israel, like the goal of society, is the Kingdom of God. But in history the goal will always remain illusory, because the condition for its achievement is contradictory: Israel must cease to be in order to reach his destiny. The way to life is through death. Only by total surrender of his privilege, attainment, dignity, and position can Israel fulfil his destiny. But the separateness, tradition, religion, and culture are the very life of a nation. Israel cannot and must not die; he cannot surrender. We shall never grasp the problem of society unless we grasp the problem of historic Israel. Both stand before the same challenge—the challenge of the Cross. For this is the principle of life: unless the wheat fall into the ground and die it cannot bear fruit (cf. John 12. 24).[3] Such extremity neither Israel nor society can accept. Plato's solution outlined in the *Republic*, or Karl Marx's solution as outlined in *Das Kapital*, or Israel's solution as outlined by rabbinic Judaism, are the only possible solutions in history.

Yet historic Israel, like society, is an instrument in God's hand. In the life of Israel we see election work itself out on the plane of history. Historic Israel is the vehicle of revelation. He is the guardian of the Bible; he is the personification of law and order; he is the instrument of salvation.

It is in Israel that the Messiah is born; it is in Israel that the Church comes into existence. It is Israel who first carries the message of the One God to the Gentile world. It is from Israel that the Church receives the "oracles" of God, her spiritual tradition, her liturgy, her music, her psalms, yes, even her vision of the Kingdom of God. Yet Israel who sees the Kingdom cannot enter.

Israel's "signs" of election are a puzzlement to the world. Historic Israel is a messianic people. For this reason Gentiles frequently experience Israel's presence as a ferment[4]; but in reality, his craving for social justice, his striving after the absolute, is part of his historic function. Israel as a community is the harbinger of the Kingdom of God. The peculiar feature of Jewish existence ties Israel with a thousand bonds to the order of this world. Ignaz Maybaum rightly said: "We are deeply engulfed in secular history."[5] It is Israel's vocation to live closely to this world. The Jewish people, whom Maritain calls "a mystical body", is closely knit by a "community of earthly hope". For it is Israel's task to strive after the Kingdom of God *here* upon earth. This is a prophetic task which has been handed on to the Jewish people by the great seers in the O.T.:

> Israel passionately hopes for, awaits, wants the advent of God in the world, the Kingdom of God here *below*. It wants with an eternal will, a supernatural and unreasonable will, justice in time, in nature, and in the community. Greek wisdom has no meaning for Israel: neither its reasonableness nor its felicity in form. The beauty Israel seeks is ineffable, and Israel wants it in this life of the flesh, to-day.[6]

In Israel we meet on the plane of history something of the leaven of eternity. Jewish life takes place under the pressure of the messianic ideal. Israel refuses to accept the *status quo*. "The Jew", says Maybaum, "is the messianic man, he is waiting for a time to come."[7] Israel thus lives for the future and he presses towards a goal.

Israel is also a priestly people; to be a Kingdom of priests is his original vocation. Not only in the past, but even to-day, and this in spite of his secularism and this-worldliness; the Jew remains the great protestant against idols. He has performed and still performs an important iconoclastic function in history. In this he has also rendered great service to the Church. Whenever the Church sank into mere "Christianity", both the voice and the presence of the Jew reminded her of the One Invisible God; of the Ten Commandments, it is the first two which are indelibly written on the heart of Israel. Jews have suffered and died in thousands *'al-ḳiddushat ha-Shem*—for the sanctification of the Name, i.e. for the witness that God is One and that there is none beside him. Maritain is therefore right when he says, "The people of Israel remains a priestly people." To him, even the bad Jew remains a priest, a "kind of bad priest".[8] But here we must be careful not to overstate the case. The individual Jew participates in the historic task of Israel only in proportion to his integration into the *kelal Yisrael*. Splintered from the community he is merely a drifter without a haven.

Jewish writers, in an effort to define Israel's historic mission, have concluded that the mere existence of the Jewish people is already a witness to the Gentile world. What Maybaum says of the Jewish mission has been said over and over again: "The Mission of the Jew is to be a Jew"[9]; but he adds one important detail: the Jew by being a Jew is already a priest—the Jew can never be a "layman", he is and remains a "lay priest".

There is one more point about historic Israel to complete the picture: Israel is the soil of God's revelation in Christ. Without Israel revelation is only a myth; with Israel revelation is anchored in history. The Jewish people is the living witness to the God of Abraham, Isaac, and Jacob. He is thus not a philosophical concept, but the God of history, the God who *makes* history. In Israel there is maintained a vital and living connection between past and present. Israel is the link not only with the O.T. but also with the N.T. But Israel is also the link between the Church and the world: he is that part of the Church which is in closest touch with the world. The Church would lose herself in other-worldliness but for historic Israel, for Israel is the Church in time *par excellence*.

In Israel is thus foreshadowed the answer to our question: What is the ultimate meaning of a people's togetherness? The answer is: Amidst trial and error, sorrow and heart-ache, pressing forward towards the Kingdom of God, to the End of time.

(*b*) "*The Israel of God*"

We have already seen that in the Pauline view the joining together in the Messiah of Jews and Gentiles on a footing of equality inaugurates the Messianic Age. The Israel of God in Gal. 6. 16 is a reference to messianic humanity, i.e. the new man who has found in the other man his brother because Jesus Christ is the Lord of both. Ideally expressed, we call Messianic Man in his togetherness the Church of Jesus Christ.

The Israel of God is Israel in his new togetherness in the Messiah. But here we meet with a strange discovery: on the plane of history (and we know no other), everything that has been said about historic Israel is applicable to the "Israel of God". The reason is obvious: the analogy stems from the fact that both live in the dimension of time. They thus share in the same failures, sins, and errors. There is nothing that historic Israel is guilty of, that the Church is not. The Church, as we have already seen, suffers from the same ambiguity as the historic people of God. Here too, the will to live prevails over the consideration of the Kingdom of God. Here too, as in Israel, the absolute is mixed up with earthly hopes. Israel has become Judaism; faith in Christ has become "Christianity"—a term which covers culture, civilization, a period in history, a certain outlook on life, as much as faith in Jesus Christ. The analogy of the position between Israel and Church goes as far as to the analogy of their respective names: Israel—the people connected with the spiritually re-born Jacob; *Christianoi*—the followers of the risen Christ. Both names carry the signification of the new life—they point to the world to come. When defining historic Israel's self-awareness,[10] we were in fact defining the self-consciousness of the Church. Church history is in fact Jewish history against a different background and on a wider geographical scale. The resemblance extends even to the "rejection" of the Christ, if not by actual deed then at least by moral implication. But at one point the similarity breaks down:

the Church knows herself guilty of the death of Christ. It is this that makes her the Church; she lives by this knowledge. Without it she would be just the Synagogue. Whenever she loses knowledge of that guilt she ceases to be the Church. The Church is thus the togetherness of people, both Jews and Gentiles, who put themselves humbly under the judgement of God and accept the verdict: Guilty. The Good News is that in spite of the verdict of guilt, God in his royal mercy offers eternal life. This is the meaning of forgiveness.

Thus the Church, like Israel, is a *corpus mysticum*: kept together by the grace of God, she lives by promise. Her persistence in history is as miraculous as that of historic Israel. Her influence upon the nations of the world goes far beyond her geographical limits. She has changed the course of history and literally transformed the face of the earth. As a ferment in the life of humanity her effectiveness goes far beyond that of historic Israel. She, too, has a priestly vocation which she has exercised and still exercises to the blessing of the nations. In her, too, human frailty and God's grace combine in such a way that the one is never without the other. She, too, stands in the tension between present and future, keyed up for the End. The Church, like historic Israel, is waiting. But here again we come upon the difference: the Church is waiting for Jesus of Nazareth to return in glory. She knows whom she expects; she knows his name, she knows his character, she knows his purpose. She will be able to recognize him by the nail prints on his hands, for these hands were once nailed to a Cross. The One she expects is no stranger: she may feel ashamed at his coming, but she knows whom she will meet.

Historic Israel is in a different position: he is expecting, waiting, he does not know for whom.

This, then, is the second mark of the Israel of God: forgiveness is known only in and through Jesus Christ. When it is not so known the Church ceases to be the Church and becomes the Synagogue again. In the Synagogue, too, there is knowledge of God's forgiveness, but that is entirely independent of and separate from Jesus of Nazareth. How the Jew receives forgiveness the Church does not know; this belongs to the innermost mystery of historic Israel and is of the same order as the experience of forgiveness among non-Christians; but this she knows: her own experience of forgiveness depends upon the Cross. This is her most precious knowledge which she dare not lose, without losing her life. The Church knows that Jesus suffered under Pontius Pilate for the sins of the world.

The Israel of God, like historic Israel, knows and dreads death. The world calls death a "natural" phenomenon, but Israel has never reconciled himself to it, because he knows God to be the God of Life. Death is a contradiction of God; it denies his goodness, it denies his power, it denies his life. The Jew rebels against death; dying is his greatest trial of faith. The pagan does not mind dying; he makes dying a cult. To the Jew death is unnatural and he looks to God for the resurrection of the dead: "Blessed art thou, O Lord, who quickenest the dead."[11] But his faith in the God who raises the dead is a pious assumption; there is very little in the O.T. to warrant it. It is based more upon the power of God than on his will to do so. That God *can* raise the dead no one doubts; but that he wills that the dead be raised is another matter. The Israel of God knows about the Resurrection in quite a different way. In the centre of the Church's faith stands the risen Christ. To her he is the Resurrection and the Life. A Church which does not know Christ in his risen Power is not the Church of Christ. A Church which forgets the empty Cross and the open grave, and dwells upon the broken body on the Crucifix, denies an essential element of her faith. In doing so she reverts to the Synagogue and loses herself in morbid contemplation of the misery of death.

We can thus see the close link between Church and Synagogue: historic Israel and the Israel of God are indissolubly linked to one another. They live by the same hope, press towards the same goal, are entrusted with the same task; they carry the seed of the same revelation and yet are not the same. Their difference derives from their attitude to Jesus Christ. He is the divider between Israel and Israel, the Israel of history and the Israel of God. To know about the division is to know the secret of Church and Synagogue. Neither knows about herself unless she knows it in the difference from the other. Here Professor Walter Zimmerli has seen aright; it is only in juxtaposition that they understand themselves.[12]

For the Church it means that by discovering the position of historic Israel she discovers herself in reflection. It is her own picture in her unbelief: the community under judgement. Israel, which is *'ammi* and *lo-'ammi* in the same person, is also at the same time Church and Synagogue, Israel in history and the Israel of God.

If the Church by looking upon historic Israel discovers her own superiority, then she has *not* seen aright; she is like the man who beheld his natural face in the mirror and went away and immediately forgot what manner of man he was (cf. James 1. 23 f.). For historic Israel is not a sect, a heresy, he is the Church, i.e. man who is called by God in his togetherness to accept the Kingdom of God, but instead accepts the trappings of the Kingdom and rejects the King. Historic Israel is the Church in her religious autonomy before God. Karl Barth, by including the Jews into the framework of the Church, has opened up a new vista into biblical theology.[13] The correlation of Church and historic Israel puts the Israel of God in history in a tension which must never be resolved.

For Barth the Church exists in a twofold manner: historic Israel and the Christian Community. The two are inseparable and belong together: their relationship is like that of the Resurrection to the Crucifixion, or that of God's mercy to God's judgement.[14] The one cannot be seen without the other. The mirror, i.e. historic Israel, is thus not only a reflection of God's wrath but also of his mercy.[15] It means that rejection and election go hand in hand: God rejects the sinful community, and yet elects it in his Son for the Kingdom of God. To leave out historic Israel from the election of grace means nothing less than leaving out the Church of history because of her failure. This would result in a completely different concept of Church: a Church of those who live by merit and not by grace; a Church, in fact, which is a Synagogue. But the Israel of God in history is the failing, ailing, humbled Church. To separate her from historic Israel is to deny her historic reality as a community.[16] But her connection with historic Israel is also important for another reason: in the schism between Church and Synagogue is reflected the schism which makes the Body of Christ a broken body.[17]

Thus the link between the Israel of God and the Israel in history is both real and necessary: both exist only by co-existing. But at this point we seem to be forced to depart from the Barthian standpoint. For it seems to us inaccurate to speak of either Israel as constant in his relationships and in his separation. To us the dividing-line, though real, remains fluid: the Church is frequently Synagogue and the Synagogue is sometimes Church. Historic Israel becomes the Israel of God, not in his totality, but by reason of the "remnant" (cf. Rom. 11. 5); but the Church, too, becomes the Synagogue, not in her totality but by reason of her corporate faithlessness, her autonomy, and her Christless character; and yet they both remain Israel—by reason of the Promise.

In this interchange of Church and Synagogue, historic Israel and the Israel of God, lies the tension of personal faith. We thus come to the "Israelite"—the individual as the believer in the God of Israel.

(c) *The Individual Israelite*

Though the Community plays an important part in the O.T., the individual occupies an equally important and legitimate place. It may well be that in the older strata of the O.T. documents Jahwe worship was a tribal affair, but in the Prophets we already have a highly developed individualistic approach to the questions of morality and religion. Here the tension between the individual and the community breaks out in all its acuteness. Such tension is the usual phenomenon in all history. The Bible denies the pagan assertion: *vox populi, vox dei*; the Prophet is the *lonely* man who utters the Word of God and as a result becomes unpopular. The Synagogue in her insistence on the supreme right of the community is in constant danger of violating the right of the individual; but the Church too finds herself in a similar situation.

Originally the Christian faith was a movement of individuals. Men and women became "Christians" by a personal decision for Jesus Christ. This was not a popular thing to do. To decide for Jesus was to go against the majority. The same applied to Gentile believers, who had to reject their pagan past and join themselves to a foreign faith and a foreign people. The early Church thus, both on Jewish and on non-Jewish soil, consisted of men and women who had not inherited a tradition, but who personally decided about the truth, as they saw it. It was only after Christianity degenerated into a mass movement and became the religion of a majority that a radical change took place; from a movement of individuals it became a movement of the mass. From henceforth entry into the Church ceased to be a matter of personal decision. "Christianity" became a question either of birth, or of fashion; or worse still, it was decided by the reigning prince, or else imposed by political and military pressure.[18] Finally, the Church faced the anomalous situation of whole nations pretending to be Christian. At this point the approximation of Synagogue and Church becomes closest.

It is the will of God that historic Israel should be the Israel of God; it is also the will of God that nations should be Christian; but in history totality is a fallacy and savours of hypocrisy. In the realm of moral and spiritual values only the individual counts. To miss this basic fact is to overlook the most essential element in the spiritual history of mankind. That historic Israel should overlook and by-pass the deep personal implications of faith is understandable, for he is first and foremost a community in the generic sense. But that this should happen to the Church reveals again the thin line which divides Church from Synagogue.

Historic Christianity slipped easily back into a primitive, tribal concept of religion. The once personal conviction became an heirloom to be passed on from father to son. Whereas originally a man had to decide personally whether to follow or reject Jesus Christ, it now became the prerogative of birth to be a "follower". Infant baptism became the biological safeguard for the continuance of the "Christian race". The stake and the inquisition saw to it that no one was exempt from being a "Christian".

Here we meet not only the same fusion between Church and world which is a characteristic of Judaism, but also the same pressure towards totality at any cost. Seen in this light "Christianity" becomes Judaism in a new dress. The terminology is different but the characteristics are the same: religion, culture, and civilization so combine that they become indistinguishable. Man thus can live, develop, and fight for "Christian culture" without necessarily being a Christian.

Once again we find repeated the same dialectical situation we meet in historic Israel and which must remain insoluble on this side of history.

The balance between Israel in history and the Israel of God is kept by the individual; he is the factor that decides how much the Church is Church and how much she is "world". Here the difference between Jew and Gentile is nil, they are both in the same position. Let us look at the Jew first.

The individual Jew belongs to the chosen community. He is a member of a people with a great tradition. In the Pauline view it was no mean privilege to be born of that people (cf. Rom. 3. 1 f.); but it is also no ordinary temptation to live as a Jew by "proxy", i.e. to dwell on the past, to take pride in his origin, to take shelter behind his dignity, and to evade *personal* responsibility before God. Wrapped in his *tallit* (prayer shawl), with the phylacteries upon his left arm and his forehead, bowed before the Ark of the Law, a member of the praying community of historic Israel can harmlessly repeat with everyone else: *attah veḥartanu mikkol ha-'ammim*—"Thou hast chosen us from all the nations"—without ever facing the implication of that choice! Are we to assume, as he already does, that the election of Israel is his guarantee for his personal salvation? This we must categorically deny unless we make faith a mockery. Christians know that man cannot be saved by nobility of birth, but only by the Cross of Jesus Christ.

Before God the individual Jew stands in exactly the same position as every other human being; he can plead no privilege and no merit, save the merit of the Son of God. For him too, and most specially for him, God's grace must remain his only plea. Neither his moral superiority over his Gentile brother, nor his great spiritual tradition, can bring him into the Kingdom of God. Before the Cross he can only stand empty-handed, with nothing to offer and no excuse. All he can plead is his own need and God's mercy. If he has advantage at all, it is only in the sense of great responsibility: to whom much is entrusted from him much shall be required (Luke 12. 48). Here the parable about the Talents is most apposite. Those who claim for the Jew special privileges unwittingly circumvent the Cross. This was Simon Peter's great discovery: God is no respecter of persons (Acts 10. 34); he has no favourites and accepts no bribery. That the Jew should want to enter into the Kingdom of God in any other way but by the way of the Cross, i.e. by the way of forgiveness and grace, is in itself an expression of human *hybris*. It only reveals the abysmal depth of man's need in his pretended self-sufficiency. Those who claim that Jews can enter the Kingdom of God by a different way than that of the Cross have never grasped the meaning of the parable about the "holier than thou" Pharisee (Luke 18. 9–14). Spiritual pride is the most subtle and deadly form of pride.

Let us now look at the Gentile.

In essence his temptations are the same, though his situation looks different. He belongs not to the Chosen Community but to the community to be chosen. But he, too, brings with him all the pride in tradition, race, and achievement peculiar to every nation. To renounce his gods for the God of Israel is the greatest trial of his faith. He asks with offended pride: Why should God remain tied to the people of Israel, he who is the Creator of the world? In his own mind and heart he therefore separates the God of history from historic Israel and turns him into a "universal concept". The conceptualization of God for the sake of "universalism" is the Gentile's greatest snare. Behind the desire to depart from the particular to the universal, is the effort to evade personal and concrete responsibility before God. God thus becomes a Truth instead of a living Person *vis-à-vis* man. The Gentile thus speaks about the "Truth of Christianity" instead of the real presence of the Risen Christ. But by turning the living Christ into a concept of "truth" he has evaded the personal issue: personal decision and responsibility before God.

With the prayer book in his hand, in the dim light of a church, turning towards the east, the individual Gentile Christian repeats with the rest of the congregation: "I believe . . ."—but he only believes what the Church believes; he has little personal faith. Personal faith can never be the result of a collective decision: here only the individual can decide.

But if the decision is entirely in the hands of the individual, what need is there of Israel as a community? Let the isolated, detached, Israelite suffice as the symbol of God's election. It is here that we discover once again the insoluble link between Israel and Israel: Israel as a community and Israel as the individual.

Apart from the community the individual's choice would have meant self-election. If man's salvation is made to depend upon his decision, then in fact he saves himself. Man, however much he may decide for God, is not elect, except in the community. It is the election of the community which makes for the individual's election. He lives only by reason of the community, which lives by the Promise of God. Apart from Israel, the individual is a pious hypocrite who elects himself to sonship because he knows himself better than the other man. Without Israel there is no personal election; only in Israel, the Chosen Community, are we elected to be sons of God.

This brings us to the next aspect of Israel.

(*d*) *Eschatological Israel*

In the human mind, for the sake of clarity, concepts have to be kept separate, though genetically they exist only in connection. It gives us an illusion of intellectual grasp once we have segregated and defined what is in fact indivisible and non-definable. To this category belongs the concept of Israel in history. By splitting Israel into Church and Synagogue we think we have come closer to the secret of election. But it becomes immediately obvious that our division is artificial once we go beyond the outward form and begin to operate in terms of inward attitudes. Here the dividing line ceases to be horizontal and becomes vertical. What St Paul said of the Jews applies with equal force to the Christian: He is not a Christian who is one outwardly, but he is a Christian who is one inwardly. There are "Christians" in the Synagogue, as there are "Jews" in the Church.[19] Jacques Maritain has expressed it in a different way, though it amounts to the same thing: "There are many Jews who prefer God to the world and many Christians who prefer the world to God."[20] This means that the demarcation-line of the Church cannot be drawn horizontally. Church, Synagogue, and world intersect at many points. So it must remain to the End.

This also means that Israel as the *completed* community does not belong to time and history, but to the End of time, to the *eschaton*. Israel here is an eschatological concept; he is not yet, as the Kingdom of God is not yet, as the End is not yet. The difference between Israel in history and Israel in his completion is like the difference between Jerusalem which now is and which is in bondage (Gal. 4. 25) and the Jerusalem which is above, the Golden City, the abode of the Saints (Rev. 21. 2, 10). While history lasts, Israel can never be complete. The continuation of Israel in history is only with a view to the End, when God will make up his peculiar treasure (cf. Mal. 3. 17). Meanwhile Israel is an ideal to pray for, to strive after, to try to realize. Israel belongs to the same category as the Kingdom of God: it is and is not; it is present and is to come; it is here and not here, at the same time. The reason for this peculiar dialectic lies embedded in the nature of time: time means suspense.

Eschatological Israel is thus Israel in his fullness; this refers to the End when all Israel will be saved (Rom. 11. 26). Gutbrod rightly distinguishes between "all Israel" and all Jews.[21] For St Paul to claim that all Jews would be saved just because they are Jews would mean to make nonsense of faith. "All Israel" is here the Church of God in her completion, the Church in heaven. On the Day of Judgement, when the last thoughts of men shall be exposed, then Israel will be revealed as Israel, the true People of God. This will be the last act in the story of revelation: the uncovering of the *mysterion* about God's people. But this will not be a revelation of human integrity, personal worth, or achievement, but a revelation of God's immeasurable grace.

Eschatological Israel is thus the hope of God's ultimate triumph over history; he stands as a sign of the completion of God's purpose: the Kingdom of God. But Ultimate Israel would remain a theological fiction if it were isolated and kept separate from Israel in history, in his threefold aspect: historic Israel, the Israel of God, and the individual Israelite. The connection lies not in history, but beyond it, in the Promise of the Word of God. In the same way as God uses Israel's blindness for the blessing of the Gentiles (Rom. 11. 25),[22] so God uses the Church's fall, for the blessing of the world. How God turns the world into Israel we do not know, but one thing we do know: that God so loved the world that Christ died for it. Thus in the question of Israel is involved the salvation of the world. Here lies the closest link between the Israel of the End and the Israel in history: in the will of God to save the world.

But the triumph of God's sovereign grace in no way detracts from the fact that within the experience of man salvation is always offered but never imposed. God does not treat man as an automaton but as a person. For this reason the Word of God became flesh in the form and fashion of a man. God limits his freedom by allowing man to choose, and though he cannot choose without the grace of God, his grace is enabling but not compelling grace. If it were otherwise neither human personality nor moral values would have any meaning. This leads us to the next problem in relation to Israel.

(*e*) *The Individual between Israel and God*

Collectivity which overlooks the basic importance of the individual is of pagan origin. Biblical humanity begins with one single man. It is the individual who is the bearer of the *imago Dei*. Christian theologians have been so captivated by the pagan concept of the mass that they find it difficult to retrieve the basic "Christian category": the individual. In the controversy regarding Israel this fact has greatly helped to confuse the issue. Professor Vischer would have reached quite different conclusions had he paid due respect to the importance of the individual in his exegesis of Rom. 9–11. The πᾶς Ἰσραήλ in 11. 26 he interprets to mean that the Jewish people will be saved in their totality. His contention is that if the Apostle had believed otherwise, there would have been no point in writing the three chapters. To him the mystery of Israel which St Paul tries to expound to his Gentile readers lies in this very fact that God triumphs even over unbelief.[23] This in itself is quite correct, but overlooks several important problems:

1. If Professor Vischer's interpretation of πᾶς 'Iσραήλ is correct, Israel is saved *en masse*, irrespective of the attitude of the individual Jew to Jesus Christ.

2. If πᾶς 'Iσραήλ is limited to the Jewish people, Israel and the Jews are coterminous; but St Paul held that not every one of Israel is Israel and that not everyone who is a Jew outwardly is one inwardly.

3. Again, if πᾶς 'Iσραήλ means the totality of the Jewish people, all generations which have passed are of necessity included. In this case salvation is already assured by reason of birth.

4. Once again, if πᾶς 'Iσραήλ is the whole Jewish people, God saves Jews by decree whereas Gentiles he saves by faith.

It is obvious that however we may try to look at the problem, Vischer's interpretation is impossible.[24] Whatever the Apostle may have had in mind when he spoke of "all Israel", he could never have implied that God is a respecter of persons, or that personal faith did not matter. As a missionary he knew too well the importance of personal decision; as a theologian he refused to accept the difference between Jew and Gentile in relation to the Cross. The answer, therefore, must be somewhere else; in our view it lies in the peculiar position that the individual occupies between Israel and God.

It is here that we meet the dialectic between history and eternity, between election and rejection, between judgement and grace, in all its acuteness. In fact we hold that all the dialectic of history is centred in the individual; he is the clue to every human problem.

The first proposition we want to lay down is this: whereas nations are the instruments of his will, God deals with individuals as *persons*. This is essential for a proper understanding of the biblical concept of election. Faith, therefore, does not relate a nation to God, but only the individual; for faith in the biblical sense can be defined only in personal terms. Before God, man is an individual and not one of millions; this is an essential part of the Gospel. This does not mean that in the eyes of God the individual is more precious than the mass, but only that the individual is *nearer* to God who is also One and who in his only begotten Son reveals the true meaning of the relationship between

Father and child.[25] In this uniqueness of the God-man relationship lies the mystery of the human personality. It is for this reason that the individual takes precedence before the community.[26] He, the individual, is singled out as the object of God's concrete love, for divine love is essentially practical. God does not love "humanity" but *the* particular man and through him the community. This is the position of the individual as we meet him in the Bible from Genesis to Revelation.

We are thus told that God created *Adam* and not just a "species of man". Man in the Bible is one, unique, a self, a person, the bearer of the image of God. Right through the story of revelation we encounter man not as a species but as a person: he has a name, he hears God speak and responds to his call as an individual—Abraham, Moses, each of the Prophets. In the Gospels the importance of the individual is even more emphatic: many of the parables deal with individual responsibility. The value of the individual is repeatedly stressed, and Jesus seems to address himself almost exclusively to him: "He who hath ears to hear, let him hear."

In the Synoptic Gospels particularly, Jesus seems to draw a dividing-line between the one and the many, the individual and the crowd. Not that he despises the crowd, but he treats it differently. He knows of the need of the multitude (cf. Matt. 9. 36 ff.), but his attention is always fixed upon the individual: the one sheep which goes astray, the prodigal son who returns, the coin which a woman loses, the one sinner who repents, illustrate this fact. He contrasts the narrow path of the few with the wide gate of the many; and though he knows that many are called, he stresses the fact that few are chosen. He speaks lovingly of his little flock, and hides himself from the crowd. His relationship to his disciples is of friend to friend. In his circle no one is a cog or a number; every one is a person with a name, a son or daughter of Abraham. The despised publican, the harlot, the little child, the woman of Samaria, the criminal on the cross—they are all persons.

This is the unique dignity of man. Herein lies his advantage over the beast. But this being a person puts him in the paradoxical position of belonging to two worlds: the world of spirit and the world of matter. Man in history walks on the narrow line between these two worlds. He carries that line of division within him: he is a split personality. Upon his forehead are two marks: the mark of God and the mark of Cain; he is sinner and saint in one person; he is the son of God and the son of the devil at the same time. In this twofold existence, as the servant of God and the servant of mammon, as free and slave, as believer and disbeliever, he walks through life. He is the battleground of the opposites and under the sign of contradiction. With his eye he can look beyond the Milky Way and in imagination reach the end of the universe, yet the slightest physical disorder can rob him of his life.

In this paradoxical position man faces God. Man faces the Creator not only as his creature but also as his son: chosen, elected, predestined to be man. But he also faces the thrice-holy God who rejects the sinner. Man is thus chosen and rejected at the same time. He is chosen as a son and rejected as a rebel. This is not a theological fiction, but the deepest awareness on the part of man when face to face with God. In the presence of God man knows himself a wastrel, who has thrown to the wind his dignity, who has left the Father's house and frittered away his heritage. He knows that he has forfeited his right to sonship; between him and God there is a gulf, the gulf of sin. His separation from God has separated him from his brother. Between man and man there is a gulf, the gulf created by selfishness. He has lost the art of fellowship. He bands together with other men for defence and robbery, but in essence he remains a lonely creature. Godless man is not only without God but also without the enjoyment of human fellowship, for without God as the Father there is no brotherhood. Without God, man remains a stranger to the other man, no matter how closely related they may be biologically. This is the story of history: *homo homini lupus*.

This is the position: on the one hand, man's eternal destiny is in the bosom of his Father; on the other hand, the empirical fact of history: lonely, God-less man.

Into this paradoxical position we must place the Gospel: the enduring faithfulness of a Father's love. It means that at the deepest point in the gulf of separation, the Other Man, Jesus of Nazareth, took his stand. He stands there in the mire of human sin to form the link between God and man. This is the *other* Son, obedient, faithful, and true to the Father's love, sacrificing his life and dignity for the sake of the brother. This is the true Son of God, and because he is the Son of God, he is also the Son of man. In him God and man are become reconciled, are at-one. This is the meaning of atonement in the Cross. The Cross is the place where God's greatest love meets man's deepest need. Here God in his infinite love identifies himself with the sinner and takes his place. This is no ordinary statement; in the eyes of the Synagogue it amounts to blasphemy, in the eyes of the Greek philosopher it is folly. This, man cannot know of himself. How can he know that there is a way out of despair? How can he believe that God really stretches his hands out to sinners and justifies the godless? How can man know that Jesus of Nazareth is the Saviour of sinners?

There is a double witness to this supreme fact in human history: the witness of historic Israel and the witness of the Church.

Israel's witness is indirect. As a people the Jews deny the Cross and their part in it. They desire to dissociate themselves from its symbolism and its implications. In fact they remain enemies of the Cross. Yet in the story of their election is included the drama of the Crucifixion. Israel was chosen to give birth to the Messiah and to become the instrument of his death. We have already seen that on the historical plane the story of Israel and the story of Jesus of Nazareth go together: Jewish history is the background for the story of revelation. That Jesus was born in Bethlehem of the house of David, that he was brought up in Nazareth, that he was condemned in Jerusalem and died upon Golgotha, is part of Jewish history. That the same Jesus who died a criminal's death is believed by millions of people to be the Son of God, is part of general history.

Jewish history these last nineteen hundred years has taken place under the shadow of this fact. Jews may try to reinterpret its significance, but from the fact itself they cannot escape.

From the Christian point of view there is something sinister about the fact that the initiative against the Christ was taken by the Church and not by the world. That it should have happened in Israel, in the holy city of Jerusalem, in full view of the Law, with the co-operation of the priesthood, with the support of pious opinion, that Jesus of Nazareth was condemned to death, reveals the position of the Church in history, but it also reveals the power and freedom of God. God turns Israel's failure to man's blessing, and God is not tied to Israel so that he depends on him. He can raise up out of the stones in the desert children unto Abraham (Matt. 3. 9).

This is the indirect witness to Jesus Christ.

But there is also a direct witness to Jesus Christ. From the day that the Gospel was first proclaimed to this present day, there have been men and women, both Jews and Gentiles, claiming to have experienced atonement through the crucified Messiah. The fact of their togetherness is a miracle in itself. Apart from the Master there is nothing to unite them; he is the one basis of their fellowship. In this fellowship they have become related to the God of Israel. They strive to be loyal to his moral standards, they submit to his Word, they accept and believe his Promises. Like historic Israel they live in suspense waiting for the consummation of the ages. Their togetherness is not based upon land, race, language, or culture; the only thing they have in common is loyalty to Jesus Christ. Their secret is their faith in the Gospel; because they believe in Jesus Christ, they believe in the God of the Promises. They *want* to be Israel and they believe that they have been called to *become* Israel, not because they merit the dignity but only because they put their trust in the grace and love of God. The token of such grace and love they find in Jesus Christ. It is by his sacrifice that they know themselves to be the sons of God, not by right but by adoption. They can make no claims upon the God of Israel, but they know that God has stretched out a hand of reconciliation to them in Jesus Christ. They have *heard* the Word of forgiveness and have thus become the Church.

This is the direct witness to Jesus Christ.

Between this double witness the individual stands, be he Jew or be he Gentile. Caught between this double front, Israel and Israel, no man stands as a member of a people, but as a "private" individual in the challenge of decision. In the dialectic tension between Israel and Church he discovers the tension of his own life; for the Cross and against the Cross, with Christ and against him.

No individual ever stands *between* Israel and Israel, he belongs to both. If we accept the definition of Israel not as a racial entity, but as an historic consciousness, and that in Israel's election is portrayed the election of the human race, then the conclusion is near at hand that in history being a "Jew" and being a "Christian" are constantly alternating possibilities in a human life. It is expressed in the clash between nature and grace. The Jewish "No" to Christ is the constant possibility of the same man who also says, "Yes"; and *vice versa*, the human "Yes" also carries the possibility of "No" at the same time. For man's response to the Gospel can never be a final response while he moves in time and space.

In the relativity of time, neither man's "No" nor his "Yes" can be final, once and for all. In every situation and to every challenge he has to respond afresh. But Barth is right when he denies the possibility of ontological godlessness; the last word is not with man but with God. Even though man says, "No", and repeatedly says, "No", to Jesus Christ, God's "Yes" counts for more; for God's Word is the last word and it is a word of salvation.

But even man's "Yes" can be only a humble "Yes", a sponsored "Yes", prompted and encouraged by the Holy Spirit of God. By himself, with his insincerity, unbelief, mixed motives, lust for power, he can hardly say "Yes" or "No". His "No" expresses his lack of security, his confusion, his pull downwards; his "Yes" expresses his desire for salvation, his need of forgiveness, his need of God. His "Yes" is therefore not completely "Yes" and his "No" is not a final "No". He therefore needs the Church, to say, "Yes", and the Synagogue, to say, "No". In his togetherness with others his decision takes on new meaning and carries greater weight. His voice joined to the voice of others takes on historical significance, it becomes history. Not only so, but in his decision for or against, he joins into the fellowship of all those who have made a similar decision even though they are entirely outside the domain of Church and Synagogue.

Man thus stands between the two signs: plus and minus, yes and no, Church and Synagogue. But over against his "Yes" and his "No", there is the great "Yes" of God in Jesus Christ (2 Cor. 1. 19 f.); and because of him there is and remains an eternal connection between historic Israel, the Israel of God, the individual believer, and Israel of the *eschaton*, when God will be All in all.

In conclusion, one more remark is necessary.

The connection between Israel and the individual is that of a triangle: the individual—Christ—Israel. Only in his relatedness to the Messiah does the individual become related to the community. At no point can the triangle be broken; his physical relatedness to Israel, in the case of the Jew, is important only inasmuch as history is important, but this does not exempt him from the dialectic of faith. He finds the other man and he finds the community only in the Messiah. Without him, he remains in suspense.

(*f*) *Correctives*

Every people lives a twofold life: it moves on two different planes, the spiritual and the physical. It is a characteristic feature of Judaism that it is impatient of this dualism and presses towards a synthesis. In this way it tries to evade the ambiguity of history, which springs from the dualism inherent in the human position. Christian writers are often fascinated by the specific Jewish monism and try to introduce it into the Christian outlook. But such monism can be justified only with a view to the End, not on the plane of history. The Christian view of history can be seen only from the Incarnation and the Cross, which reveal the clash between time and eternity and not its fusion. The Incarnation means that God invades the world vertically and not horizontally; in other words, Jesus Christ is not the peak of humanity but the Word become flesh. This breaking into history of the Other World reveals the dialectic of man's situation: he is here and he is there; he belongs to the world which passes away and also to the world of the Spirit. In this tension Jewish history stands, and so does all other history. But in the case of the Jewish people that tension is more visible and at a higher pitch. Here egocentricity and theocentricity are in a closer relationship because of revelation. Historic Israel's twofold existence is therefore more marked than in the case of other nations: every Jew lives a double life, as a man and as a Jew. Because this is so, the Jewish people lives a double life: as a people and as God's People. The Jewish people is therefore burdened with a double historic consciousness: it has an ethnic consciousness and a "*theological*" consciousness; it knows itself torn between the demands of history and the Law of God. Its Messianism, as its monism, is to a large degree the quest for a synthesis between the two opposites. This occasionally happens to other nations but never to the same degree.[27] We have already dwelt on the fact of the unique Jewish awareness of election.

i. *The Jewish Position.* We thus must recognize the fact that being a man and being a Jew is not the same thing; the Jew is a Jewish man, that is to say a *special* man. To interpret the adjective "Jewish" in a purely ethnic or racial sense is to violate the facts of history and to dissociate the Jew from his past. The tension which so markedly pervades Jewish history springs from this source: the Jew is a man and a Jew in one person; he belongs to the world and he belongs to God. This is the peculiar burden of the Chosen People, and it expresses itself in the constant challenge to make a choice. An interesting example is afforded by the case of Samuel when the Elders of Israel ask the prophet to give them a king so that they may be like the other nations (1 Sam. 8. 5,

20). Their motive is important: they do not wish to be a special people with the God of Israel as the Invisible King. To have God as King divides a people's loyalty; it imposes upon its life an aspect of eternity; it puts its strivings and quests under a question-mark. To place authority into the hands of a visible king is to remove the ambiguity of its existence and provide it with a definite, attainable purpose.[28] Here lies the fascination of the political aim over against the Kingdom of God.

But no man has ever managed to escape from the inherent dualism in history, not even the Jew. Intellectually this is a possibility; man can construct a system of thought in which every form of dualism is excluded and where either monotheism or monism is the rule. But in life, in history, in the realm of moral decision, there is always polarity, there is always tension. In the context of history the Jew is therefore both: the ordinary man and the *special* man; the man of the world and the man of God; the man of this age and of the age to come.

Because of this ambiguity there is a special difficulty in defining a Jew. Many writers have been greatly puzzled by this fact. Not only Gentiles, but Jews themselves have never decided what is meant by "Jew". Jacques Maritain, who carefully discusses the problem, arrives at the conclusion that the Jews are not a people in the ordinary sense, but "the people of peoples, the people of God. They are the consecrated tribe; they are a *house*, the house of Israel."[29] This is not really a definition, but only a description with a view to the Bible. Apart from the Promises, the Jews are just a people, with special traits of its own, but all the same a people as any other people. It is only in the biblical context that the Jew becomes a *special* man and Israel a *special* people. The Bible is thus the area where the man becomes a Jew and the Jews become Israel. Mere birth, tradition, blood-relationship, Hebrew culture, historic consciousness, etc., do not make the Jews into Israel; only God does. In other words Israel is Israel by Promise. The "inwardness" of the Jew in the Pauline definition has nothing to do with circumcision of the flesh or natural disposition; it is the grace of God. But because grace is given and cannot be taken, not every one of Israel is Israel and not every one who is a Jew outwardly is one inwardly. In this tension between being called and being chosen, the Jew stands, the Church stands, man stands. To remain there in humble faith is man's only possible response to grace.

To speak of historic Israel as a "race" or a nation is quite legitimate in the historic sense. To call the Jews the "chosen race" is theologically a misconception. God does not choose one "race" before another. The distinctive mark of Israel's election is not "race" but Promise. But it is not a promise given to the Jews, it is God's Promise to mankind given to Abraham and sealed in Jesus Christ.

ii. *Jewish Rejection.* We have already dealt with this subject in another connection.[30] Here we will view the question in the perspective of history. Christians usually affirm that the Jewish people had rejected Jesus Christ, and that as a punishment they have been rejected by God. We thus have before us two propositions, the one dependent on the other; we will deal with them separately, considering first the Jewish rejection of Jesus Christ.

The question of the legality of the court which decided to deliver Jesus into the hands of Pilate does not concern us here, because no court, no matter how representative, can speak for a whole people.[31] The story of the rejection finds its climax in the story of the Crucifixion: the mounting opposition in Jerusalem led to a quick arrest, a hasty trial, and the verdict to deliver Jesus into the hands of the Roman Governor. On Good Friday, an excited crowd, instigated by the High Priest and his henchmen, demanded the death penalty for Jesus. The Master from the Cross prayed for his persecutors (cf. Luke 23. 34).

The question we now have to ask is this: Does the crowd in Jerusalem truly and factually represent the decision of the Jewish people? It is obvious that such a question can be answered only in the negative, and this for the following reasons:

1. No crowd is a *representative* crowd.

2. Even had the whole of Jerusalem taken part in the Crucifixion, this would still be a minority decision.

3. There were other crowds, also Jewish, which took the opposite view regarding Jesus of Nazareth, namely the crowd on Palm Sunday, the crowd on Pentecost.

4. The disciples, the ever-growing circle of believers, the early Church in Jerusalem to which both Priests and Pharisees belonged was almost entirely Jewish.

5. There was never a time in history when the Church was devoid of Jewish believers.

6. In later centuries, when the Gospel became obscured by

political and cultural issues, the Jewish people was never really presented with the challenge.

7. There is a growing number of Jewish Christians in modern times, a fact which belies the assertion that the Jewish decision regarding Jesus was once and final.

But these arguments must in no way obscure the most important point of all: no people can accept or reject Jesus Christ; this can only be done personally. Further, no people can once and for all decide about Jesus Christ; every generation has to do it for itself.

The glib assertion, therefore, that the "Jews" have rejected Jesus Christ belongs to those half-truths which are worse than lies because they obscure the deception. Behind it is usually the false assumption that the Gentiles have accepted him, which makes it a double lie.

We come now to God's rejection of the Jewish people. This has almost become a canon for Christendom and goes back to the earliest times of the Church, to the Epistle of Barnabas and Justin's *Dialogue*. Jewish rejection they interpret as punishment for the Crucifixion. If that were true, then the God of love is a vindictive God and of lesser stature than Jesus, who prayed for his persecutors. Such an implication is a blasphemous maligning of the character of God. But it also contradicts the very message of the Church, namely that Christ died for sinners, i.e. for the very people who crucified him.

There was good reason for Barnabas and Justin to interpret the tragic events of Jewish history of the first and second centuries in the light of the Jewish decision about Jesus; for in this world of cause and effect there is always a connection between decision and result. But though according to the Law of Moses God punishes the sins of the fathers upon the children to the third and fourth generation, he does not do so to the twentieth. To connect Jewish suffering to-day with punishment for the Crucifixion which took place about two thousand years ago, is to make of God a tyrant.

There is, however, more to it. To maintain Jewish rejection on the grounds of failure cuts the very ground from underneath the Church. If failure or success were the criterion of God's favour, then the Gospel is not the Gospel and grace is not grace. Has the Church succeeded where Israel has failed?

St Paul contradicts the assertion that God has cast off his

people (Rom. 11. 1). He does so not because of Israel's worthiness but because of God's faithfulness. God is not like man; he cannot lie (Num. 23. 19) and does not change (Mal. 3. 6), and with him there is no shadow cast by turning (James 1. 17). In St Paul's question, not only the hope of historic Israel is involved but also that of the Church and of mankind: shall their want of faith make of none effect the faithfulness of God (Rom. 3. 3)? Such is the character of God that he remains faithful even though man becomes faithless, "for he cannot deny himself" (2 Tim. 2. 13); so much so that even though our own conscience condemn us, "God is greater than our heart, and knoweth all things" (1 John 3. 20). This is the very Gospel, that God does not deal with us according to the justice of the *lex talionis*—tooth for tooth—but according to his fathomless mercy—he justifies the godless (Rom. 4. 5).

The fact is that the Church cannot afford to speak of the Jews as a "rejected" people without endangering her own position. They stand and fall together.

iii. *Jewish Suffering*. The supposed rejection of historic Israel stems not from theological consideration but from empirical observation. Jewish persistent suffering requires more than an ordinary explanation, and the rejection of the Messiah is the one nearest at hand.

It is a fact that in the long story of man's martyrdom there is nothing to equal that of the Jewish people. Jewish history is a long record of suffering from the slavery in Egypt to the gas-ovens of modern concentration camps.[32] In this terrible story of bloodshed, rape, and pillage, "Christians" have played some shameful part. It may well be that the myth of divine disfavour was invented in order to pacify a bad conscience, though the misfortunes which befell Jewry in the first and second centuries easily lent themselves to such an interpretation. That Jewish suffering was a sign of divine wrath was introduced early into the Church,[33] and has continued to this day. A typical example of how Christians viewed the Jewish people quite early in history comes from the pen of Tertullian, who describes them as:

> a race of wanderers, exiles from their own land and clime, they roam over the whole world without either a human or a heavenly king, not possessing even the stranger's right to set so much as one footstep in their native land . . .[34]

That the Jewish plight is the result of their faithlessness was obvious to Christian writers, who found their view confirmed in the N.T., where the consequences of the rejection of the Messiah are predicted (cf. Matt. 23. 37–9; Luke 13. 34, 35; 19. 41–4).[35] Gal. 4. 25 may probably be added to these passages: "Jerusalem which now is in bondage with her children", though Lightfoot sees in it a reference to spiritual bondage.[36] A similar reference is found in 1 Thess. 2. 13–16, where the suffering of the Gentile Christians is compared to that of Jewish believers at the hands of those "who both killed the Lord Jesus and the Prophets, and drave out us, and please not God, and are contrary to all men . . . *but the wrath is come upon them to the uttermost*". Here is an obvious reference to the connection between Jewish misdemeanour and Jewish suffering.

Such an interpretation is natural and in some measure justified, but it lends itself to grave misunderstanding. There is yet another aspect of suffering, which occupies the writer of the book of Job and forms the theme of the Servant Songs of Deutero-Isaiah, namely, innocent suffering. Though the law of cause and effect is as operative in history as it is in nature, yet on the moral plane responsibility for the sins of the fathers must not be placed upon the shoulders of the children. This was already the insight of the O.T. Prophets (cf. Jer. 31. 29 f.; Ez. 18. 1 ff.). In the light of the N.T., and specially in view of the Cross, suffering can never mean divine retribution. No people can be spoken of as a God-forsaken people, if God is a God of love.

There are three more aspects to Jewish suffering which are important to our theme:

(*a*) Suffering which man inflicts upon man is the visible demonstration of the reality of sin. It opens before us the real tragedy of human history, which according to the Bible begins with an act of fratricide. We repeat: *homo homini lupus* is written large over the annals of mankind. The suffering of the Jews is a part of that story. It must be seen and understood in the context of history and not in isolation,[37] save that in the case of the Jews suffering is more concentrated and continuous; this is connected with the peculiar position of statelessness in Jewish history. It is for this reason that the stark fact of the Jewish plight must serve as the most violent contradiction to every idealistic effort to gloss over human depravity. Jewish history, written in blood and tears, stands as the indelible record of the Martyrdom of Man[38] at the hands of his fellow-creature.

(*b*) All human suffering has also a vocational aspect. On the personal level this is described in an exemplary fashion by Max Eyth, in connection with the story of the building and collapse of the Forth Bridge.[39] On the corporate level it is illustrated by every major revolution in society, and by the continued sacrifice which is required to build civilization. In the case of the Jews their suffering is connected with their peculiar destiny and vocation in history. Here suffering has a positive connotation and brings a people within the close proximity of the Cross, because all such suffering is vicarious, i.e. on behalf of others.

Israel's suffering, although little understood by the Jews themselves, keeps the Messiah and his people in an intimate relationship, for he is the co-sufferer with all suffering humanity. In the case of the Jews, their suffering is also closely connected with their special vocation as God's people in history. It is the price, as Barth puts it, for the privilege of election.[40] Maritain sees it in the same light: "It is the vocation of Israel which the world execrates."[41] Gotthilf Weber, Otto Fricke, and many others give to Jewish suffering a similar explanation. "Anti-Semitism", says Weber, "is rebellion against the God of revelation."[42] The pagan in the Gentile, by persecuting the Jew, expresses his rebellion against the Other Jew who died upon the Cross for the sins of the world. Jew-hatred, in the last resort, is mutiny against God and his Anointed (cf. Ps. 2.). The very presence of the Jewish people serves to emphasize the link with the past and brings the Cross into the perspective of actuality. Jesus ceases to be a myth and becomes a challenging and embarrassing fact.

Here we see again the close link between historic Israel and Jesus Christ.

(*c*) There is yet one more aspect of Jewish suffering which we must bear in mind.

Professor Paul Tillich, in a penetrating study of the peculiar brand of German anti-Semitism, arrives at the conclusion that it springs to a large extent from a similarity of characteristic traits common to both Jews and Germans. He looks at anti-Semitism as a form of self-hatred which expresses itself by a projection of one's own baser instincts into the other man.[43] The negative traits of human nature which others so cleverly camouflage, the Jews are liable to exhibit in magnified form. These traits are not Jewish but *human*, and the Jew is only acting as a mirror. The Gentile hates to see himself in the Jew as he really is.[44] But there is the peculiar fact that the Jew is unable to keep to the middle path of mediocrity; in him both good and evil take extreme forms. This, too, is somehow related to his special function in history. Maritain wisely remarks: "Jews who become like others become worse than others."[45] The Jew, therefore, suffers for his humanity; that is, in him sin reveals itself for what it really is. The anti-Semite hates himself by hating the Jew, but it is the Jew who suffers.

Here we discover the other link which ties the Jew not only to the Messiah, but also to the human race.

In this position between the suffering Messiah and suffering humanity stands the suffering Jew. In the Jewish people is strangely concentrated the suffering of the human race. In the Jew, man suffers to the point of despair. Here we meet him at his deepest need. To preach the Gospel to Jews is therefore to apply its healing power to the most tender part of the body of humanity; it is also its greatest test.

iv. *Jewish Restoration as an Eschatological Hope.* Election does not exempt a people from the exigencies of history, but rather places it in the storm-centre of world affairs. This fact is written large over the pages of Jewish history. The Jewish people is strangely exposed to the storms which afflict humanity. To be tempest-tossed (Isa. 54. 11) seems to be the inescapable destiny of historic Israel. Here we find depicted the experience of a people when God places his hand upon it. He does not remove out of the world those whom he chooses, but places them more deeply in it. The people of God is most deeply involved in the affairs of the world. This involvement is not by fusion of interests, but by the tension of opposites. Though Israel may fail to realize it, the pull which the world has upon him is centrifugal and not centripetal; the greater centre which pulls in the other direction is the Kingdom of God. It is out of this tension that Israel's dialectic is born: the people of God is a people of the world, committed to it, engrossed in it, and engulfed by it on every side. There can be no escape from the world either by Israel or the Church. The world is the stage upon which the People of God is called to enact salvation. The Church has frequently erred in the direction of other-worldliness, but we have already seen that Judaism has moved in the opposite direction. There is an emphasis upon *this*-worldliness (*'olam ha-zeh*) in Judaism which has always been a puzzle to Christians. The pious Jew is wedded to *this* world: his food, his marital relations, his dress, his well-being, are all part of his religion. The religious Jew strives to bring God into every department of life in order to transform this world into a paradise. Buber regards this as the most essential feature of Judaism.[46]

This Promethean effort inevitably carries the danger of fusion between world and God; for this reason Pantheism is never far removed from Judaism. The characteristic monism which Judaism displays (and which the Church so frequently envies!) creates only the impression of a solution, but in reality it glosses over the tension which is inherent in the human situation. It breaks out with renewed force whenever a correlation of time and Eternity is attempted. Here the transiency of the world is only emphasized by the Word of God which endureth for ever (Isa. 40. 8). That the People of God is so essentially committed to the dimension of time[47] is the paradox of Israel's position.

The Jewish people therefore lies at the heart of the world. The Jews are an integral part of this passing age. All flesh is grass, says the Prophet, and passes away, Jew and Gentile alike. Only those who look upon the Kingdom of God as the result of evolution can speak of the total conversion of historic Israel. To us, this is theological nonsense. It overlooks the meaning of time, the contingency of history, the nature of the world. As long as history lasts, there will always be a section of Jewry unconverted, as there will always be unconverted humanity.

Eschatological redemption, of which St Paul speaks in Rom. 11. 26, remains inseparable from God's final decree over mankind. "All Israel" cannot be saved without the world. Till then historic Israel must remain the people of time, the people of the earth, the people of this transient world. As such he is the living witness of the Age to Come and to God's final triumph over death and sin.

CHAPTER 7

ELECTION IN THE DIALECTIC OF HISTORY

WE have now reached the central point in our discussion, namely, the problem of election. This is the problem which underlies every aspect of historic Israel and is at the heart of Christian theology. But this is not a problem which can be stated in any other way than dialectically; that is to say, on this side of history it can be understood only in terms of tension. To answer it in any other way would mean to give it a conceptual instead of an existential significance. But before such an answer is attempted we must be clear in our minds what is meant by a dialectical answer.

A. A THEOLOGICAL DEFINITION OF DIALECTIC

At the outset it is important that we draw a clear line of distinction between the philosophical and theological approaches to dialectic. In theology, dialectic is not a matter of method. Karl Barth, who may be regarded as the founder of the modern school of dialectic theology,[1] has proved by his own example how little theology is committed to the method; though in his earlier work he keeps strictly to the dialectical method, in his maturer writings he almost forgets the method, but retains the dialectical attitude. The fact is that dialectic theology is not a matter of eristic, though language and method remain important media. What, then, is the difference between the philosophical and the theological aspect of dialectic?

We will first glance at dialectic from a philosopher's point of view.

To the philosopher, dialectic presents itself mainly in this two-fold aspect: (*a*) as methodology, i.e. a method of reasoning; (*b*) as phenomenology, i.e. as the doctrine of opposites.

(*a*) *Methodology*

Zeno, according to Aristotle, may be looked upon as the inventor of the dialectic method of reasoning. He sometimes used it for the quaint purpose of proving the impossible, as he does in the case of unity and multiplicity to show the contradiction of existence: there can be no multiplicity, for this would imply the infinite small and the infinite large in either direction, which is impossible. He deals with the question of unity in a similar fashion. By the same token of logical deduction Zeno gives four reasons why motion is only an illusion and does not really exist.[2] Here reasoning leads to the absurd, and yet as a method it is of great importance in the art of thinking. Kant rightly describes it as a "*formallogisches Entwicklungsprinzip*". Eisler knows of at least four different methods which can be employed in the use of the dialectical argument. John Scotus, who was no mean master in the method of the dialectical procedure, describes it as *communium animi conceptionum rationabilium diligens investigatrixque disciplina.*[3] As a discipline it is therefore a form of logic which must be treated carefully for, as Kant describes it, it is both *ars sophistica* and *disputatoria* at the same time. A theology which is not concerned with "proving truth" can in no way be wedded to dialectic as a method.

(*b*) *Phenomenology*

The phenomenologic aspect of dialectic is more complex. The doctrine of the opposites is a well-known philosophical theme. Every phenomenon appears to have a dialectical aspect to it, and because of its antinomian character in relation to the Absolute it derives the quality of contradiction.[4] Liebert therefore regards what he calls the "criso-crisis" situation[5] as the essence of philosophy. But naturally enough, to Liebert as to every dialectical philosopher, the "crisis" is not really a crisis in the radical sense, for it serves only as a means to a higher form of development; it is, as Liebert puts it, "*ein notwendiges fruchtbares Moment*" for the furtherance of his philosophical idealism.[6] These opposite ideas become linked to form a unity akin to the Platonic concept of κοινωνία.[7] Logically such a method ought to lead to a dead end, as in the case of the Aristotelian world which moves in a closed circle of concepts from which there is no escape because there is no loophole. Here dialectic as a department of logic operates with data already deposited and demonstrable as universal truths. The apodeictic procedure already assures us of the result in advance: the last suppositions in the chain of our reasoning remain undemonstrable. In the last resort, this is the vicious circle of all philosophical systems. The revolt against medieval scholasticism which expressed itself in abandoning "formal" for "natural" dialectic was an effort to break out from the iron grip of the logical system into the world of reality. It is of great significance that neither Kant nor Hegel ever managed to regain their freedom without a violent breach in logic. Kant's transcendental dialectic leads to an endless chain of reaction in the process of cognition which by its very nature is incapable of an ultimate result.[8] Hegel finds himself in exactly the same position, though he arrives there by a different route. J. O. Wisdom has managed to uncover the logical contradictions which underlie Hegel's historical philosophy.[9]

There is here an obvious breach between being and thinking, however much perennial philosophy may try to overcome it. The synthesis after which Hegelian philosophy strives may well be a subconscious way to camouflage an inherent weakness by utilizing it to arrive at a "higher truth".

B. A THEOLOGICAL APPROACH TO DIALECTIC

Since Kierkegaard a new dialectic has become established in theology, which is quite different not only in form but also in essence from the scholastic discipline. But it also contradicts the Hegelian concept of dialectic on the grounds that it misrepresents the human situation. In fact it was Kierkegaard who first registered his opposition to Hegel's philosophy because it overlooked the contradictory position in which man finds himself. Viewed in the act of living, man does not escape from the tension of decision by a synthesis of two opposites, but only by a leap of faith, which in itself is a paradox. Here dialectic is not a conceptual approach which deals with propositions, but an existential approach to life itself. Life, however, always exceeds the sphere of logic, for life means tension, whereas logic is the dissolution of tension and therefore operates in the realm of the abstract. Man knows no other life but the life of tension; in the world as in the Church, in society as at home, within and without, he is always *in between*: suspended between one decision and the next. No synthesis can release him from such suspense. The question whether Brentano's criticism of Hegel's philosophy is justified or not, is of little consequence to the theologian.[10] His main concern is that the human situation be recognized for what it really is—life in tension from which there is no escape. Here there can be no "down" nor "up", no "progress" nor "regress", here there is only a question-mark under which man stands as a challenge to decision. For the theologian, therefore, dialectic is not a method which yields results, or a system of reasoning in which life can be resolved in concepts, but a *situation* in which man is challenged to act and *does* act in faith or disobedience.

The challenge comes from the speaking God, but God's Word is never heard in a state of quiescence. Only living man can hear God's living Word; but to live means to stand between life and death, between time and eternity, between God and the devil, between one decision and another. But man can decide only in the instant of the moment, he cannot decide once and for all. To decide once and for all would mean to step out of time into the dimension of eternity where past, present, and future coincide. On the plane of history man is a changing creature to whom no situation is like the previous one. But more so: man does not change only with the passing of time, but in every given moment he is more than one thing, he is a complex entity: pious and impious, believer and disbeliever, God-fearing and God-less, at the same time. Man lives in contradictions: he seeks God and mammon, he follows Christ and the devil, he worships God and idols. True, there is a difference between saints and sinners, but only at our level, not at God's. Even here every saint has his temptations and every sinner his moments of saintship. This is not a "pessimistic" view concerning man, but a factual one. It is borne out by the results of modern psychology and by the daily experience of ourselves. This the saint knows better than the sinner, for he acquires his self-knowledge as a result of his confrontation with the Word of God. The more man knows about God the better he is able to assess the reality of his situation: a rebel before God.

(*a*) *Christian Anthropology*

Anthropology and theology are indivisible subjects; they belong together. Our ideas about God largely depend upon our assessment of man. An idealistic approach to man inevitably leads to a humanistic concept of God. The result is a God who is less than the God of Israel, and man who is more than his own stature. Outsize man is an idol whose image is worshipped by pseudo-theology.

Christian anthropology can be determined only from underneath the Cross of Jesus Christ. Here we meet man with his mask down: upon his forehead which once bore the *imago Dei* is superimposed the mark of Cain. A theology of salvation must start at this lowest point if it is to avoid the pitfalls of a facile idealism. Our anthropology will therefore always be determined by our interpretation of the Cross. If the Cross stands as a sign that Christ died for sinners, then it means that man is a God-less creature who is in desperate need of salvation. But in man's dialectical position salvation can never mean a state, a condition, but must always mean motion. It means that there can be no security before God. God-openness is not something which can be achieved once and for all. Here the words of forgiveness can never be heard in advance, nor can they be taken for granted; they must be heard repeatedly in an act of faith, if they are heard at all. Such hearing of the Word of God takes place in the double context of personal and corporate life, for man never stands alone, he always stands with others. The individual lives only by reason of society; the Kingdom of God presupposes the other man. The Church is never one person, but two or three must unite, to warrant the Presence of the Risen Christ. Election therefore must have a twofold aspect: election of the individual and election of society. The Church gives the pre-eminence to the individual; herein it differs fundamentally from Judaism. To the Synagogue, election begins with the community; the individual is only elected inasmuch as he is a member of the community. To the Church, the individual experiences election and the Church comes into existence by reason of elect individuals. But in history individual and community do not stand in direct but in dialectical relationship—society pointing to the End and the individual pointing beyond it.

(*b*) *The Dialectic between Personal and Corporate Salvation*

St Paul uses an interesting argument to show how corporate and personal salvation do not coincide. Embedded in this argument lies the clue to our understanding of the difference:

> For I would not, brethren, have you ignorant, how that our fathers were all under the cloud, and all passed through the sea; and were all baptized unto Moses in the cloud and the sea; and did all eat the same spiritual meat; and did all drink the same spiritual drink: for they drank of a spiritual rock that followed them: and the rock was Christ. Howbeit with most of them God was not well pleased: for they were overthrown in the wilderness. Now these things were our

> examples, to the intent we should not lust after evil things, as they also lusted. Neither be ye idolaters, as were some of them; as it is written, The people sat down to eat and drink, and rose up to play. Neither let us commit fornication, as some of them committed, and fell in one day three and twenty thousand. Neither let us tempt the Lord, as some of them tempted, and perished by the serpents. Neither murmur ye, as some of them murmured, and perished by the destroyer (1 Cor. 10. 1–10).

This passage is important, for it clearly reveals the inherent tension between the individual believer and the group. The passage refers back to a definite historical situation: God intervenes in a dispute between two nations. He takes sides with the oppressed against the oppressor. By a mighty act, in which a whole people becomes involved, he delivers Israel from the hands of Pharaoh. Here there is no distinction made between the worthy and the unworthy, the good and the bad. Israel in his totality experiences the saving and helping hand of God. The whole of Israel passes through the sea, eats the same spiritual meat and drinks the same spiritual drink. The whole people, without distinction, is called, dedicated, and saved; yet it never reached the promised land but was overthrown in the wilderness. This is St Paul's argument.

A somewhat comparable situation we meet in world history since the death of Jesus Christ. According to the N.T., Jesus died for the sins of the world. This is therefore a world already "saved". It is saved because, as Christians believe, the Son of God gave his life for it. It means that the whole of humanity has become involved in this supreme act of God's saving grace. There are visible and historically verifiable results "of the travail of his soul". The Gospel has made an impact upon world history and has changed its course. Psychologically, morally, culturally, the nations of the world have "eaten" and have "drunk" from the spiritual rock which is Christ. Almost two thousand years of Church history, in spite of all its ambiguity, cannot easily be crossed off as of no consequence. Not only believers, but humanity at large, has been profoundly affected by the Christmas and Easter stories. Whole nations have been brought out of the darkness of paganism and immorality as a result of the Gospel. The Birth of Jesus is like a light which has shined into the darkness of the night with the promise of the coming dawn. The fact that Jesus lived and died some two thousand years ago is still affecting millions of human lives. In terms of spiritual and moral values the benefits humanity has derived from the coming of Jesus Christ are too immense to contemplate. There is hardly a human being whose life, in one way or another, has not been affected by the fact that Jesus lived upon this earth. Yet the world is still unsaved. Why? Because salvation can be experienced only personally, in spite of the fact that the whole of humanity is the object of God's love.

This brings us once again to the Church.

We must here understand Church in the widest sense, perhaps a better description is "Christianity". With "Christianity" we describe the impersonal, traditional, historic, deposit of the Christian faith in society. It is popularly spoken of as the "Christian heritage" and rightly so, for it is inheritable. It can be passed on from father to son, as any other family tradition. The "Christian tradition" (another name for it) is not the Christian faith as professed by believers, but a cultural, national, semi-moral, semi-religious attitude which has some association with historic Christianity. It is religion in the mass against a vaguely Christian background. It serves the purpose of supplying a social need and giving a certain tone of respectability to a nation. But it also serves another purpose: it is a stepping-stone from mere Christianity into personal faith.

Here we have yet another analogy to the position of historic Israel. Israel as a people is like Christianity in history: the national, the cultural, the religious elements all combine to give to Judaism its specific texture; with its help the Jewish people keeps in touch with the past, and keeps alive the Promises for the future. But the individual Jew is not saved by the mere fact of belonging to the Chosen People. He can be saved only by returning, by believing, by submitting to the regenerating power of the Holy Spirit of God. Here we see demonstrated the difference between being called and being chosen.

The Church in the more narrow sense is not "Christianity", but the fellowship of believers. These are individuals who have been "splintered" from their social background to be placed in a new relationship to one another. The community of believers is the People of God in the process of becoming. As there is an antinomy between historic Israel and the Israel of God, so there is an antinomy between the Christian Church and the People of God: history never achieves, never completes, never finishes, but never stops trying.

The same applies to the individual: he is never ready. Both he and society stand under the sign of eschatology. It means that history points Godward, beyond itself. *Here* there can be no absolutes; "salvation" in history is only a partial experience. Completed salvation, i.e. salvation in its fullness, can take place only outside space and time. Within history everything must remain relative. Here we can see only "as in a glass, darkly"; on this side of history man can live only by promise of the world to come. This means walking by faith and not by sight. Here even the Holy Spirit can be received only as an "earnest" (2 Cor. 1. 22; 5. 5) and not in his fullness. Such is the pilgrimage on the way to the City of God.

In the tension between time and eternity, historic Israel, the Israel of God, and the individual remain in a relationship of constant motion: they cross and recross each other's paths. Whenever faith becomes alive they react upon each other like an electric current. In separation they are dead and live with the past; by the quickening effect of faith they spring to life and point to the End. Sometimes it is the faith of historic Israel, sometimes it is the faith of the individual, sometimes the corporate faith of the Church.

The individual is not a Christian without the Church, and the Church is not Christian without historic Israel. To move in this threefold relationship of interdependence is the destiny of the believer's life through time.

(*c*) *The Dialectic between Rejection and Election*

It is a peculiarity of the Bible and specially evident in the prophetic message that judgement and mercy are inseparably wedded. There is scarcely an instance when judgement is not accompanied by the offer of mercy, and *vice versa*. In most cases judgement and grace are pronounced simultaneously. Here is a striking example:

> Except the Lord of hosts had left unto us a very small remnant, we should have been as Sodom, we should have been like unto Gomorrah. . . . Therefore saith the Lord, the Lord of Hosts, the Mighty One of Israel . . . I will turn my hand upon thee, and throughly purge away thy dross, and will take away all thy tin [alloy]: and I will restore thy judges as at the first, and thy counsellors as at the beginning: afterward thou shalt be called The city of righteousness, the faithful city . . . (Isa. 1. 9, 24–6).

Here we have an interesting continuation of promises and threats. God rejects and elects at the same time; he makes demands and supplies himself what is lacking in man. A classical example is provided by these two passages in Ezekiel:

> Cast away from you all your transgressions, wherein ye have transgressed; and make you a new heart and a new spirit: for why will ye die, O house of Israel? (Ez. 18. 31);

and:

> A new heart also will I give you and a new spirit will I put within you: and I will take away the stony heart out of your flesh, and I will give you an heart of flesh . . . (Ez. 36. 26; 11. 19).

Here "receiving" and "having" do not seem to stand in the usual relationship of cause and effect; those who receive never "have" and those who have never receive. Our emptiness and poverty seem to be a condition for life and our affluence and fullness the cause of death. When we are weak we are strong, and when we are strong we are weak (2 Cor. 12. 10). The terrifying void of godlessness can become a more blessed state than the religious self-satisfaction of the pious. For only those who have experienced the judgements of God know of his grace, but woe betide the man whom God refuses to judge. Only those who have stood under his condemnation know the grace of his pardon, but those who have never experienced forgiveness know nothing of his mercy. This is what Luther meant when he spoke of the "terror of conscience" which leads to the acceptance of God's free pardon, for only by it do we realize that there is "nothing else to lean unto, but the precious pearl Jesus Christ".[11]

We will now understand why Law and Gospel, though opposites, are yet complementary: there is no Gospel without the Law and there is no Law without the Gospel. Only man under the Law can truly grasp the glory of the Gospel and only man under the Gospel can truly perceive the terror of the Law. The Law is God's voice of judgement; the Gospel is the *same* voice of the all-righteous and all-holy God, offering grace. In view of the Law, God rejects the sinner; in view of the Cross, God *elects* the self-same sinner to be his son.

It is not the case that the Gospel is effective in the Church and the Law in the world. Law and Gospel operate in the Church and in the believer, who carry the world in their bosom and from which there can be no escape. There is some good reason for the theological distinction in reference to the *primus, secundus, et tertius usus legis*: the first applies to the world, the second to the function to convince of sin; and the third serves as a reminder to the Christian of his own worldliness. For the "Christian is not only a new man, but also at the same time the old man; not only saved, but also at the same time sinner; not only spirit but also flesh".[12]

As a sinner, the Christian is under the wrath of God; as a redeemed sinner he is under his grace and favour. But it is the peculiarity of the human situation that he is both sinner and saint at the same time. He is sinner by virtue of transgression and saint by virtue of the atoning Sacrifice on the Cross. This is the peculiar strain under which every Christian believer lives. For this reason the full Gospel can be presented only in the twofold message of repentance and grace. No one knew it better than Luther: "We must preach neither one nor the other alone, but both together. . . . For repentence flows from the commandments of God, and faith flows from his promises."[13] Thus Law and Gospel, judgement and pardon, rejection and election must remain ever-present experiences in the life of the believer. The alternating factor in this fluid situation is not God but man. As far as God is concerned, in Christ is all Yea and Amen (2 Cor. 1. 19 f.), but the case with man is different. Here life can be expressed only in terms of growth, hazard, and venture. Not that salvation depends on man's desert; God saves us in spite of ourselves, but in the contingency of time it can be salvation only as an "earnest" and never complete. Only if man were "pure soul and pure spirit" could it be otherwise; but this is "a thing which will never happen before the last day", says Luther, and he adds: "There will never be anything else on earth than a beginning and a growth; these will only be completed in the next world."[14]

But there is yet another reason why the dialectic between rejection and election must remain insoluble.

God elects by reason of his free and sovereign will. He wills not that the sinner should perish, but that he should return and live (Ez. 18. 23, 32; 33. 11). But he elects man only in Christ, the Second Adam, and not in the first. As far as the first Adam is concerned man remains under the verdict of death. As such he stands rejected as the enemy of God. But though man cannot elect himself, he can submit to the election of God. It is this that we call a decision for Christ. This freedom to decide, God gives to the sinner. Without such freedom decision would have no moral value. This minimum of freedom is already implied in the concept of sin; sin would lose its moral significance without it.[15] Here again we hit upon a paradox on three scores: (*a*) because human freedom contradicts God's omniscience and *vice versa*; (*b*) because freedom and sin are already contradictory; (*c*) because a freedom which is *given* is not freedom in the strict sense. Every effort to find a logical solution out of the difficulty must be regarded as theological betrayal. The paradox stems from the dialectic of the human situation, and to resolve it is an act of disobedience; only faith can move here freely without taking offence. The only valid answer is that given by Augustine:

> Faith and good deeds are God's work within us, for he it is who has prepared our will; but it is at the same time our work, for God accomplishes it only in those who will.[16]

But it is an answer which is in itself a paradox.

Because life is continuous motion, the experience of God's judgement and grace is the continuous experience of the believer. He can never hear the Word of pardon which is spoken on the Cross without simultaneously hearing the word of condemnation which is spoken on Mount Sinai. In the believer, the Jew and the Christian meet. Here historic Israel and Church face one another under judgement and grace. They face each other not in the theological discussion on the platform of history, but in the innermost recesses of the believer's heart: to be a Christian means to hear the two voices, the voice of the Law and the voice of the Gospel, to be a sinner and "saved" at the same time. It is also here that we learn the real meaning of faith: faith is the humble attitude of allowing God to keep us in suspense—so that we lean only on his Grace.[17]

(*d*) *The Dialectic between Time and Eternity*

Time to the theologian is not really a chronological or mathematical concept. Whatever time may mean to the physicist—and his definition varies from age to age—to the theologian time is eschatologically defined. It means that here the noun has a moral connotation. To the theologian the second law of thermodynamics, by reason of which entropy brings the physical world to a standstill, is only remotely connected with the End of time. Whether the physical world continues or not, the End for theology is inseparable from him who is the Creator of time and the Great Timekeeper. He who called the world into being remains for ever the Judge of the quick and the dead.

The finitude of time indicates its transiency; it belongs to the order of this world which passes away. For the Christian believer, time is the peculiar feature of the present aeon; more especially is it confined to the duration between the two events which determine history: the Incarnation and the Second Advent. Time is therefore the canvas necessary for the pattern of history which is woven by the deeds and decisions of mankind. Time is better described as an adjective than a noun, for it is the attribute of the world in which man lives: moving towards the End.

In the direction of time is implied its most peculiar trait—it is irrevocable. It is this which gives to time its moral character; a moment gone is irretrievably lost, for the pageant of history is irreversible. Here lies the moral earnestness in the Christian concept of time; it carries with it a sense of urgency.

Eternity is not the opposite of time; the opposite of time is the End. Eternity to the Christian is not "timelessness" or "end-lessness", or a negation of time, but a dimension outside the concept of time. Time and eternity are neither parallel nor contiguous: it means that they cannot be viewed horizontally or consecutively, in the sense that the one begins where the other leaves off. Expressed in terms of motion, time and eternity move on two different planes. Theologians have used the horizontal line to signify time and the vertical line to describe eternity. These two lines intersect whenever the Word of God reaches man's ear; when this happens the End becomes visible. This breaking in of eternity into time Kierkegaard called the Instant, and defined as an atom of eternity in time.[18] The place of contact where time and eternity intersect is man and only man; it is his destiny to stand on the margin of history with one foot in eternity. But he cannot move either way; there can be no escape from history and there can be no escape from God. Man thus moves on the margin of two worlds simultaneously. But in the Instant when time and eternity clash he sees the End and he hears the Voice: "I am the Lord."

It is historic Israel's peculiar destiny to hear the Voice more clearly than any other people has ever heard it; but the vision of the End is hidden from him. The End can be seen only when the Voice which Israel hears is identified as the Voice from the Cross. In Jesus Christ End means τέλος, the goal, the end of the journey.

Israel's hearing of the Voice is the mark of his election. Israel has been chosen to hear and to repeat the burning, searing words, "I am the Lord", to the nations of the world. But this is not a sentence which can be properly uttered by word of mouth; it can be heard only amidst the exigencies of life. Israel is the living proof that God is Lord. This Word spoken into history comes as an interjection, as a disruption, as an interference in human affairs. It challenges man's purpose and puts it under a question-mark. It is for this reason that anti-Semitism must be understood as something more than ordinary xenophobia.

The people which carries in its history deeply engraven the message that God is Lord, stands in a peculiarly close relation to history and therefore to time. It is for this reason that we must accept Professor Tillich's contention that historic Israel is the People of Time *par excellence*.[19] This special time-consciousness can be explained only from an unusual encounter with eternity, for man can know of the transience of time only when he stands face to face with the living God.

Though Israel does not see the End, he knows about it. Deeply buried in Jewish tradition is the hope of the *ḳeẓ* (End), which is usually associated with the coming of the Messiah.[20] This eschatological hope has played an important part in Jewish mysticism and in Ḥasidism. Though the Synagogue fights shy of eschatology and the Talmud speaks with derision of the "speculators of the End",[21] knowledge of the *ḳeẓ* brings a jarring note into Israel's abandonment to time. Man dislikes the End, for it gives history an interim character. In Jewish thinking, therefore, time and the End have become fused, so that the End is placed in time and enacted as part of history. It has become identified with the end of the *galut* (Exile) and the Restoration to national existence.

We have already said that the End becomes visible in time in the Instant when the Voice is identified as the Voice from the Cross. This marks the Church from the Synagogue. The Church knows the End in him who is both the τέλος and the conclusion of history. In him only is the End visible. The Cross therefore disrupts time by breaking it up into moments of decision. Here time and eternity clash in such a way that the encounter with the historic Jesus becomes a personal encounter with the living God.

When eternity breaks into time, "religion" ceases to be the practice of rites, or conformity with the requirements of the Law;

it becomes encounter. When this happens, "religious experience" has left the realm of sentimental mysticism and has become decision for Christ in the Instant of time. When the same thing happens with two people simultaneously, the Church springs into being; it means that the historic Church becomes *the* Church in the instant of time—a foretaste of the world to come and the Communion of the Saints.

Here we come upon the other point of difference between the Synagogue and the Church: the Law without the Incarnation belongs to this world's order; at no point do time and eternity clash. Moses is not an eternal Presence but a person who belongs to history. The Jew looks backward to his origins and forward to the messianic age; the present is in between what was and what shall be. He moves on the plane of time without disruption from the outside; his here and now are filled with the performance of the Law. Jewish life is thus lived on the horizontal line of history. No interference from without, no break in the chain of causality, are tolerated. This explains the this-worldly, matter-of-fact rationalism so characteristic of Judaism. Confined to time and engulfed by history on every side, the Jew does not expect any other salvation than the one forged by human hands. His inveterate optimism, in spite of his bitter experience in history, is necessitated by the inward need to see meaning even in chaos. Here history, and history only, is the forge upon which human destiny is hammered out. For this reason faith in the ultimate reasonableness of man is essential to Jewish existence.

Judaism is thus closely related to every form of humanistic idealism. But this is not a specifically Jewish, but a human trait. It makes a special appeal to the Anglo-Saxon world, where Greek influence is prevalent. Fascination with the heroic element in man is a human weakness; here Jew and Greek meet. It is a reassuring discovery that man's sickness is not until death, that he is still the master of his fortune, and that he still has a chance to create a pattern out of chaos, and thus vindicate himself.

Living on the horizontal line of history is equally the experience of every Christian believer; man in time cannot live in any other dimension. But the Christian is more vulnerable to the disruption of eternity. He experiences the clash of time and eternity with greater sensitivity in proportion to his openness to the fact of the Incarnation. The collision between time and eternity is peculiar to the whole setting of the Bible. Here history and eternity are not intertwined in a blended pattern, but touch at the point of conflict. This is supremely illustrated by the Cross, but is already implied in every biblical situation when the Word from above makes itself heard. This belongs to the peculiar characteristic of the Bible. Here the dialogue is carried on in conflict: God's voice and man's voice in contradiction. It means that the Word of God never comes to us "pure"; it is always accompanied by the "echo". The "other" voice is always present in the *kerygma* of the Bible. Man can never hear God in any other way; the Voice and the echo go together. Whenever the Bible lets us hear God, it also lets us hear the voice of Israel, rejecting, questioning, arguing, defying. These two voices are intermixed and are part of the message. The hearer has to hear them both if he hears the Word at all, so that the original echo becomes his own—the hearer's *personal* resistance.

The tension between time and eternity is remarkably demonstrated in the person of Jesus Christ himself. This is more apparent in the Synoptic Gospels than in the Fourth, but even in the Johannine Gospel it is not altogether absent.

The Synoptic Gospels draw the portrait of a double personality: the Son of Man and the hidden Son of God are logically in contradiction. On the one hand there is Jesus of Nazareth who hungers and thirsts, who spends his nights on the hillside in prayer to God, who is tempted and distressed, who suffers and dies; on the other hand there is the Messiah who teaches with authority, who forgives sins, who heals the sick, who raises the dead, and walks on the sea in a raging storm.

Here we come upon the great contradiction in the person of the Messiah. In him time and eternity meet not in the Instant but during a lifetime. He endures the strain of this double existence which the believer knows only from time to time. What it means to be man and God in one person, theology will never be able to define. Behind it lies the main paradox of the Christian Faith. Although the Church has rejected the Monophysite doctrine as a heresy, the concept of the *communicatio idiomatum* in the last resort amounts to the same thing. It is an effort to relieve the tension by bringing the human and divine in closer union; but this never really works, for either the divine swallows up the human element or else God is brought down to the level of man. To speak of God as *deus natus et mortuus*, as the old Church did, is more than a sacrifice of logic, it is blasphemy. A way out was to maintain the *duae substantiae* (or *naturae*) and yet hold to *una persona*, as the "Athanasian" Creed does. But this too can be achieved only at the expense of logic.[22] There is no solution either way, except to admit the paradox: Jesus was truly Man and Christ was the Incarnation of God. How the two natures coexisted in the frail body of the historical Jesus must remain the secret of the Messiah.

If Jesus were to be exempted from the tension between time and eternity, he would not have been truly man in one vital respect. But the Gospels, even the Johannine Gospel, never attempt to convey the impression that Jesus was God walking about *incognito*. On the contrary, they picture a man who is tempted, who suffers, who dies; but at the same time, God manifests himself in him in an unheard-of way. It is, as it were, that in Jesus of Nazareth, the Instant of eternity is *extended* in time. Here the Messiah carries in his own person the contradiction of the human situation: he lives in tension between time and the Instant of Eternity. Not only so, but he kindles that tension in the life of others. Herein lies the cause of offence to Jew and Greek. In Jesus of Nazareth, as in the believer, time and eternity clash, but so that the Kingdom of God becomes visible. This is the highest triumph of faith: the Messiah is *the* Man who truly walks in faith from cradle to Cross; he tastes the bitterness of death with unshaken faith in a loving heavenly Father—"Father, into thy hands I commend my spirit."

The tension between time and eternity becomes equally visible in respect of the Kingdom of God. Here we notice two sayings which are contradictory: "Thy Kingdom come" and "My Kingdom is not of this world". We believe that the same Master who taught his disciples to pray: "Thy Kingdom come", knew that the Kingdom of God is not of this world. Here world and Kingdom stand in opposition, they can never be fused. On the plane of history God's Kingdom is always in the act of coming but can never be *here*, for the reason that it spells the end of time and the beginning of the New Aeon. God's Kingdom in its finality is the conclusion of history. Only in the experience of the believer is the Kingdom present, but this solely in the Instant of time, and so that it is not of this world.

To stand in faith is always to stand in the dialectic between time and eternity.

(e) *The Church as Event*

We have already stated that on the plane of history both Church and Israel move horizontally. "Jewish culture", "Christian civilization", are purely historical definitions. A Jew can live by "Jewish culture", as a Gentile can live by "Christian culture", without any personal relationship to God. This is possible not only outside but also inside the Church and the Synagogue. Judaism and Christianity may face each other in hostility or indifference without any awareness of their true position in the sight of God. Jewish and Christian scholars may carry on a fierce theological dispute without really speaking in the context of faith. There is a vast apologetic literature expressing the point of view of both sides, and the argument remains inconclusive. The Church "says", the Synagogue "teaches", Christianity "holds", Judaism "maintains"—thus goes the argument *about* the "truth". But in fact, if the object of man's speech is God, not just the theological concept of God, but God himself, the Holy One of Israel, then man can never "discuss" him, but only listen and obey. Such hearing neither "Judaism" nor "Christianity" can attain to; this is the prerogative of the individual.

The miracle of faith is the miracle of a personal encounter with God in question and answer. Man can hear God only as an individual (cf. Ps. 40. 6; Isa. 50. 4). In the Bible, God always speaks to the individual and through him to society, never the other way round. Israel can only hear the voice of Moses, the voice of Isaiah; but how Moses and Isaiah hear remains the secret of the believer.[23]

This lonely hearing of the word of God is essentially the experience of the prophet. The prophet is both "seer" (*ḥozeh*) and "listener"; and only because he sees and hears is he *navi*, "speaker". But it is also possible that two or more people hear *together* the Word of God and respond in obedience of faith. When this happens the Church springs into existence. Here *ecclesia* is really *koinonia*—togetherness under the Word of God; and here "hearing" always means obedience.

There is an interesting juxtaposition of Church and Temple which runs through the whole of the Bible. Temple stands for institutionalized religion with its hierarchy, symbolism, ceremonies, and sacrifices. In juxtaposition to it we see the prophetic circle with the prophet in the centre. Here religion is interpreted in terms of personal faith and obedience to God. The Temple is deeply rooted in history; the prophet depends not on tradition but on a personal waiting upon God.[24] That God will speak he cannot take for granted, but that he *does* speak the prophet knows from the depth of faith. When it occurs it is Event in the fullest sense of the word and of revolutionary significance. It creates upheaval and forces man to great adventure as it did Abraham, Moses, the Prophets, the Apostles. Abraham *heard* the call to leave his father's house, Moses *heard* the Voice from the burning bush, Isaiah *heard* the Voice in the temple, Jesus *heard* the Voice at his baptism: "This is my beloved Son . . ." This hearing of the Voice is the secret of the believer. It may come as the still small voice to Elijah or as the mighty rushing sound to the disciples on Pentecost, but it is always the same Word, an act of the living God. It is this hearing which makes the difference between Church and Temple, Christianity and faith.

The Church in history is both temple and *Ecclesia*. Seen horizontally she is and can only be what she is—"organized religion". Only in the prophetic experience of the Instant does she break away from the shackles of history and becomes *Ecclesia*. This manifestation of eternity into time cannot be organized, premeditated, conditioned; it is and remains a miracle of grace.

What, then, is the connection between Church and Church, Church as Event and Church in history? The answer is that the connection is the same as between historic Israel and the Israel of God. Church does not occur in a vacuum, in the void, but in history. Historic Israel, Christianity, "organized religion", are the indispensable background against which the "Church" becomes Church; i.e. the church of history becomes the Church of God in the Instant of time.

History is necessary to save the individual from the danger of mystical self-contemplation. It is a reminder that no man can stand before God in isolation. Man is always the representative of others, his family, his people, mankind. History is also a reminder that the individual before God does not step out of time but stands in it. Historic Israel, Christianity, organized religion, are not just trappings which can be stripped off, but are the canvas itself upon which the individual's life is woven. The Church in time therefore carries the world with her as an integral part and is never separate from it. There is never "pure" Church in history, as there is no "pure" Word of God; the echo of the human voice and the shadow of man's deed are always present.

The Church must always remain part of the world, in a position of ambiguity and under a question-mark. Here below she is never the communion of saints without being at the same time the communion of sinners. Between the Church in history and the Church as Event there is everlasting tension, similar to the tension between priestly religion and prophetic faith in the O.T.

The believer does not merely stand between "church" and Church, but he carries both within him; the one as an empirical fact, the other as a constant possibility. It means that he himself alternates between faith and mere tradition. But before God, non-faith is faithlessness, is sin. The Christian stands rejected as a sinner and accepted as a saint by reason of the righteousness which is not his own. Only because grace is stronger than the world and the Spirit of God mighty to the casting down of strongholds (cf. 2 Cor. 10. 4) is the "Church" not only "church" but the Church. She is the background, the canvas upon which God himself weaves the pattern of his Kingdom.

The "Church" as *Ecclesia* is a vertical Event. She springs into time when the Lord of the Church reveals his Presence to *two* believers. One believer and the Master is not yet the Church; the Church includes the presence of the other man who is an outsider. Without him the Church is incomplete and the Kingdom of God is in abeyance. His presence is a prerequisite for the "Church" to become what she is meant to be—a home for sinners in whom grace abounds.

(*f*) *Election in the Messiah*

We have now reached almost the end of our thesis. We began with the juxtaposition of Church and historic Israel; we have finished with the juxtaposition of "church" and Church. We have seen how the story of revelation is conditioned by the dialectic of history. We have discovered that grace and "nature" do not fuse but clash, and that only in the light of that explosion does the Kingdom of God become visible. We have seen that election always means election of sinners and that in Israel's call is implied the call of mankind. Election is therefore not a prerogative but a call to service, from which man cannot escape. Historic Israel has accomplished his task by giving birth to the Messiah even though he himself has mistaken his calling and failed to recognize the time of his visitation (cf. Luke 19. 44). But man can never wilfully fall out of God's hand, unless God himself lets him fall.

Man's failure cannot annul God's purpose. Historic Israel is therefore both chosen and rejected. He is rejected, as man is rejected, and chosen because in Jesus Christ sinners are chosen. But Israel is a collective noun; a community consists of individuals. Election in the deepest sense is election of the individual. The individual and the community represent two different centres moving on two different lines, though they both move in the same direction. The community can be seen only eschatologically, i.e. in the perspective of the End. This is how St Paul saw it when he said: All Israel will be saved. The individual must be seen differently: he moves within the God-given freedom of choice. The Jew and the Gentile, without difference, and on equal terms, confront the Cross of Jesus Christ.

Here man in his moral responsibility before God is challenged to decision: Why is that Other Man upon the Cross? Is it by mistake, is it because of judicial murder; or am I personally involved in the act of the Crucifixion? The discovery of co-responsibility for the death of Jesus of Nazareth is the discovery of personal guilt before God. It is at this stage that man discovers the terrifying fact about the holy God: that he is a burning fire (cf. Hebr. 10. 31; Isa. 33. 14; Luke 12. 5). The knowledge of God's all-consuming holiness distinguishes faith from all sentimental religion. This was the experience of Abraham, Isaiah, of the disciples on the Mount of the Transfiguration, of Saul on the way to Damascus. This was the experience of Simon Peter, when he cried out: "Depart from me, for I am a sinful man, O Lord!" (Luke 5. 8). This remains the experience of the Church in the Instant of Eternity, no matter how much the Church of history may have become familiarized with the "benevolent" God—more an indulgent grandfather, than the Holy One of Israel. Faith cries out for mercy. It is then that the miracle happens: the Cross which was the sign of guilt becomes the place of mercy. The believer knows himself forgiven for Christ Jesus' sake.

Election, therefore, is always election with reference to the Messiah. Man is chosen only because of him; in him man becomes Man and the rebel a Son. In the ordinary terms of justice this is the "scandal": that God the righteous Judge should make him who knew no sin to be sin on our behalf that we might become the righteousness of God (2 Cor. 5. 21). But to the believer, in Christ, God himself takes the penalty for *my* sin; this is the greater scandal.

Election, therefore, in the Christian sense is always ἐν αὐτῷ and in no other way: εὑρεθῶ ἐν αὐτῷ (Phil. 3. 9)—to be found in him—is to discover oneself as a son of God in spite of what one is in his godlessness. The believer has no other righteousness except that of Jesus Christ, who is made unto us righteousness, sanctification, and redemption (1 Cor. 1. 30). Man, Jew and Gentile, is under the condemnation of the Law, but Christ redeemed us from the curse of the Law, having become a curse for us (Gal. 3. 13). The believer is baptized εἰς Χριστὸν Ἰησοῦν, into his death, and partakes of his Resurrection (Rom. 6. 1 ff.). His life is hid with Christ in God who now is the believer's life (Col. 3. 3 f.), so much so that he carries about in his own body the dying of the Master, so that the life of Jesus may be manifested in him. The believer is *a* son of God, only because the Messiah is *the* Son of God; his sonship is only by adoption (Gal. 4. 4–6). The Messiah is the ἀγαπητός and we are only beloved in Him: ἐν τῷ ἠγαπημένῳ (Eph. 1. 6).

The N.T. knows of no other election except ἐν Χριστῷ Ἰησοῦ; this is basic for the Pauline argument. The ἐκλεκτοὶ τοῦ Θεοῦ derive their status from their relation to the Son of God. He is the vine and they are the branches (John 15. 1 ff.), and without him they can do nothing (*v.* 5); all they do in word and deed they do in the name of Jesus Christ (Col. 3. 12 ff.).

Election *in* the Messiah is the deepest awareness of the Christian believer. Apart from Jesus Christ he knows himself a sinner under God's wrath and condemnation, the Jew by reason of the Law, the Gentile by reason of his conscience (Rom. 2. 15). In the Messiah, Jew or Gentile knows himself united, the Jew to the Root, the Gentile to Israel. He, the Messiah, is the foundation-stone of the spiritual Temple (1 Pet. 2. 4 ff.), and because he chooses the "living stones", they are chosen.

Can historic Israel's election be viewed apart from the Messiah? Here lies the crux of our problem.

It is true that at least in one passage St Paul connects Israel's election with the Patriarchs and not with the Messiah: "As touching the election they are beloved for the fathers' sake" (Rom. 11. 28). But this passage must be read in the context of the whole argument. His reference to the "remnant according to the election of grace" (11. 5) and his affirmation that "the election obtained it, and the rest were hardened" (11. 7), considerably weakens the former statement.

Let us look at the argument once again. The Apostle tries to explain the curious fact that Israel, God's Chosen People, turned his back upon God's chosen Servant, the Messiah. He gives not one, but several answers: Israel's falling away serves the purpose of bringing the Gentiles into fellowship with God; Israel's hardening is only for a time; that because of the Promise to the Fathers, Israel, in spite of his unbelief, is still beloved; that because of his function in the story of revelation, Israel's position remains unique; that God in his own time will graft them in again and that in the end all Israel will be saved.

But the fact remains unaltered: they are hardened. There seems to be no possible way of reconciling the two contradictory facts: the fact of Israel's election and his hardening. Both facts are true, and Jewish life has ever since taken place within the orbits of these two facts. Israel thus stands where man always stands, between rejection and election: he is condemned as a sinner and chosen in the Messiah.

Scholars have tried to show that St Paul has radically changed the concept of election. In the O.T. and with the rabbis, election has a national connotation, whereas with St Paul election is individual and means election to eternal life.[25] But such a view over-simplifies the case. From Rom. 11 it is quite clear that the Apostle held to both views without any effort to reconcile them. For him, Israel is the elect people of God; the election of the individual is the basis of salvation; neither Israel nor the individual deserves the favour, it is the free gift of God. God gives it to man in the Messiah.

Because it is God who elects, and not man himself, even Israel's hardening is part of his election and serves to the greater glory of God. As Israel's casting away has been the means of the reconciliation of the world, so, in the end, will his receiving back be life from the dead (Rom. 11. 15).

Here we have the history of mankind summarized in the life of one single people. In St Paul's argument Israel and the world go together; to isolate them is to overlook his main concern—salvation for mankind. In Israel's election is anchored the election of humanity. In the hope that all Israel shall be saved lies the hope for mankind. The Apostle refuses to give the world over to the devil—it is God's world and belongs to him. Rejected and unworthy as the world is, God so loved it that he gave his only begotten Son that man should be saved. God in his infinite Wisdom has shut up all (Israel included) in disobedience, that he might have mercy upon all (Rom. 11. 32).

If there is hope for Israel there is hope for humanity. In ourselves we stand condemned, but in the Messiah we are chosen for eternal life.

CHAPTER 8

THE HEBREW CHRISTIAN POSITION[1]

To conclude our thesis a special word must be said about the Jewish believer in Jesus Christ. He occupies an intermediary position between historic Israel and the Gentile world. Seen in the aspect of history, in him is re-established the position of the first century when the Church mainly consisted of a small Jewish minority. But his position needs special understanding, for in him is reflected the relation between Israel and the world.

The issue which divided the early Church turned round a basic principle, the catholicity of the Christian message. Was the Gospel to remain tied to a special people or was it to free itself from all national limitations? The answer lay in the question regarding the significance of the Cross: Did Jesus die for Jews and for those who became Jews, or for the world? For St Paul there was no question that Jesus died for the world, for he died for sinners. There is no *difference*, was his cry. Had his opponents won the day, the messianic movement would have remained an insignificant sect within the confines of the Synagogue. But under God's providence, the Pauline vision of a universal Church, in which Jews and Gentiles, bond and free, are united in a common brotherhood, triumphed.

Unfortunately, the old divisions reasserted themselves in the course of history. The Church repeatedly fell apart into ethnic and sectarian groups. In the West the national distinctions became specially emphasized as a result of the Reformation. But the division between Jew and Gentile is of a different order. This is not merely an ethnic division. In the Bible, humanity is divided into only two parts: the people of God and the "nations". It is this peculiar division, the basic division, which Jesus Christ came to heal, according to St Paul.

In assessing the Hebrew Christian position we shall have to keep the Pauline concern constantly before us. The fact of origin can be understood in two ways. It can be taken as a special privilege, and become a source of pride,[2] or else it can be accepted as a fact, in humble acknowledgement of God's will and purpose.

This is the choice before the Hebrew Christian believer. He cannot vaunt his origin, but at the same time he cannot, and must not, escape the destiny of his people. He acknowledges his origin not to emphasize his difference from his Gentile brother, but to declare his readiness to carry the burden of the Jewish destiny with the rest of his people. Faith in Christ must not become for him a means of escape. Behind his positive attitude to the people of his origin is the acknowledgement that all "accidents" of life are not fortuitous but have teleological significance. The facts of colour, race, nationality, are the God-given framework into which the believer is meant to weave the pattern of Christian service. The humble acceptance of our origin is part of our human obedience to the will of God.

But the Hebrew Christian has yet another reason why loyalty to his position is important. This is connected with his special witness to the Jewish people and the Gentile Church. This is somewhat different from the usual Christian witness which every believer owes the other man.

(a) The Special Position of the Hebrew Christian Believer

C. S. Lewis, in a foreword to a little book by a Hebrew Christian, makes the following remark:

> In a sense the converted Jew is the only normal human being in the world. To him, in the first instance, the promises were made, and he has availed himself of them. He calls Abraham his father by hereditary right as well as by divine courtesy. He has taken the whole syllabus in order, as it was set. . . . Everyone else is, from one point of view, a special case, dealt with under emergency regulations. . . .[3]

Though C. S. Lewis may have overstated the case, in essence his perception is right: in the Hebrew Christian is kept alive the historical continuity of the early Church. He thus stands as the symbol of Israel's election in the Messiah and of God's continued mercy with his People. This we think is in accordance with the Pauline view: "I say then, did God cast off his people? God forbid. For I also am an Israelite, of the seed of Abraham, . . ." (Rom. 11. 1). As the Gentile believer is the "first-fruit" of the nations, so is the Hebrew Christian the "first-fruit" of historic Israel. But in respect of history there is a difference between Jewish and Gentile believers in Jesus Christ, though theologically there is none. The Gentile, by turning to Christ, renounces his heathen heritage; he turns away from idols to serve the God of Israel. The Jew, by turning to Christ, *re*-turns to the God of Israel, the God of his fathers. The Gentile therefore always remains the "proselyte", whereas the Jew is only a returner. This is the very meaning of "repentance"—*teshuvah.* The Jewish believer returns to his greatest spiritual heritage by returning to the Messiah; he thus "normalizes" his own position and that of his people. To this return to "normalcy" belongs the acknowledgement of God's special purpose with his people, the humble acceptance of Jewish failure, and the willingness to carry the burden of Jewish destiny. The same can be said of every Gentile believer in respect to his own people, only that in the case of the Hebrew Christian there is an added historical and theological aspect.

Thus the Jew who accepts Jesus as Messiah and at the same time affirms his connection with historic Israel re-establishes the missing link in the story of revelation and connects the past with the *eschaton.*[4] He maintains the historical continuity between promise and fulfilment with a view to the End. In the Hebrew Christian the end of Israel's pilgrimage becomes visible at the point where all history ends—in him who is the End of time. Hebrew Christianity therefore stands from the beginning under the sign of eschatology.

(*b*) *The Hebrew Christian Witness*

As is the case with the Jewish people, the Hebrew Christian is a witness, though he may personally not be engaged in missionary work. His witness is implied in his position as a Jewish believer in Jesus Christ. As long as he maintains this position he is a witness in a special sense to his own people and to the Gentile church.

i. *The Hebrew Christian Witness to the Jews.* It has become *minhag* (custom) in Jewry to regard the decision reached by a small minority on Good Friday, some two thousand years ago, as final. Every individual and every generation is expected to accept the verdict as a matter of course. The Jewish concern to prove their innocence in the Crucifixion is to the Jews not a matter of conscience but expediency. They have suffered too long from the accusation of being the "Christ-killers". Only half-witted and ignorant "Christians" could have ever blamed the Jews for the Crucifixion and at the same time claim the "benefit of his passion" for themselves. To the Church, the death of the Messiah is the free sacrifice on the part of the Son of God for the sins of the world;[5] if it were otherwise there is no Gospel. A Church which does not know herself as co-responsible for the death of Christ can hardly claim to be a Christian Church. In fact, in the death of the Messiah, the Church is deeply and personally involved together with the Jews and the world. It is noteworthy that the early Church apportioned the blame in equal measure to Herod, Pontius Pilate, the Gentiles, and the people of Israel (Acts 4. 27). The Jew who turns to the Messiah does not dissociate himself from the guilt of his people, but accepts it as his own. But his decision about Jesus is strictly personal; his children will have to decide for themselves. This is an important issue, for on it hangs the question of a "national" decision once and for all. The Hebrew Christian thus denies that any people can decide about Jesus summarily. Herein lies his challenge to his Jewish brother. The Jewish believer refuses to accept that there can be a final and ultimate decision about Jesus of Nazareth. He claims the privilege and the right to decide for himself; there have always been and there always will be Jews to make such a choice.

Implied in the Hebrew Christian position is the prophetic freedom of the individual. As already stated, *vox populi, vox dei* is a pagan concept. The Bible contradicts it on almost every page. The true prophet in the Bible is "the voice in the wilderness", unpopular, rejected, and scorned. He only becomes "true" in the perspective of history when seen in the context of God's higher purpose. The "true" prophet for the mass is the false prophet who knows how to gain popularity at the expense of truth.

The Hebrew Christian is thus a challenge to prophetic freedom. His Jewish brother sees in him a living protest against the enslavement of public opinion. Here is a man who dares to challenge hallowed custom for the sake of conscience. When the writer to the Hebrews exhorted his fellow-believers to go outside the camp[6] and bear the reproach of the Master (Hebr. 13. 13), he acted within the prophetic tradition of the O.T.

The clash between public opinion and personal conscience underlies the whole struggle of the early Church and goes right through history. It is against this background that we learn the meaning of personal faith.

Ideally, Israel was meant to be a theocracy, the Jewish people, the People of God, every single Jew a son of God. But in practice a theocracy can degenerate into the most vile form of tyranny.

It is possible for the "people of God" to lose its soul in self-adulation and to become hardened to the call of repentance. For Professor Schoeps to overlook this fact is to fly in the face of history.[7] The Hebrew Christian position implies a contradiction of every form of that tribalism which is the most subtle form of idolatry.[8] The Hebrew Christian refuses to accept his people's destiny in terms of "fate". Franz Werfel, by limiting the individual's freedom to decide about Jesus in advance of his people, argues for a fatalistic and non-biblical attitude. His argument is that the individual must not evade the suffering which came to Israel as a result of rejecting the Messiah.[9] Such an attitude stands in direct opposition to the prophetic concept of *teshuvah*: "To-day, oh that ye would hear my voice!" (Ps. 95. 7; cf. Hebr. 3. 7 ff.). For the individual to submit to Israel's "fate" is to neglect the day of opportunity and despise the grace of God. No Jew dare wait for the rest of his people so that he can make the journey in company. The road to God is a lonely path and can be undertaken only by a decision of faith.

This implies personal responsibility before God: "Here am I; send me" (Isa. 6. 8). This is the second characteristic of the prophetic attitude. The Prophet shares in the guilt of his people, but he also carries the burden of that guilt in personal responsibility before God. He is *ẓofeh*, watchman, the keeper of his people's conscience. It is his task to give warning, and if he fails he is to be held guilty of negligence (cf. Ez. 3. 17 ff.). By an inward compulsion the Prophet is driven to act as the mouthpiece of God (cf. Jer. 20. 7–10). The fact that because of loyalty to his vocation he finds himself in the minority, detracts nothing from his position; it only enhances it. Unlike the false prophet, the true Prophet is a lonely man: "I sat alone because of thy hand; for thou hast filled me with indignation" (Jer. 15. 17). It has been said that one man with God constitutes a majority—this is the Prophet's position. The Hebrew Christian is in a somewhat similar position.

The parallel goes further.

The Prophet is an iconoclast, not because he delights in revolution, but because he abhors idols. These idols need not necessarily be of foreign origin to outrage the prophetic conscience. The temple, the sacrifices, the priesthood, even the prophetic office itself, become idolatrous when they cease to serve the main purpose, i.e. to point to God. Once these institutions are used as false securities, they assume the character of idolatry. In post-exilic time the Law became such an idol; in having become an end in itself, it served as a security to assure autonomy before God. The Hebrew Christian, like the Prophet of old, has to face the issue and recognize its danger. Not that he is without Law (cf. 1 Cor. 9. 21); he carries it deep in his soul, but he also knows of the freedom of the children of God for whom love is the fulfilment of the Law (cf. Gal. 5. 14). He refuses to accept precepts of men as the oracle of God; to him rabbinic Judaism is false and he has the courage to say so.

There is yet another point which is of great importance not only to the Jews but specially to the Church. The "two-way" theory is a modern invention to explain away the all-sufficiency of the Gospel. According to it, God uses two ways in dealing with mankind. In the case of the Jews, he employs the Law, in the case of Gentiles, the Gospel. It is the same Voice, but Jews hear it at Sinai and Gentiles on Golgotha,[10] and they thus need not walk the same path to be saved. The logical consequences of such a view touch at the very heart of the Christian message, namely that Jesus carried upon the Cross the sins of the world. It also drives a wedge through humanity and divides Jewry from the rest of mankind. It denies the universality of the human need and the uniqueness of the Incarnation. The Hebrew Christian stands as the living witness to the fact that God is no respecter of persons, and that there is no other way than the one which leads from Moses to the Cross and from Good Friday to Easter Day. He represents the other voice in Israel which humbly acknowledges that there is only one name given unto men, and only one way whereby man can be saved—the way of the Cross.

ii. *The Hebrew Christian Witness to the Gentile Church.* It is peculiar to the Hebrew Christian position to stand between two camps. In one respect this is the position of every believer, but in the case of the Christ-believing Jew, his origin takes on special significance.[11] In him is the schism healed which divides historic Israel from the Church. He belongs to both and in him both are united. He is not so much the bridge from the one to the other, as the focus of the eschatological promise: All Israel shall be saved. The presence of the Hebrew Christian in a predominantly Gentile Church serves as a reminder that God is still the God of Israel, of the Covenant, and of the Promises. In him the Church finds the visible demonstration of the faithfulness of God.

But the Hebrew Christian is also a reminder of another fact.

Not only is there a dichotomy between his people and the Church, but there is another dichotomy which must be uncovered for the sake of the Gospel.

The clash of loyalties imposes unbearable strain upon the historic Church. To avoid it she everlastingly seeks to compromise. Her main concern is to gloss over the fact that she is at war with the world. She is thus in constant search of a formula which would make a *modus vivendi* possible without too much of a sacrifice. Her theologians are engaged in proving the commensurability between the Kingdom of God and the world; her divines write learned dissertations on "religion and science", "reason and revelation", "natural theology and revealed religion"; her preachers show the usefulness of the "Christian religion" to society and the desirability of being good.

The historic Church has lent herself to ambiguities which are worse than lies; she baptizes infants of pagan parents; she gives Christian burial to men and women who have never been inside a church; she marries couples in the name of the Holy Trinity who have never heard of the rudiments of the Christian Faith. She protects the State, blesses the army, dresses her clergy in military uniform, and tries to give dignity to the order of this world. In doing this she knows that God claims the world for himself, that Christ died for it, that God seeks to reign over it. She knows it from the Cross of the Master and from the prayer: "Thy will be done on earth, as it is in Heaven." But in her zeal to win the world, she forgets that the path to salvation is narrow, that many are called but few are chosen, that the love of the world is enmity to God, that the order of this world passes away, that this world lies in wickedness.

This is her dilemma: to mix with the world and retain her integrity. She has to keep her doors open for sinners and to remain the Communion of Saints. She must guard against becoming a religious club on the one hand, and a conventicle of self-righteous bigots on the other. But for her, the middle path is not virtue, but weakness; to compromise is not a sign of sagacity, but infidelity. In the Hebrew Christian she finds reopened the whole issue in its original force.

The Hebrew Christian does not enter the Church by reason of birth but by personal decision. For him to decide for Christ entails suffering. From the day of his Baptism he is stigmatized a *meshummad* and becomes an outcast. Thus a Jewish decision for

Christ means to-day what it meant in the first century and what it will always mean to the believer, a rift, a break.

First, it is a rift with national tradition. The Hebrew Christian becomes a "protestant", a rebel. He finds himself in conflict with established authority. He makes a decision which runs against the majority view. Secondly, he steps out into the unknown in his venture for God; he takes the risk which is implicit in faith. Thirdly, he finds himself divided from his family. He learns from bitter experience the meaning of the Master's words: "He who loves father or mother more than me is not worthy of me." For him to be a Christian means to pay the price in terms of suffering.

The sacrifice on the part of a Jewish believer is often such that both Jews and Gentiles suspect him of ulterior motives. They cannot comprehend such inward compulsion which would make a man decide at so great a cost. It is the price of loyalty which a Gentile Christian pays only in non-Western lands. This can be explained, unless it is feigned faith, only in terms of personal conviction. The Hebrew Christian is a "convert" in the truest sense—not from Judaism to Christianity, but from sin to God.[12]

The presence of the Hebrew Christian in the Gentile Church has also definite theological significance. It demonstrates St Paul's argument in a contemporary setting:

1. That not all of Israel are Israel. This applies as much to historic Israel as to historic Christianity. Neither worship, nor doctrine, nor Church order, nor liturgy, nor orthodoxy are sufficient guarantees that the church is the Church of Christ. This is precisely St Paul's argument in relation to Israel. The Church cannot take herself for granted. Here the Master's word is decisive. "Not every one that saith unto me Lord, Lord, shall enter into the Kingdom of Heaven, but he that doeth the will of my Father" (Matt. 7. 21).

2. That if God spared not the natural branches, the Gentile Church must take heed lest she also suffer a similar fate (Rom. 11. 21). That Hebrew Christians are but a remnant of God's Chosen People is an everlasting warning to the Gentile Church. Here she learns afresh that the God of Israel is not committed to Israel, but is Israel's God.

3. That salvation is by grace and not by works. With all his zeal for God, Israel yet misses the mark. The Church cannot take her election for granted; neither her "orthodoxy" of doctrine nor her "validity" of sacrament, nor her "apostolicity" of priesthood,

nor her "catholicity" of liturgy make her to be the Church—she is Church only by the miracle of grace.

4. That the first shall be last and the last first. This reversal of order is peculiar to the Kingdom of God. It demonstrates the sovereignty of the Lord of Hosts. The Lord God is no man's debtor. Those who are the "first" here are the "last" there, and *vice versa*. The last word is with God and not with man. Israel who is last to enter may yet be the first to inherit the Kingdom of God.

5. That there is a difference between called and chosen. It is not only the Temple in Jerusalem which God suffers to be destroyed; it is also the Church of Laodicaea which he spews out because she is unworthy (Rev. 3. 14 ff.). There is no hiding from God and there is no evasion of his judgements. He calls all, but not all are fit to be chosen.

6. That God does not depend on man for his purposes. He can make out of the stones of the desert children unto Abraham. If the prophet refuses to see, his ass does (Num. 22. 22 ff.); if the wise and the prudent prove to be blind, he reveals his glory unto babes (Matt. 11. 25). He by-passes the mighty and establishes strength out of the mouth of sucklings (Ps. 8. 2; Matt. 21. 16); "he puts down the mighty from their seats and exalts the humble and meek" (Luke 1. 52). God's purposes cannot be frustrated either by Israel or by the Church. If Israel proves unworthy to enter the Promised Land, he perishes in the wilderness. God is and remains the Lord of history, and his ways are past finding out.

7. That there is always a faithful remnant. God's word never returns void but accomplishes that which he pleases and prospers whereunto it is sent (Isa. 55. 11). At all times and in every nation God has his faithful remnant of those who have not bowed their knees to Baal (1 Kings 19. 18). The power of the Holy Spirit works as effectually in Jewish as he does in Gentile hearts. God knows no frontiers, no colour-bars, no privileged classes. No one has the monopoly of God's grace, there are no favourites with him.

8. That salvation is only by faith. Man's hope is not here but there—at the End of the journey. The world is not saved while Israel is still absent; the fullness of the Gentiles is not yet. The Church is a waiting Church, if she is the Church at all. She prays, "Thy Kingdom come", which means that salvation is not complete, that she still walks between the times, between Christmas and Advent. She is not an end in herself, but a preparer of the way, a Church in between the times.

9. That she does not bear the root but the root her. The Gentile Church is only a grafted plant; she therefore can live only by grace. God is still the God of Israel, for he is and remains the God of the Promises.[13] The Hebrew Christian's presence is a sign and token that he is a Covenant-keeping God.

10. That if historic Israel with all his privileges has failed in his vocation, so that only the remnant found grace, what of the Gentiles who are strangers and aliens to the Promises? Karl Barth thinks that to keep this fact constantly before her eyes is the Hebrew Christian's main function in the Church.[14] He stands as a sign of man's utter insufficiency and the unsearchable riches of God's grace.

11. That God is able and willing to do what man can never accomplish of himself—to save to the uttermost. He accomplishes the impossible (cf. Rom. 11. 23; Luke 1. 17). The birth of Isaac, the delivery from Egypt, the return from Exile (cf. Zech. 8. 4–8), the spiritual regeneration of Israel (Jer. 31. 33), the triumph over sin and death (Isa. 25. 4–8)—are all within the province of God's mighty power. The restoration of primeval peace in the Messianic age as depicted in Isa. 11 is prompted by a deep faith in the power of Almighty God. Exactly the same conviction we meet in the N.T.: all things are possible with God (Mark 10. 27; Matt. 19. 26; Luke 18. 27). God is not only able but willing to perform his Promises (Rom. 4. 21) to save his people. The Hebrew Christian is a token and pledge of the coming age.

12. That God in his dealing with Israel exemplifies his dealing with mankind. In the Hebrew Christian we have a visible illustration of God's great forbearance. He is indeed a God slow to anger and full of mercy and truth (Ex. 34. 6). He does not leave man in his stubborn disobedience, but claims him for his child. God, who was defeated on Calvary, triumphs in history. This is the very paradox of the Cross. The Hebrew Christian stands as a sign of resurrection, first of his own people (Ez. 37) and secondly of mankind. He is the link between his dying people and the Risen Christ. The Messiah is the opener of Israel's grave, and the Victor over death on behalf of humanity (1 Cor. 15. 26).

The Hebrew Christian reminds the Church that the last word is God's, and that it is a word which has already been uttered on Easter Day: Life from the dead (cf. Rom. 11. 15).

CHAPTER 9

THE ECONOMY OF ELECTION

BIBLICAL election does not correspond to the usual connotation which goes with the noun. It cannot be explained empirically or in terms of hope. It is not the election of the deserving; if it were, Christ would have died for the just, and not for sinners (cf. Rom. 5. 7, 8). Election in the Bible is not an ethical, but a strictly theological concept. It carries a paradox and therefore defies logic: it means the election of sinners first and foremost. For this reason it cannot be explained in terms of the usual values which rule society. Biblical election is inseparably linked to the sovereign will of God. It is the keynote of God's testament, his manifesto to mankind. He reveals himself as the One who chooses sinners: this is meant by the proclamation of the Gospel. Not *because* man is a sinner is he chosen, but because God is what he is in Christ Jesus: the Saviour of sinners. In choosing sinners, the rejection of sin is already implied. The Holy God chooses sinners to clothe them with righteousness. In the centre, therefore, of God's saving act stands Jesus Christ. Man is made acceptable only in him (Phil. 3. 9); apart from him he stands under the verdict of death.

It is at this point that we come to the mystery of predestination.

The concept is, unfortunately, heavily weighted with theological prejudice. Because of its history it is not an easy task to recover its original Pauline meaning. It has become a theological tradition to understand under predestination "the separation of a part of the human family to eternal life, while the remainder are left, or consigned to eternal death".[1] But such a definition obviously contradicts St Paul's triumphant conclusion: not only will all Israel be saved, but God hath shut up all unto disobedience, that he might have mercy upon all (Rom. 11. 32). It is with this final conclusion in mind that election and predestination must be viewed.

1. We shall find in Rom. 8. 29, 30 a useful starting-point for our discussion. This passage is important, for the whole controversy regarding election and free-will here has its origin. Sanday

and Headlam have shown how the Pauline concepts have been misunderstood partly as a result of the controversy with Gnosticism, and partly from a desire to work out a reasoned system from mutually contradictory statements.[2] The Apostle himself never intended to reconcile the contradiction; in fact he seems to take pleasure in the antinomy and regards it as part of his argument. To him the antinomy seems to belong to the economy of election. The πρόθεσις τοῦ Θεοῦ according to which man is called is not, and was never meant to be, an abstract statement to invite further theological discussion. It is a concrete affirmation of faith in God, uttered for the sake of other believers in need of reassurance.[3] It is to definite people in a concrete situation that the Apostle addresses himself to tell *them* that God called them to faith; that he already foreknew their circumstances; that he has already pre-ordained (πρό + ὁρίζω) their destiny, i.e. to become assimilated to the image (εἰκών) of his Son. Here "predestination" is nothing less than supreme trust in God: "he who hath begun a good work in them will bring it to perfection with[4] the day of Jesus Christ" (Phil. 1. 6). In other words, the Apostle, from his knowledge of God in whom he believed (cf. 2 Tim. 1. 12), concludes not only about his own, but his readers' salvation. He knows God to be supremely trustworthy. It is a reflection upon the vagaries of the human mind to have constructed a most rigid system of predestination from a text which in itself is the deepest expression of faith in a loving God.[5]

The believer, however, knows God in the double experience; he knows him to be the God of judgement and grace at the same time. Judgement is rejection and grace is election, and between this double verdict man always stands. In the pattern of the Bible, as we have already seen, judgement and grace go hand in hand: the word of judgement is a word of succour and the word of succour a word of judgement. But in the Cross, grace prevails over judgement, for here only is God's "Yea" louder than his "Nay". In Jesus Christ is "Yea" and "Amen" (2 Cor. 1. 20). This means that we do not elect each other, but it is and remains God's prerogative to elect sinners in Christ. He does the choosing: "Ye did not choose me, but I have chosen you and appointed you, that ye should go and bear fruit" (John 15. 16). No one comes to Christ except God draws him (John 6. 44), and no one knows the Father but the Son and he to whomsoever the Son willeth to reveal him (Matt. 11. 27). That the Father draws men to Christ and that Christ draws men to God is not just a theological quibble but the deepest experience of the believer. Behind it is hidden the secret of *hearing* the Word of God. In this act of *hearing*, man becomes in the truest sense an individual. This is the Kierkegaardian concept of the basic Christian category. Christian election, says Barth, is essentially individualistic.[6]

2. But in the Bible, election is never entirely a matter of the individual alone. The elect people, the People of God, the community, is of equal importance. The two go together and presuppose one another. God does not elect the individual to enjoy bliss; he elects men for one another. Only in his togetherness with the fellow-man is the individual elected. The Kingdom of God does not consist of isolated individuals, but in the fellowship of the Saints. The perfect communion of the Holy Trinity must extend to those who want to be children of God, for the Kingdom to become reality: "The effect of the Incarnation upon man is that the Son may be surrounded by a multitude of the redeemed."[7] Seen ideally, Israel is the family of God in perfect fellowship with God and one another. The "community" (*Gemeinde*)[8] is chosen for that very purpose; its task is to strive after the realization of the communion of the Saints.

This is the pattern of biblical election. Into this pattern is woven the story of Israel. It is the story of God's people, which is *not* God's people at the same time. With a view to God's Promises Israel *is* God's People: with a view to Israel's faithlessness and blindness,[9] Israel is *lo-'ammi*—"not my people". Here the story of the individual is multiplied on a national scale. But there is one essential difference between the individual Jew and collective Israel: Israel as a people cannot hear the word of the Cross; it can be heard only personally by the individual Jew. The same applies to the Gentile world. The "mass" is always *massa perditionis*—not that God has decreed its destruction, this would contradict the heart of the Gospel that God loved the world—but that the mass is impersonal, an abstraction, the invention of the mind; God deals only with real people.

3. There is a curious relationship between historic Israel and the Israel of God. That relationship is part of the pattern of biblical election. The one cannot exist without the other; only together they form a whole. It is the same relationship as there is between Christianity and Church, or between the Bible and the Word of God. These are not interchangeable; they are never the

same; yet they never exist in separation; either they go together or are not at all.

This "doubleness" of phenomena is conditioned by the nature of things; it underlies the order of our world which consists of "things visible and invisible". Israel is both *'ammi* and *lo-'ammi*—the Church is both the Church of God and mere Christianity; Jesus is both, the son of a carpenter and the Son of God; the Bible is both a book and the Word of God; election is both election and rejection at the same time; the bush which Moses saw is both an ordinary bush and a bush which is not consumed by fire. They become the *other* thing only by the miracle of faith, which is a sovereign act of God.

4. But the pattern of election is incomplete without the eschatological perspective. The Christian theologian can never forget that Christ died for the world. Election in the biblical context is election of unworthy, godless, rebellious men and women to become children of God. Here there is no difference between Jew and Hottentot. This is the very heart of the Gospel that Jesus is the Lamb of God who takes away the sins of the world. To the believer, the prophetic vision of universal bliss is not a poetic phantasy but a Promise by God who is faithful and true. Eschatology is the vindication of God's promises; it is the successful conclusion of the human drama in which God has the last word. This means that Christ did not die in vain; that the curse which he took upon himself has become a blessing to mankind. He carried the burden of sin on man's behalf so that man should become a child of God.[10]

There can be no bliss for the saints without the salvation of the sinners; there can be no real heaven as long as there is hell. That God will be all in all, is the believer's ultimate hope (1 Cor. 15. 28). In the pattern of election the golden thread of εὐδοκία is the foundation of the whole design. The Gospel is not really Good News if it is Good News only for some and not for all.

When death has been swallowed up in victory and every tear from human faces has been wiped away, then shall the reproach of God's people be removed from off all the earth (Isa. 25. 8). Israel's humiliation, his fall and his blindness, is the humiliation, the fall, and the blindness of mankind.

Israel's salvation is inseparable from that of humanity. Israel's election is the election of man. As long as there is hope for Israel there is hope for the world.

Man, Israel, and the Church are one; in front of them stands the One who died that they should live. Election to life is the Christian meaning of election. The road to it, on the plane of history, may lead through Judgement and Death, but at the end of the road is a loving Father waiting for the prodigal son.

A treatise which deals with the problem of election in the context of the Gospel can fittingly end only with the Apostle's cry of wonder: "O the depth of the riches both of the wisdom and the knowledge of God!"

NOTES TO CHAPTER I

1. Cf. Karl Barth, *Dogmatik*, I, 2, 505 ff.

2. Here is a typical remark which we flatly contradict: "If Christian theology, in its central department, cannot pretend to set forth *truth*, it proclaims itself bankrupt. It can live upon nothing less than the truths regarding God and His purposes which He has been pleased to make known to us" (so Robert Mackintosh, *H. Dict. of Christ and the Gospels*, 726, para. 4). We reply for theology to declare itself bankrupt is its only salvation; only in weakness is its strength; it has lived too long upon "truths", instead of the living God.

3. Barth, op. cit., I, 2, 563 f.

4. Cf. J. Jocz, *The Jewish People and Jesus Christ*, 275 ff.

5. Cf. the apt remark by Emmett McLoughlin in reference to the Roman Catholic system, *People's Padre*, London, 1955, 96 f.

6. J. Jocz, op. cit.

7. Martin Buber, *The Two Types of Faith*, E.T., 12. We know of only one modern Jewish writer who speaks contemptuously of Jesus, but from other than religious motives; cf. Oscar Levy, *The Idiocy of Idealism*, 1940. He mocks at the Gentile world which has chosen "this minor specimen of Jewry for its god". But the writer has no standing in Jewry and was obviously suffering from the strain of the war. His destructive cynicism extends to all the higher aspirations of mankind.

8. Edmond Fleg, *Jesus: told by the Wandering Jew*, 1934.

9. Asch's books have aroused prolonged and bitter strife in Jewry. He was decried as a crypto-Christian and accused of surreptitious missionary motives. Asch, though he has never retracted what he has written, has given repeated assurances of his loyalty to Judaism. The controversy is too extensive to be quoted in full. Here we can indicate only some of the literature:

Hillel Rogof, "Sholem Asch and Christianity", Yiddish, *Forward*, 31 December 1950; also *Jewish Chronicle*, 20 November 1953; ibid., 6 January 1955.

"Sholem Asch denies Conversion", *Jewish Chronicle*, 2 September 1949.

"Jewish Attack on Sholem Asch", *Daily Telegraph*, 28 November 1953.

"Sholem Asch's Explanation", *Jewish Chronicle*, 9 May 1952.

"Sholem Asch's Confession", *Jewish Chronicle*, 10 December 1954.

"Sholem Asch's Judaism", *Jewish Chronicle*, 15 April 1955.

Also the special interview for the *Jewish Chronicle*: Sholem Asch—"I am a good Jew", 4 December 1954; also Sholem Asch, *Jewish Chronicle*, 14 May 1955.

10. Franz Werfel, *Paul among the Jews*, E.T. by P. P. Levertoff, 1928.

11. For a more detailed discussion, see Robert Brunner, "Franz Werfel's theologisches Vermächtnis", *Judaica*, III, 1946. Unfortunately, Robert Brunner did not succeed in working out Werfel's more positive relationship to Jesus Christ, which in fact underlies much of his thinking.

12. H. F. Rubinstein, *Hated Servants*, 1944. Eight one-act plays, six of which deal with primitive Christianity. Cf. also his play, *The Fifth Gospel*, 1946.

13. Nathan Bistrizki, *Jesus of Nazareth*, Hebrew, Tel Aviv, 1950.

14. There are several lives of Jesus written by Jews. One of the earliest is by Joseph Jacobs, *As Others Saw Him*, 1895. A very popular but superficial one is by E. Ludwig, *Der Menschensohn: Geschichte eines Propheten*, 1928.

15. Cf. Cornelia and Irving Süssman, "Marc Chagall, Painter of the Crucified", *The Bridge*, ed. John M. Oesterreicher, 1955, 96 ff.

16. The most moving poem comes from the pen of the outstanding Polish Jewish poet, Juljan Tuwim: *Chrystusie* . . . "Yet in my sorrow will I turn to Thee, O Christ . . .", *Wiersze Zebrane*, 1936, p. 53.

17. Cf. *Der Weg* (Yiddish), Jan.–Feb. 1933, Warsaw, C.M.J. publication.

18. Cf. J. Jocz, "Roman Hebrew Christianity", *The Hebrew Christian*, Autumn 1954.

19. In addition to Oesterreicher's essay on Bergson, see also Jacques Chevalier, *Bergson et le Père Pouget*, 1955.

20. Cf. his review of Oesterreicher's book, *Jewish Chronicle*, 19 March 1954.

21. For evidence see his autobiographical work, *My Dear Timothy*, 1952; also the 2nd vol., *More for Timothy*, 1953. His close discipleship can best be seen in his impassioned plea for the abolition of capital punishment in connection with the sad case of Derek Bentley, ibid., II, 259 ff.

22. Louis Golding, *The Day of Atonement*, 1924.

23. *Redeeming the Time*, 104 ff.

24. Cf. S. J. Hunter, *Outlines of Dogmatic Theology*, 1909, I, 263 f.

25. Aug., *De Capt. c. Donat.*, VII, 77.

26. Ibid., III, 4.

27. Maritain, op. cit., 125.

28. Ibid., 135.

29. Cf. Maimonides, *Yad ha-ḥazaḳah, Shoftim*, the two last chapters; also J. Jocz, op. cit., 281 ff.

30. For an interesting chapter on non-Jewish Messiahs, see René Fülöp-Miller, *Leaders, Dreamers, and Rebels*, 1935; also Ronald Matthews, *English Messiahs*, 1936. For the Jewish Messianic hope, see J. Klausner, *The Messianic Idea in Israel*, E.T., 1956.

31. H. L. Ellison, "Jesus and the Pharisees", *Journal of Transactions of the Victoria Institute*, Vol. LXXXV, 1953. Mr Ellison's otherwise excellent article is unfortunately vitiated by his effort to explain away "hypocrites" by giving it the meaning of "play-acting", as if this were more acceptable; an idea he borrowed from Lukyn Williams (cf. *Talmudic Judaism and Christianity*, 1933, Appendix).

32. Cf. J. Jocz, op. cit., 304.

33. This is the argument forwarded by Philip Cohen, *The Hebrew-Christian and his National Continuity*, London, n.d.

34. Cf. the impassioned plea by Dr Felix Propper: *Zum Leben berufen*, 1955.

35. For the spiritual issues involved in the Hebrew Christian position see Robert Brunner, "Judenchristliches Dilemma", *Judaica*, IV, 1948. For a survey of contemporary Hebrew Christianity, see Gerhard Jasper, "Der Judenchrist als Zeichen Gottes für Israel und die Kirche", *Judaica*, III, 1955.

36. The question of infant Baptism of non-believing parents is increasingly becoming a burning issue; cf. K. Barth's indictment in his *The Teaching of the Church regarding Baptism* (*Die Kirchliche Lehre von der Taufe*), E.T., 1948.

NOTES TO CHAPTER 2

1. Cf. Otto Pfleiderer, *Philosophy and Development of Religion*, Gifford Lectures, II, Lecture VIII, "The Christianity of the Alexandrian Fathers", 258 ff.

2. "Dieser Gedanke der Offenbarung des göttlichen Wesens im Menschen, der die innere Verwandtschaft der verschiedensten Glaubensformen darstellt, ist nicht bloss als spekulatives Prinzip lebendig gewesen: er hat das religiöse Gefühl genährt und die Herzen der Menschen aufs tiefste bewegt"; Prof. Herambachandra Maitra, "Die Sehnsucht des Menschen nach dem Unendlichen", *Fünfter Weltkongress für freies Christentum*, Berlin, 1910, 390.

3. J. Jocz, "Religion and the Gospel", *Journal of Transactions of the Victoria Institute*, Vol. LXXXIV, 1952, 77 ff. In this essay the relationship between religion and gospel is dealt with at some length.

4. The same is true of Judaism, though Judaism too has its mysticism, cf. Ernst Mueller, *A History of Jewish Mysticism*, 1946. In the eighteenth century the revival of mysticism split the Synagogue into *ḥasidim* and *mitnagdim*. Ḥasidism is connected with the name of Israel ben Eliezer, better known as Ḃaal-Shem-Tov (The Master of the Good Name, i.e. God); cf. I. Günzig, *Die Wundermänner im jüdischen Volke*, Antwerp, 1921; see also P. Levertoff, *Die religiose Denkweise der Chassidim*, Leipzig, 1918, 130 ff. It is an inconsistency in Prof. Martin Buber's attitude that he is a mystic as well as the great exponent of the I–Thou relationship.

For Ḥasidism, see T. Ysander, *Studien zum B'ešṭschen Ḥasidismus*, Uppsala, 1933.

5. This is important, for Jewish scholars frequently present the Christian faith as based upon mysticism.

6. "Ecclesia Christi visibilis est coetus fidelium, in quo verbum Dei purum praedicatur . . ." (Article XIX, The Thirty-Nine Articles of the Anglican Church).

7. Cf. Rom. 8. 29; Matt. 23. 8; Matt. 12. 49 f.

8. So H. Loewe, *Vallentine's Jew. Encycl.*, 336 b.

9. Cf. Augustine, *Conf.*, VII, 10, 17.

10. *De fide et symbolo*, 1.

11. Cf. Augustine, *Ep.*, 120, 3.

12. Cf. Augustine, *Enchiridion*, VIII.

13. But cf. Loofs, *Dogmengeschichte*, 1906, 386, who maintains that the *sola fide justificamur* principle was common to the theological outlook of the time and was by no means Augustine's special contribution.

14. Be it noted that "the holy temple of the Lord" in Eph. 2. 20 f. is not a dogmatic edifice like Thomas's *Summa*, but the living organism of believers.

15. *De unit.*, 25. 74.

16. *De doctr.*, 3. 32, 45.

17. *W.A.*, VI, 300, 37–301, 6.

18. Note, however, Loofs' remark: "Luthers Lehre von der 'Sichtbarkeit' wird m. E. falsch verstanden, wo verkennt wird, dass es mehr um eine Sichtbarkeit für den Glauben sich handelt" (op. cit., 733, n. 6), but cf. H. H. Kramm, *The Theology of Martin Luther*, 69 f.

19. Quoted by the Editor of the 1953 edition of Luther's *Commentary on Gal.*, p. 9, n. 5.

20. Cf. Kramm, op. cit., 69.

21. Luther held, in spite of Prof. Loofs' remark (cf. note 18), that there was a remnant of the true Church on earth in visible existence, as is evident from the answer in the Great Catechism: "Ich glaube, dass da sei ein heiliges Hauflein und Gemeine auf Erden eitler [i.e. lauter] Heiligen unter einem Haupt, Christo, durch den heiligen Geist zusammen berufen . . ." (G. Holz, *Luther's Grosser Katechismus*, 1933, 91).

22. Cf. Optatus' answer to the Donatists: *deus lavat non homo. . . .*

23. So F. W. Farrar, *Lives of the Fathers*, II, 532.

24. Cf. Loofs, op. cit., 376 (8).

25. H. Heppe, *Reformed Dogmatics*, E.T., 665. Cf. the whole chapter dealing with the subject of the Church.

26. Cf. H. F. Woodhouse, *The Doctrine of the Church in Anglican Theology, 1547–1603*, 1954, 46. Woodhouse rightly points out the inconsistency which we have already noticed in the case of Luther.

27. It may well be that much of Christian impatience with the Jews springs from the Jewish question: Where is the holy, catholic, apostolic Church to be found? One of the most gentle voices to ask the question is that of Baruch Spinoza: "I have often wondered, that persons who make a boast of professing the Christian religion, namely, love, joy, peace, temperance and charity to all men, should quarrel with such rancorous animosity, and display daily such bitter hatred. . . ." The gentle philosopher finds it strange that in the manner of life there is no real difference between Christian, Turk, Jew, and Heathen. (Cf. The Preface to the *Theologico-political Treatise*, E.T., by R. H. M. Elwes, 6 f.)

28. Hooker, III, I, 8.

29. Cf. *Jewish Encycl.*, Vol. XI, 619 b. (Hereafter referred to as *J.E.*)

30. Cf. J. Jocz, "Die Juden im Johannesevangelium", *Judaica*, Heft 3, 1953; cf. also Gösta Lindeskg, *Die Judenfrage im neuzeitlichen Judentum*, 140 ff. Some Jewish scholars admit that Pharisaism is a development from a previous position. The pioneer of the idea is Geiger (*Sadducäer und Pharisäer*, Breslau, 1863). A step further was made by S. Schechter in his *Documents of Jewish Sectaries*, 1910. The hypothesis has now found new support from the Dead Sea Scrolls (cf. A. Dupont-Sommer, *The Jewish Sect of Qumran and the Essenes*, 1954); cf. also D. Daube, *The N.T. and Rabb. Judaism*, 1956, 92.

31. The many efforts on the part of Jewish and Gentile scholars to prove the contrary we find unconvincing. For the appropriate literature see J. Jocz, *The Jewish People and Jesus Christ*, ch. II, and notes; also Lindeskg, op. cit., 220 ff.

32. W. D. Davies, *Paul and Rabbinic Judaism*, 259. Davies is much too cautious on this matter. We hold that the Sacrifices and specially the Paschal Lamb were of supreme importance in the Pauline interpretation of the Cross.

33. Cf. *J.E.* article: "Synagogue".

34. Cf. A. Schlatter, *Geschichte Israels*, 1925, 51 ff. The Temple erected in Leontopolis (Egypt) for the Jewish garrison is unparalleled in Jewish history and will have had political as well as religious reasons; see *J.E.*, VIII, 7 b f.

35. Cf. Ellenbogen in *Religion in Geschichte und Gegenwart*, 1931, V, 947. It

is reasonable to assume that in the first place the "Synagogues" were communal centres of sacred study and that only gradually did they become places of worship. To this day every more important Synagogue has a "house of study" attached to it.

36. Cf. Singer, *Annotated Prayer Book* (hereafter referred to as "Singer"), cv f.

37. Cf. *Rosh ha-shanah*, IV, 1, 2.

38. Singer, 14, etc.

39. Singer, xxv; cf. pp. 9–13.

40. Cf. Singer, 262.

41. *Yoma*, 54b. We assume that "Zion" is here synonymous with "Temple". This is usual in Jewish tradition, though topographically inaccurate. For Jerusalem's position as the centre of the world, see *J.E.*, VIII, 497 b.

42. Singer, 245.

43. Cf. Oesterley and Box, *Religion and Worship of the Synagogue*, 359 ff. Cf. Singer, xxvi.

44. Cf. L. N. Dembitz, *Jewish Services*, 406, note 2.

45. Solomon Hirschell's *Prayer Book for German and Polish Jews in England*, p. 9 (early 19th c.).

46. Cf. Singer, 145.

47. Prof. Daube says: "The concept of the priesthood must have played a greater part than might appear from our Talmudic sources", but this is an understatement; cf. D. Daube, *N.T. and Rabb. Jud.*, 124.

48. *Judaica*, Heft 3, 1953.

49. Cf. J. Jocz, op. cit., 209 f.

50. Cf. Ferdinand Weber, *Die Lehre des Talmud*, Leipzig, 1880.

51. The fact that the writer of Hebrews uses the Tabernacle rather than the Temple in his argumentation we put down to an ancient Hebrew tradition which maintained a certain hostility to city life; cf. Schoeps, *Theologie und geschichte des Judenchristentums*, 220 ff.

52. Cf. Streeter, *The Four Gospels*, 422 f.; also Strack and Billerbeck, II, 835.

53. D. Chwolson, *Das letzte Passamahl Christi und der Tag seines Todes*, 1892; cf. Strack and Billerbeck's Excursions: *Der Todestag Jesus*, II, 845 ff.

54. This is contradicted by Strack and Billerbeck, who maintain that ἑτοιμάζειν τὸ πάσχα, φαγεῖν τὸ πάσχα, θύειν τὸ πάσχα are all references to the Paschal Lamb; cf. op. cit., II, 837.

55. On the date of the Crucifixion both the Synoptic and the Johannine traditions coincide; cf. Strack and Billerbeck, II, 841.

56. Cf. Edersheim, *The Temple*, 102.

57. Cf. Strack and Billerbeck, IV, B, 1146 f.

58. The Hebrew Bible ends with the second book of Chronicles; the Massoretic Bible therefore has no ending. The Hebrew Scriptures are left without a sequel. But even if the Synagogue had rearranged the order of the books and had adopted the Christian pattern, the result would be the same. The O.T. is left in suspense—waiting for Elijah and the fulfilment of God's promise (cf. Mal. 3. 23 f.).

59. For the meaning of *'am segullah*, see H. J. Schoeps, *Aus frühchristlicher Zeit*, 191 f.

60. Cf. Singer, pp. 4, 64, etc.

61. "Die frei schenkende und wählende Liebe Gottes ist der Kausalgrund, der Auserwählung Israels", *Schoeps*, op. cit., 197.

62. The עֲקֵדַת יִצְחָק plays a very special part in Jewish piety; cf. Singer, 252.

63. Cf. Singer, 258.

64. Here, as throughout, Law means Torah, though we are aware of the inadequacy of such a translation; cf. *Judaism and Christianity*, III, 50 ff.

65. Singer, 207.

66. This is the way becoming for the study of Torah: a morsel of bread with salt shalt thou eat, and water by measure shalt thou drink, upon the (bare) ground shalt thou sleep, and a life of sorrow shalt thou lead—while thou toilest in the Torah. *Pirke Abbot*, VI, 4; cf. Singer, 206.

67. There are many superstitious practices attached to the pronouncing of the Ineffable Name. In magic and mysticism the Tetragrammaton plays an important part. In order to avoid the mention of the Name, the Synagogue invented many substitutes (cf. Dalman, *The Words of Jesus*, E.T., 204 ff.). A more rational attitude to the Name is taken by Maimonides, *Guide for the Perplexed*, E.T., 1947, 95 ff. For an interpretation of the Tetragrammaton in connection with Ex. 3. 14, see L. M. v. Pákozdy, *Judaica*, 4, 1955.

68. Cf. A. Marmorstein, *The Old Rabbinic Doctrine of God*, I, 17 f.

69. Maimonides, op. cit., 95: "the *shem ha-mephorash* is not an appellative", it does not "denote any attribute of God, nor does it imply anything except his existence".

70. Cf. Singer, xxii.

71. Cf. *Laws and Customs of Israel*, E.T. by Gerald Friedländer, 251, § 13.

72. J. H. Hertz, *The Pentateuch*, 770.

73. So the Engl. transl. by the Jewish Publication Society of America, 1917.

74. Cf. C. G. Montefiore and H. Loewe, *Rabbinic Anthology*, 4, note 1.

75. Martin Buber und Franz Rosenzweig, *Die Schrift*, *Das Buch Reden* (no date).

76. Singer, 89.

77. Cf. Moses Maimonides, *The Guide for the Perplexed*, chapters LVII ff.

78. Hertz, *Affirmations of Judaism*, 12.

79. Martin Buber, *Two Types of Faith*, 58.

80. Buber, *Der Heilige Weg*, 42: "der zentralste Jude".

81. "Die Wahrheit als Tat!", op. cit., 71.

82. Cf. *J.E.*, IV, 180 b.

83. The literal meaning of *mizvah* is commandment, but it has the overtone of meritorious deed and of privilege.

84. The traditional phrase of every benediction uttered before the fulfilment of a *mizvah*; cf. Singer, 4.

85. Singer, 44, and note on p. lix.

86. Singer, 50.

87. Cf. the note in Singer, cxxiv f.

88. Cf. Singer, 90.

89. Ignaz Maybaum, *Man and Catastrophe*, 58 f.

90. Cf. Lewis N. Dembitz, op. cit., 281 f.; also Oesterley and Box, *The Religion and Worship of the Synagogue*, 382.

91. Oesterley and Box, op. cit., 402. The Synagogue celebrates the anni-

versary of the Giving of the Law on the Festival of *Shavuot*, which Festival corresponds to Whit-Sunday.

92. Cf. Oesterley and Box, 380 ff.

93. Joseph Bonsirven, *On the Ruins of the Temple*, 89 ff.; S. Daiches, *Aspects of Judaism*, 66 ff.

94. Cf. his poem: *Das neue israelitische Hospital zu Hamburg*:

"Behaftet mit den bösen drei Gebrechen—
Mit Armut, Körperschmerz und Judentume
Das schlimmste von den dreien ist das letzte. . . ."

95. The exception is the frightful persecution under German Nazism, when race and not religion was the deciding factor. Cf. Lord Russell of Liverpool, *The Scourge of the Swastika*, 1954.

96. Jos., *Wars*, VI, 2, 1.

97. Cf. *Rabbinic Anthology*, 136.

98. Ibid., 269.

99. *Num. R.*, 31, 2.

100. Cf. also *Sab.*, 32 a; *Bab. M.*, 30 b, 88 b; *'Arak*, 16 b; cf. also *Rabbinic Anthol.*, 492.

101. Cf. J. Jocz, op. cit., 167.

102. Singer, 245 f.

103. Ibid., 62.

104. Jehuda Halevi, *Kuzari*, II, § 24.

105. I. Maybaum, *The Jewish Mission*, 144.

106. I. I. Mattuck, *What are the Jews?*, 196 f.

107. We touch here upon an important difference between orthodox and Reformed Judaism. Whereas the rabbis have always understood Judaism in religio-national terms, Reform Jews cling to the "non-nation religious concept of Jewish life". The Reform Synagogue believes herself to aim "at a larger survival" than that of the Jewish people. (Cf. Mattuck, op. cit., 240; also ibid. 211.)

108. Cf. *Rabbinic Anthol.*, 158 (427).

109. Cf. M. Fishberg, *The Jews, A Study of Race and Environment*.

The *Jewish Chronicle* produced a photograph of two small boys playing—one as fair as any Slav could possibly be, the other as dark as an Ethiopian—both Jews.

110. We read in *Lev. R.*: God said to Moses: Go tell the Israelites my children, as I am pure, so be ye pure; as I am holy, so be ye holy; as it is said, "Holy shall ye be, for I your God am holy". (*parush*, of which word Pharisee is derived, is here used instead of holy; lit. "to be separated".)

111. *Sifra* to Lev. 19. 2.

112. *Sot.* 14 a. The rabbis quote texts from the O.T. to prove that God did all these things. Maimonides insists, however (*Guide*, i, 52), and so does *Sifre* (Deut. 49), that these attributes relate to God's activity and not to his Essence.

113. *Rabbinic Anthol.*, 279.

114. *Die Lehren des Judentums*, edited by S. Bernfeld and F. Bamberger, Vols. 1–3.

115. *Rabbinic Anthol.*, 89.

116. *Deut. R.*, 5. 3.

117. For the whole subject, cf. the excellent chapter by A. Cohen *Everyman's Talmud*, 203–9.

118. The same apostle who was so emphatic on the importance of faith, says: Be not deceived, God is not mocked, whatsoever a man soweth, that shall he also reap (Gal. 6. 7). Herein lies the essential Jewishness of St Paul.

NOTES TO CHAPTER 3

1. It is noteworthy that Mark begins with a quotation from Isaiah, which is soon followed by another quotation from Ps. 2. Our Lord begins his ministry with the announcement πεπλήρωται ὁ καιρός (Mark 1. 15) in reference to the time anticipated by the Prophets. Mark 14. 49: ἵνα πληρωθῶσιν αἱ γραφαί, is undoubtedly a Dominical expression. A comparison between Mark 14. 49 and Luke 18. 31 ff. is most instructive. The Lucan version: "all the things . . . written by the Prophets", points to the Church's increasing need to verify its statements by reference to the O.T.

2. Cf. J. Jocz, "Das exegetische Problem und die Judenmission", *Judaica*, I, 1956, 8. 17.

3. "Christus est punctus mathematicus sacrae scripturae." For the whole subject of Luther's attitude to the O.T., cf. Heinrich Bornkamm, *Luther und das Alte Testament*, 1948.

4. Quoted by Bornkamm, op. cit., 175, n. 3.

5. Cf. J. Jocz, *Judaica*, I, 1956.

6. So M. Buber; cf. Schoeps, *Jüdisch-christliches Religionsgespräch*, 154.

7. Cf. Ludwig Diestel, *Geschichte des Alten Testaments in der christlichen Kirche*, Jena, 245.

8. Be it observed that some of Justin's arguments, and of many others, both ancient and modern exegetes, belong to the same order of reasoning.

9. The O.T. "proof" of the Virgin Birth is still an important issue between Jews and Christians. But it seems to us rather precarious to pin so great a matter on the philological argument of one single word. If the doctrine of the Virgin Birth was made to depend entirely on העלמה in Isa. 7. 14, then it truly rests upon a very slender basis. Even the R.V. offers, as an alternative for "virgin", "maiden", and Basilius Magnus did not hesitate to translate העלמה with νεᾶνις, instead of the usual παρθένος; cf. *Judaica*, I, 1956, 20 f.

10. *Dial.*, 89. 1.

11. Rabbiner Dr Seligmann Pick, *Die auf Jesus gedeuteten Stellen des Alten Testaments*, 1923, 84: "Es ergibt sich aus unseren auf Grund von Quellenstudien geführten Untersuchungen, dass keine der untersuchten alttestamentlichen Stellen christologischen Inhalts ist."

12. J. H. Hertz, *Pentateuch and Haftorah*, 201 f. Dr Hertz goes much further in his denial of messianic texts than does Dr Pick, who at least differentiates between messianic and Christological prophecies, denying only the existence of the latter. For the whole subject cf. Klausner, op. cit., 519 ff.

13. Ed. Riehm, *Die messianische Weissagung*, 1885, 160.

14. Cf. *Judaica*, I, 1956, 6 f.

15. An interesting example is the case of Luther. He readily accepts many of the Jewish objections and yet he is able to carry through a consistent Christocentric exegesis of the O.T.; cf. Bornkamm, op. cit., 98, 169 ff.

16. Cf. Loofs, op. cit., 102. Loofs rightly distinguishes between the "*öko-*

nomische-trinitarisch" monotheism of Ignatius and the "pluralistic" monotheism of later apologists, like Theophilus.

17. Cf. Singer, VII. "Inconceivable" is inaccurate, נֶעְלָם means hidden, like Isa. 1. 15, where the same verb is used.

18. Singer, 3.

19. Cf. his *Sefer ḥizzuḳ emunah*, chapters 9 and 10.

20. Cf. Saadia, *Emunot ve-deot*, II, 5; Hasdai Crescas, *Bittul ikre ha-nozrim*, 23; Albo, *Ikkarim*, III, 25.

21. Lukyn Williams, writing as a Christian apologist, admits that some of R. Isaac's objections to O.T. "proofs" are well justified. Cf. *Christian Evidences for Jewish People*, I, 94 ff., 184 ff., etc.

22. Maimonides, *Guide for the Perplexed*, Engl. ed., 67 (ch. L).

23. For Luther's perception of the problem of language in relation to the Trinity, see Loofs, op. cit., 750 f.: "*Trinitas*", "*Unitas*" *sunt vocabula mathematica.*

24. *Rabb. Anthol.*, 7. For other references to the subject see Montefiore, *The Old Testament and After*, 28, 561.

25. Cf. Hertz, *Affirmations of Judaism*, 19 ff.

26. Lukyn Williams, op. cit., 93.

27. The story of Christian argumentation in favour of the doctrine of the Trinity would require a separate treatise. The arguments sometimes advanced were so far-fetched as to be ridiculous. We venture to suggest that a fragment of such an argument has survived in *Shab.*, 87 b, though Rabbi H. Friedman interprets the passage differently: A certain Galilean lectured before R. Ḥisdai: Blessed be the Merciful One who gave a threefold book (i.e. Torah, Prophets, and Hagiographa) to a threefold people (i.e. Priests, Levites, and Israelites), through a third (born) (i.e. Moses who was born after Miriam and Aaron), on the third day (i.e. on their separation from their wives), on the third month. With whom does this agree?—with the Rabbis.

Now H. Friedman suggests that the mysterious "Galilean" is merely acting as a "*meturgeman*" (cf. *Babyl. Talmud*, E.T., Vol. II, 416 f.), but his argument is unconvincing. We suggest that the "Galilean" is a Jewish Christian and that his exposition is a typical midrash on the Trinity. Unfortunately, we have here only part of the argument.

28. Lukyn Williams, op. cit., 95.

29. "A material possession . . . inheritable by reason of blood-relationship", op. cit., 143.

30. Cf. H. J. Schoeps, "Weiteres zur Auserwählung Israels", *Judaica*, Oct. 1946.

31. On the subject of proselytes, see J. Jocz, op. cit., 302 f.

32. Judah Halevi holds that the proselyte is equal to the born Jew in every respect, save one: he is denied the privilege of prophetic utterance.

33. Cf. Schoeps, *Judaica*, Oct. 1946, 201, note 15.

34. Schoeps, op. cit., 192 f.

35. In our view Hans Kosmala has gone too far in giving Judaism a racial bias, though the racial element is by no means absent; cf. *The Jew in the Christian World*, 1942, 47 ff.

36. *Cant. R.*, 6. 12.

37. Cf. *Rabb. Anthol.*, 38 f., 72.

38. He describes it as "die vorausetzungslose Gnadenhandlung Gottes", *Judaica*, Oct. 1946, 190.

39. A. Feldman, *Parables and Similes of the Rabbis*, 200.

40. A. Feldman, op. cit., 163.

41. Schoeps, *Judaica*, III, 1946, 192.

42. Judah Halevi calls it: ענין אלהי, Schoeps translates: *res divina*.

43. חכמים וחסידים—the חכם is the "sage", a student and a competent teacher of Torah (Kuzari, I, 115, 5). According to *Ab. Z.*, 3 a, a heathen who studies Torah is equal to the High Priest.

44. Cf. J. Jocz, op. cit., 309 and notes.

45. They relate to idolatry, incest, shedding of blood, blasphemy, injustice, robbery, the cutting of a limb of a living animal; *Gen. R.*, 34. 8. For the whole subject see H. Kosmala and Robert Smith, *The Jew in the Christian World*, 93 ff.

46. For a review on the subject see Oepke: *Das neue Gottesvolk*. It is unfortunate that this otherwise most erudite book is marred by typical German prejudice. We quote one sentence as an example: "Und doch wird der Synagoge ihre Religion zum Fluch und ihre Moral zum Verbrechen" (op. cit., 14. 2). How does Professor Oepke justify this? Cf. also Goppelt, *Christentum und Judentum*, who deals with the same subject.

47. Cf. J. Jocz, "The New Theological Orientation regarding Israel", *The Hebrew Christian*, IV, 1951, 96 ff.

48. Karl Barth, *Die Kirchliche Dogmatik*, II, 2, 218 f.

49. Cf. pp. 134 f.

50. The Yigdal Prayer, Singer, 2.

51. Singer, 90.

52. Cf. H. Loewe, in his Introduction to *Rabb. Anthol.*, lxix f.

53. This is the very question which Trypho is asking of Justin; cp. *Dial.* 10.

54. Cf. Strack and Billerbeck, I, 905 ff.

55. Cf. Justin, *Dial.* 19: Irenaeus, *Adv. haer.*, IV, 15. It would be a profitable study to investigate the Patristic interpretation of the Law.

56. A classical instance is the way Barnabas used the Law; cf. ch. 10.

57. For a short summary, see H. H. Kramm, *The Theology of Martin Luther*, 60 ff.

58. *Sanh.*, 10, 1.

59. The concept of a *new* Torah is not foreign to rabbinic Judaism, cf. H. Loewe, *Judaism and Christianity*, I, 117 f., 175 ff. Loewe observes: "Torah cannot be abrogated; when it has permeated the hearts of all men, its outward symbols will cease automatically", ibid., p. 177. This is an important statement, for it tallies with the Pauline view that the moral law having been written upon the hearts of the believers the "outward symbols" are of no importance any more (2 Cor. 3. 2–12). See also J. Jocz, op. cit., 21–7, 286–91.

60. Herbert Loewe, who writes as an observing Jew, says: "No human being could 'change' the Torah, only God could do so", op. cit., 175.

61. Cf. *T. J. Meg.*, 1, and see 7 f., quoted by Loewe, op. cit., 176. Loewe suggests that Esther is exempted because of the example of self-sacrifice. We doubt the explanation. A more recent attitude to Esther is that of Shalom ben Chorin, *Kritik des Estherbuches*, Jerusalem, 1938.

62. J. Denney, *H.D.B.*, III, 74. For a more recent discussion of the subject, see H. Ljungman, *Das Gesetz erfüllen*, Matt. 5. 17 ff., Lund, 1954. Ljungman's

interpretation is not very different from our own. For a criticism of his book, see *Judaica*, II, 1955, 123 f.

63. The editor of the Gospel does not seem to be aware of a contradiction between Matt. 5. 18 and 19. 8; did he not notice it, or is there none?

64. Cf. J. Jocz, op. cit., 36 ff.

65. J. Weiss, A. Mayer, Lietzmann, Holtzmann, and many others are inclined to think that Jesus uses the expression "Son of Man" in a general sense; cf. Dalman, *The Words of Jesus*, E.T., 261 ff. But C. G. Montefiore sees more correctly when he says: "The 'Son of Man' is here used in its final Messianic sense. The Messiah is the Lord of the Sabbath . . ." (*The Synoptic Gospels*, 1909, II, 618).

66. J. Klausner, *Jesus von Nazareth*, 510; but Schoeps gives a different construction, cf. the chapter: "Jesus und das jüdische Gesetz", in his *Aus frühchristlicher Zeit*, 219 f.

67. Cf. Strack and Billerbeck, I, 241.

68. A. Edersheim, *The Life and Times of Jesus the Messiah*, I, 537.

69. Montefiore, *The Synoptic Gospels*, I, 492.

70. J. Klausner, *From Jesus to Paul*, 355 f.

71. Ibid., 393.

72. Cf. J. Gresham Machen, *The Origin of Paul's Religion*, 18 ff.; 93 ff.; etc.

73. Schoeps misunderstands the Pauline position by supposing the Apostle reduced the Torah to ethical Law. Justification of sinners, which the Law cannot accomplish, is not an ethical but a forensic concept. It is God's prerogative to justify sinners, but he does so only on the basis of the death of Christ. Cf. Schoeps, "Paulus als rabbinischer Exeget", *Aus frühchristl. Zeit*, 229.

74. *H.D.B.*, III, 79 a.

75. Ibid., 81 b.

76. Ibid., 82 a.

77. Cf. Irenaeus, *Adv. haer.*, IV, 15, 1.

78. Ibid., IV, 16, 4; for a similar rabbinic tradition see Daube, *The New Testament and Rabbinic Judaism*, 65.

Irenaeus, 79. op. cit., IV, 9, 1.

80. Cf. P. S. Minear, *Eyes of Faith*, chapter 6: God appoints times.

81. Cyprian, *Test. adv. Judaeos*, I, 8, 9, 10, etc.

82. Cf. Origen, *De principiis*, IV, 17, etc.

83. R. P. C. Hanson, *Origen's Doctrine of Tradition*, 104.

84. Origen, *Contra Celsum*, VII, 25.

85. Hanson, op. cit., 89; for Clement's exegetical methods see ibid., 61 ff.

86. Cf. *Contra Celsum*, VII, 25.

87. Ibid., VII, 26.

88. Cf. T. F. Torrance, *The Doctrine of Grace in the Apostolic Fathers*, 116 ff.

89. Cp. pp. 43 f.

90. Strack and Billerbeck, index: "Tage des Messias"; also the learned excursus: "Die Welt und die Tage des Messias", ibid., IV, 2, 799 ff.

91. Martin Buber, *Jewish Mysticism*, E.T., 157.

92. *The Jewish Caravan*, "Pangs of Messiah", 721 ff.

93. Cf. Isaac of Troki, ספר חזוק אמונה, ch. I.

94. A. Lukyn Williams, *A Manual of Christian Evidences*, I, 27–62.

95. Maimonides, *The Guide*, E.T., 1947, 325.

96. *De praedest. Sanct.*, 3.

97. *C. duas epp. Pelag.*, II, 21.

98. Oscar Cullman, *Christ and Time*, E.T., 145 f.

99. Cf. W. Lowrie, *Kierkegaard*, 445, 525 f.

100. Franz Rosenzweig has seen this more clearly than many a Christian writer (cf. *Der Stern der Erlösung*).

101. To our knowledge Professor H. J. Schoeps is the only professing Jew who admits the possibility that Israel's Messiah may have the face of Jesus of Nazareth; cf. his article "Möglichkeiten und Grenzen einer jüdisch-christlichen Verständigung", *Unterwegs*, 1948, No. 3.

102. Maimonides, *Ḥilkot melakim*, Amsterdam, ed. 1702, IV, 307.

103. Cf. M. Buber, *Die Stunde und die Erkenntnis*, p. 153: "Wir wissen aber auch, wie wir wissen dass Luft ist . . . dass Raum ist . . . tiefer, echter, wissen wir, dass die Weltgeschichte nicht bis auf ihren Grund aufgebrochen, dass die Welt noch nicht erlöst ist. Wir *spüren* die Unerlöstheit der Welt."

NOTES TO CHAPTER 4

1. Cf. James Parkes, *Judaism and Christianity*, 1948, 21: "Sinai and Calvary are two events not one". Parkes, in order to keep the Bible together, is, however, forced to the view that though these are *two* events they did not occur in isolation, but that they are related, yet must not be fused (cf. op. cit., 25, 30, etc.). It is difficult to assess the exact meaning of his view. For the Jewish point of view, see J. Jocz, op. cit., 315 ff.

2. Cf. the excellent appendix provided by R. H. Murray, *Erasmus and Luther*, 424 ff.; also his book *Science and Scientists*, 122 ff.

3. Justin, *Apologia*, II, 13.

4. V. Harnack, *Dogmengeschichte*, Grundriss, 1883, 87.

5. Clement Alex., *Stromata*, I, 5.

6. Augustine, *De doctrina christiana*, II, 61.

7. H. H. Gowan, *The History of Religion*, 3.

8. Robert H. Murray goes as far as attributing to Augustine the modern concept of progress; cf. *Erasmus and Luther*, 424.

9. *De fide et symbolo*, III, 4, 5.

10. Lactantius, *De vita beata*, VII, 7.

11. So V. H. Stanton, *A Companion to Biblical Studies*, ed. W. Emery Barnes, 1916, 284.

12. The same contradiction vitiates Emil Brunner's theory, which works on the principle of progressive revelation but limits it to the coming of Jesus Christ; cf. *Revelation and Reason*, E.T., 133 ff.

13. *De agone christiano*, VIII, 9.

14. Cf. Edwyn Bevan, *Sibyls and Seers*, 1928.

15. Cf. V. Harnack, op. cit., 90.

16. Charles Gore, *The Philosophy of the Good Life*, 300; cf. also Professor Andrew C. Zenos, *Standard Bible Dic.*, 1909, art. "Revelation".

17. Emil Brunner, op. cit., 318 f.

18. Ibid., pp. 36, 178 n.

19. Cf. Martin Buber, *I and Thou*, E.T., 1937.

20. The article on revelation by H. L. Goudge is a typical example of the traditional approach to the subject. Goudge speaks of "accommodation in revelation", which is another way of expressing the much-discussed *Anknüpfungspunkt* in German theology and means that revelation is given according to capacity. One sentence is rather puzzling: "To assert the reality of the higher is in no way to deny the reality or value of the lower . . ." The logic of the sentence is not self-evident. Cf. *Encycl. Religion and Ethics*, X, 745 ff.

21. W. R. Inge, *God and the Astronomers*, 180.

22. Jacques Maritain, *Redeeming the Time*, 229.

23. Ibid., pp. 227, 246 n., 247 n. We feel sure that Brunner would be surprised to discover in Maritain a kindred spirit!

24. Cf. Rudolf Otto, *The Philosophy of Religion*, E.T., 143 n.

25. Ibid., pp. 23, 126, 134, 143 n., 165 f.

26. E. Troeltsch, *Glaubenslehre*, 1925, 54.

27. N. Söderblom, *The Nature of Revelation*, E.T., 1933, 8.

28. Ibid., 120.

29. Cf. J. Jocz, op. cit., 278 ff.

30. Cf. C. G. Montefiore, *Rabb. Anthol.*, xxxiii.

31. Sanh. 99 a (E.T., 672 f.). For גורה שדה see Jastrow's *Dic.*, 232.

32. *Ab.*, 2, 18 a.

33. *Bat ḳol*, lit. daughter of the Voice; a curious expression, perhaps coined to avoid an anthropomorphism? The rabbis explain that one did not hear the Voice itself, but only the echo of the Voice; cf. Strack and Billerbeck, I, 125.

34. *Yoma*, 9 b.

35. *Ber.*, 51 b; cf. *Er.*, 7 a; *Baba Mez.*, 59 b.

36. Clement, *Stromata*, VI, 8.

37. Quoted by Brunner, op. cit., 315, n. 9.

38. Cf. Tertullian, *Apologeticus*, 17 f.

39. For Brunner's "not yet" which he applies to the Prophets we would substitute "never"; cf. Brunner, op. cit., 199.

40. Cf. the splendid section on "Gott der verborgene und der geoffenbarte", Theodosius Harnack, *Luthers Theologie*, 1927, 84 ff.

41. Cf. E. Brunner's apposite remarks regarding the "name" of God and the "face" of God; op. cit., 88 ff.

42. For the derivative of אל see Brown, Driver, and Briggs, 41 f. It is an oversight on the part of Thorleif Boman not to have paid due attention to this important noun. Cf. *Das hebräische Denken im Vergleich mit dem griechischen*, 1952, especially pp. 45 ff.

43. Cf. Loofs, op. cit., 535.

44. The idea of the "suffering God" in the person of Jesus Christ has its roots in the O.T., especially Isa. 63. 9.

45. Though we reject some of Boman's conclusions (see our review in the *Hebrew Christian*, Autumn, 1953), on this particular question Boman sees aright: "Dass Gott in der Person Jesu Christi war und sein Wesen durch ihn offenbart hat, ist griechisch gedacht; dass er seinen Sohn gesandt und seinen Willen durch ihn verwirklicht hat, ist israelitisch gedacht". Boman, op. cit., 154.

46. Ps. 15 is already a "rationalist" approach where moral integrity takes precedence over Levitical purity; usually in the O.T. they go hand in hand.

47. There is some controversy as to the rendering of *Yahveh-yireh*; cf. *H.D.B.*, II, 563 a. For the traditional Jewish translation see Rashi and Onkelos. Cheyne's translation is too hypothetical to commend itself. Cf. *Encyc. Biblica*; for a more balanced view see *The Expositor*, II, 3rd series, p. 7.

48. For the adverb פני see Brown, Driver, and Briggs, 816 b.

49. In translation the preposition עד is lost; "unto the Lord" does not really convey the forcefulness of the challenge. It can only be paraphrased: Turn, O Israel, until thou facest the Lord thy God!

50. It is interesting to note the individual aspect of the same theme as stated in Rev. 21. 7. Here it is not any longer the people as a whole, but the individual who becomes a son of God.

51. For a definition of idolatry see Otto Weber, *Jahwe der Gott und Jahwe der Götze*, 1933.

52. A. Roy Eckhardt, who has much to say about the danger of idolatry in the Church, is completely ignorant of such a danger in the Synagogue; cf. *Christianity and the Children of Israel*, 1948.

NOTES TO CHAPTER 5

1. Cf. Gal. 3. 6–9, 29.

2. Cf. Midrash *Ex. R.* 28. *v.* 8. Dr Hertz says: "The Covenant is one which must be held to bind not only the living who were present on that day, but their distant posterity as well"; *The Pentateuch and Haftorahs*, on Deut. 29. 13 f.

3. Schoeps shows remarkable insight when he says: "Auf der Vergleichnisebene stehen sich nicht Kirche und Synagoge, sondern Kirche und Volk Israel gegenüber"; *Juden-christl. Religionsgespräch*, 149.

4. With the exception of the Karaites and a small Hebrew Christian minority scattered in the Gentile Churches, all spiritual conflicts within Jewry were fought out within the walls of the Synagogue (cf. Maurice Simon, *Jewish Religious Conflicts*, 1950). This does not apply to the modern situation.

5. Cf. J. Jocz, *Judaism and the State of Israel*, 1950.

6. This is a sentence from the third collect on Good Friday, in the Anglican *Book of Common Prayer*, when the Church prays for the Jews in conjunction with "Turks, infidels, and heretics". In the Roman Missal there is a separate prayer for the Jews. It begins with the words: "Oremus et pro perfidis Judaeis . . ." which the English Missal translates as "faithless Jews". Cf. on the question of *perfidia Judaica* the note by Maritain, *Redeeming the Time*, 134. That Rome prays only grudgingly for the Jews can be seen from the fact that this is the only prayer which is said without kneeling; the rubric explains that the solemn prayers on Good Friday are said "for all humanity, Christian and pagan; even the Jews are not excluded" (!).

7. Cf. Eugène Sue, *The Wandering Jew*, 1845.

8. Cf. G. H. Joyce, art. "Revelation", *The Catholic Encyclopædia*; and Aug. Paulain, art. "Private Revelations", ibid.

9. For a typical Protestant definition of revelation, see M. Köhler, *The New Schaff-Herzog Encycl. of Relig. Knowledge*, Vol. X, 3f.; "Revelation is the act of God in disclosing or communicating truth to the human soul". If that is so, why should it stop with the N.T.?

10. *Shabb.*, 88 b.

11. *Ab. Z.*, 3 a.

12. *Sanh.*, 59 a.

13. Tamar, Rahab, and Ruth; cf. Matt. 1. 3, 5.

14. Cf. Josephus, *Bell.*, II, 17, 1–2; *c. Apionem*, II, 6. Philo, *Leg. ad Caium*, 157, 317.

For the sacrifice on behalf of the nations see the many references by Strack and Billerbeck, II, 551, 811.

15. Cf. *Cant. R.*, 1. 15: "As a dove atones for sins, so the Israelites atone for the nations, for the seventy oxen which they offer on the festivals represent the seventy nations (of the world) . . ."

16. Cf. Strack and Billerbeck, II, 549 f.

17. Cf. Edersheim, *The Temple*; particularly his sketch of the courts, p. 23.

It is not true to say, as do Sanday and Headlam, that "later Judaism denied all hope to the Gentiles"; cf. *Romans* (*I.C.C.*), 1900, 337.

18. Cf. Moses Hadas, *Aristeas to Philocrates*, 42, 71 n.

19. Hadas, op. cit., 111 n.

20. Cf. P. E. Kahle, *The Cairo Geniza*, 158.

21. So Montefiore, *The Synoptic Gospels*, II, 728.

22. *Bikkurim* 1, 4.

23. Ibid., 1. 5; if baptism really means new birth in the rabbinic view then this is an obvious inconsistency; cf. D. Daube, *The New Testament and Rabbinic Judaism*, 113.

24. Cf. J. Jocz, op. cit., 296 ff.

25. Cf. A. V. Harnack, *Sprüche und Reden Jesu*, 1907, 99.

26. Cf. Montefiore, *The Synoptic Gospels*, II, 559.

27. This must not be taken as an attempt to exonerate Peter or to explain away Paul's accusation that Peter acted in a cowardly manner.

28. Cf. Sanday and Headlam, op. cit., 249 f.

29. *A New Commentary*, ed. by Gore, Goudge, and Guillaume, 479.

30. Cf. Sanday and Headlam, 330.

31. Ibid., 327.

32. Ibid., 331 f.

33. Cf. ibid., 253.

34. Alford's *Greek N.T.*, 1886, 430.

35. Cf. Strack and Billerbeck, I, 65; cf. also ibid., II, 334, f., 346 ff.; III, 626. Though Strack and Billerbeck deny that the ancient Synagogue knew of a pre-existent Messiah, the *Jewish Encycl.* takes the opposite view. Cf. VIII, 511.

36. Cf. Isa. 11. 1; Jer. 23. 5; 33. 15; Zech. 3. 8; cf. also Edersheim, *Life and Times*, I, 222.

37. Delitzsch suggested that Ναζωραῖος originally read: כי נצר שמו, "For Nezer (i.e. Branch) is his name"; cf. *Zeitschrift für Luther. Theol.*, 1876, III, 402.

38. *Encycl. of Rel. and Ethics*, VIII, 136 a.

39. In the controversy between Church and Synagogue over messianic texts this fact creates much difficulty. To this day, Jewish exegetes maintain that in Isa. 53 the whole people is meant and not just one single person. This they infer from the fact that other deutero-Isaiah passages plainly indicate that the whole people is the Servant of God. Cf. J. Klausner, *The Messianic Idea in Israel*, E.T., 161 f.

40. Cf. Edersheim, I, 161 f.; also Strack and Billerbeck, I, 85 f.

41. Wilhelm Vischer in his splendid exposition of Rom. 9–11 equates the 'root" with God's grace. This seems to us a rather forced picture; cf. *Judaica*, II, 1950, 126.

42. *The New Commentary*, 479.

43. Prof. W. Zimmerli, "Biblische Grundlinien zur Judenfrage", *Judaica*, 1945, II, 110: "Abgesehen von diesem Annehmen der freien Gnade ist es nie Gottes Volk gewesen".

44. Cf. J. Cohen, *Deicides*, 1872. The book is a pathetic effort to justify the Jewish people, but the title speaks for itself.

45. It is odd that the question of responsibility for the Crucifixion is still a subject of heated discussion between Jews and Christians. Whatever the Jewish contention, from the Christian point of view every sinner is guilty of the Master's death—how otherwise are we to understand that Jesus Christ died for the sins of the world?

46. On the question of Responsibility, cf. D. Daube, *Studies in Biblical Law*, 155 ff.

47. Sanday and Headlam, op. cit., 317.

48. *Tanh. B. Debarim*, 2 b fin.; quoted from *Rabb. Anthol.*, 564.

49. Cf. A. v. Harnack, *Die Mission und die Ausbreitung des Christentums*, chap. IV: "Jesus Christus und die Weltmission nach den Evangelien."

50. Harnack was too great and honest a scholar to feel happy about it; he thus admits, at least in one place, his indecision; cf. ibid., 26, n. 3.

51. In this respect Oepke is a laudable exception. Cf. op. cit., 160–2, 235.

52. All that Harnack admits of the Lord's Prayer is the petition for daily bread, forgiveness of sins, and deliverance from temptation; cf. *Sprüche und Reden Jesu*, 1907, 47, 94, 178; cf. also Streeter, *The Four Gospels*, 277 f.

53. Cf. *Mission und Ausbreitung*, 26, n. 3.

54. Harnack, ibid., 27, n. 1.

55. Harnack includes Matt. 8. 11 f. in Q; cf. Sprüche, 59, 99.

56. Harnack, *Mission*, 27, n. 3.

57. Cf. Schürer, op. cit., E.T., II, 2, 307 ff.

58. Cf. Streeter, op. cit., 190, 211, 217.

59. Oepke, op. cit., 157; Goppelt similarly subscribes to the traditional view that Jesus founded the new Israel; cf. *Christentum und Judentum*, 60, and note.

60. Streeter, op. cit., 4.

61. The reading is doubtful. Some MSS. omit καινὴ in Mark 14. 24 and Matt. 26. 28. Luke 22. 20 has a more uniform tradition. But if we accept 1 Cor. 11. 25 as the most ancient evidence, then καινὴ διαθήκη is undoubtedly original.

62. Behm takes classical Greek as an example in contrasting καινός, "neu der Art nach", with νέος, "neu der Zeit, dem Urspring nach"; Kittel's *Theol. Wörterbuch*, III, 452; 30.

63. *Theol. Wörterbuch*, II, 137; his definition of διαθήκη as "Verfügung" (cf. ibid., II, 127, 20) is insufficient to cover the Hebrew concept of *berit*.

64. Cf. T. C. Edwards, "'Testament' or 'Covenant' ", *Expositor*, 3rd Series, III, 370 ff.

65. This rule is attributed to R. Demi; cf. *B.B.*, 135 b. דייתיקי is a Hebraized form of διαθήκη.

66. Behm mistakenly speaks of "zwei verschiedene, einander ablösende διαθῆκαι", *Theol. Wörterb.*, II, 133 f.

67. Cf. Gustaf Dalman, *Jesus-Jeshua*, E.T., 1929, 163.

68. That "grace and truth came by Jesus Christ" (John 1. 17) must not be understood to mean that there was neither grace nor truth before Jesus Christ. The gift of the Law is as much grace as the gift of the Gospel. Moses and Jesus stand not in opposition but in completion to each other. Cf. Schlatter's excellent note, *Der Evangelist Johannes*, 32 f.

69. If our view is correct, then the effort on the part of some scholars towards a "bridge-theology" with a view to a synthesis between Judaism and Christianity is a departure from the N.T. attitude.

70. Αἱ διαθῆκαι (pl.) in Rom. 9. 4 is important, for by stressing that there were more than one Covenant the "new" Covenant was placed in the perspective of history—the last of several: the Covenant with Abraham (circumcision); the Covenant through Moses (the Law); the Covenant through the Messiah (the New Birth). Cf. W. D. Davies, op. cit., 120.

71. Lightfoot, *Galatians*, 148.

72. Cf. E. De Witt Burton, *Galatians* (*I.C.C.*), 1921, 201.

73. Cf. Isa. 42. 9. Here *rishonot* and *ḥadashot* are contrasted: "the former things" refer to God's providence over Israel's past; the "new things" speak of yet greater things to come.

74. Cf. Alford's *Greek N.T.*, II, 647.

The name of "O.T." for the Hebrew Bible must have derived from this Pauline text, though there was as yet no "N.T." when Paul wrote. Cf. Oepke, op. cit., 207, n. 5.

75. Oepke's conclusion that for St Paul "die leibliche Abstammung ist ohne Bedeutung" (op. cit., 202) is ill-founded; we shall return to the subject at a later stage.

76. Op cit., 217.

77. Cf. op. cit., 76 f., 183, 207, 229, etc.

78. Cf. op. cit., 170–2, 179, 182, 197.

79. We quote Ephesians as representing the Pauline view. Though the authorship of the letter is under question, it is generally agreed to represent St Paul's point of view. Cf. K. L. Schmidt, *The Church*, E.T., 1950, 20: "Ephesians is in fact thoroughly Pauline—whether it was written by the apostle or by one of his disciples."

80. Cf. the excellent article by F. Lovsky, "The Christian Hope and the Mystery of Israel", *The Ecumenical Review*, April, 1955, 244.

81. Cf. K. L. Schmidt, op. cit., 14.

82. Read in the context, Luke 17. 21 must mean "The Kingdom of God is in the midst of you"—ἐντὸς ὑμῶν ἐστιν. There would be little point in announcing the Gospel of the Kingdom if the Kingdom was already in the hearts of the listeners. This is a typical Greek fallacy.

83. For this reason we choose to read: Marana tha!—"Our Lord, come!"—instead of the usual: Maran atha—"Our Lord is coming!"

84. Cf. H. Schlier, quoted by K. L. Schmidt, op. cit., 17.

85. It is important to stress that "prophets" are here a reference to the O.T. in spite of the wrong sequence: "apostles and prophets". This we hold to be more in keeping with the context, against H. M. Gwatkin, *H.D.B.*, IV,

128 a; and Eric Graham, *New Comm.*, 544. But cf. J. A. Selbie, *H.D.B.*, I, 499 b.

86. Gottlob Schrenk, "Was bedeutet 'Israel Gottes' ", *Judaica*, II, 1949, 93 f.

87. N. A. Dahl, "Zur Auslegung von Gal. 6. 16", *Judaica*, III, 1950, 168.

88. Cf. Schrenk, "Der Segenswunsch nach der Kampfepistel", *Judaica*, III, 1950, 170 ff.

89. We use the name Ἰουδαῖοι as we believe it is used in the Fourth Gospel, namely in distinction from Israel. Cf. J. Jocz, "Die Juden im Johannesevangelium", *Judaica*, III, 1953.

90. Cf. the article by the Hungarian Hebrew Christian, Josef Éliás: "Erwählung als Gabe und Aufgabe", *Judaica*, II, 1955, specially 91 f.

NOTES TO CHAPTER 6

1. Gutbrod, in Kittel's *Theol. Wörterb. zum N.T.*, III, 385. 45.

2. Ibid.

3. Cf. H. H. Rowley, *Israel's Mission*, 1939, 95.

4. There is a large literature on this theme. In the minds of some Gentiles all revolutionary movements seem to be associated with Jewish influence; cf. the book published anonymously in 1920 and supplied with a preface by the Editor of *The Morning Post*, H. A. Gwynne, *The Cause of World Unrest*. According to this book Jews take the blame for all revolutionary movements in Europe. Hilaire Belloc's book, *The Jews*, 1922, is written in the same spirit though with greater restraint. It is the main tenet of anti-Semitism that the Jewish people is a "destructive force", but psychologists are agreed that anti-Semitism springs from the need for a scapegoat. Yet the Jewish people is a "protestant" force. For their considerable influence on the Reformation, see Louis I. Newman, *Jewish Influence on Christian Reform Movements*, New York, 1925.

5. Ignaz Maybaum, *The Jewish Mission*, 8.

6. Jacques Maritain, "The Mystery of Israel", *Redeeming the Time*, 134 f. In this connection Buber's Messianism is of special interest; cf. Franz v. Hammerstein, "Martin Buber's messianische Hoffnung und ihr Verhältnis zu seiner Philosophie", *Judaica*, II, 1954.

7. Maybaum, op. cit, 28.

8. Maritain, op. cit., 153.

9. Maybaum, op. cit., 59 f.; cf. also J. Jocz, op. cit., 317 f.

10. Cf. pp. 39 ff.

11. Cf. Singer, "The Burial Service", 319.

12. Cf. Walter Zimmerli, "Biblische Grundlinien zur Judenfrage", *Judaica*, II, 1945, 95: "Die Diskussion um die jüdische Frage hat die Kirche . . . zu einer ganz intensiven *Selbstbesinnung* zu treiben. Indem sie zu verstehen sucht, was nun das Volk der Juden ist, kann sie allein wieder recht verstehen, wer sie selber ist."

13. It is interesting to note that Jacques Maritain comes very near the Barthian view but fails to draw Barth's conclusions.

14. Cf. *Dogmatik*, II, 2, 233.

15. Ibid., 231; Goppelt, who refuses to see in historic Israel the "heils-

geschichtliche Voraussetzung" of the Church's existence, is out of tune with the Barthian point of view; cf. Goppelt, op. cit., 124.

16. Cf. ibid., 221 f.

17. Ibid., 229.

18. An extreme example in history is the "conversion" of the old Prussian tribes by the Teutonic Knights.

19. Cf. J. Jocz, op. cit., 322, and note 375.

20. Maritain, op. cit., 132.

21. Cf. Gutbrod, in Kittel's *Theol. Wörterbuch*, III, 390.

22. Cf. G. Molin, "Mysterion Israel", *Judaica*, IV, 1954, 242 f.

23. Cf. Wilhelm Vischer, "Das Geheimnis Israels, eine Erklärung der Kapitel 9–11 des Römerbriefs", *Judaica*, II, 1950, 127 f.

24. Goppelt's interpretation is even more contradictory; cf. Goppelt, op. cit., 119, 122.

25. Cf. Barth, op. cit., II, 2, 344 f.

26. This is the distinctly Christian insight as against the Jewish position, where the order is reversed.

27. An interesting example was Polish Messianism, which was developed by the national poet Adam Mickiewicz (1798–1855). At a time of national humiliation, Mickiewicz explained the suffering of his people as vicarious suffering for the sins of the West. He called Poland the "Messiah of the nations" which was being crucified for the sake of a better future. The view affected only a limited circle, and failed to penetrate the consciousness of the Polish people.

28. Deut. 17. 14 ff. presents a compromise. The king is here placed under the jurisdiction of God. His power is limited; he is a "constitutional monarch"; he owes allegiance to the Law. Hos. 13. 10 f. presents the institution of the monarchy as a form of punishment. Professor Geo. Widengren's presentation of the position of the king in Israel seems to overlook evident hostility to the monarchy in the O.T. Cf. his *Sakrales Königtum im Alten Testament*, 1955.

29. Maritain, op. cit., 129 f. For a more theological definition of what is a Jew see Erica Küppers, "Widerstehet dem Antisemitismus!" in *Die Juden und wir Christen*, ed. by Hans Kallenbach, 1950. For a Jewish definition in the demographic sense, see *A Minority in Britain*, ed. by Maurice Freedman, 1955, 60, 150 f., 206.

30. Pp. 17 f; 96 ff.

31. On the question of legality see Giovanni Rosadi, *The Trial of Jesus*, E.T., 1904, specially ch. XI; also J. Klausner, *Jesus von Nazareth* (German ed.), 469; cf. also Carl Becker's reply to Rabbi Ludwig Philippson, *Ja; die Juden haben wirklich Jesum gekreuzigt*, Berlin, 1872.

32. Something of the Martyrdom of European Jewry can be gauged from Lord Russell's book, *The Scourge of the Swastika*, 1954. For a short historical survey see J. Jocz, "A Suffering People", *The Moody Monthly*, May, 1955.

33. Cf. Barn, 4. 14, etc.; Justin, *Dial.*, ch. 16; *Apol.*, I, 47.

34. Tertullian, *Apologeticus*, 21.

35. Montefiore is forced to admit that at least part of the Lucan passage must have belonged to Q (cf. *Synoptic Gospels*, II, 733); most scholars hold a similar view; see Streeter, 253 f.

36. Cf. Lightfoot, *Galatians*, 181; Ramsay accepts Lightfoot's argument,

cf. *Historical Comm. on Gal.*, 433 f. But commentators overlook that Jerusalem even prior to A.D. 70 was, in the eyes of Jewry, a city in bondage under foreign rule. They overlook the political aspect which gives pungency to the Apostle's argument. For the whole subject cf. Leonhard Goppelt, *Christentum und Judentum*, 1954, 67 ff.

37. Wilfred T. F. Castle's book, *Syrian Pageant*, provides an excellent background to the story of Jewish suffering as far as Palestine was concerned.

38. It is a pity that so grandiloquent a title as the *Martyrdom of Man* should for ever be associated with the shallow and superficial effort by Winwood Reade. It is not accidental that Reade has so little sympathy with and understanding for the most moving spectacle of Jewish martyrdom.

39. Max Eyth, *Die Brücke über die Ennobucht* (Berufstragik), Reclam Ausgabe, 1955.

40. Cf. Barth's radio broadcast at Basel on 13 December 1949: "Der Jude bezahlt dafür, dass er der Erwählte Gottes ist." The whole broadcast is to be found in *Die Juden und wir Christen*, ed. by Hans Kallenbach, 1950, in the series "Kirche und Welt".

41. Maritain, op. cit., 143.

42. *Die Juden und wir Christen*, 27; for Fricke's view see ibid., 45.

43. Paul Tillich, *Die Judenfrage, ein christliches und ein deutsches Problem*, 1953. Tillich speaks of the "Strukturähnlichkeiten zwischen dem deutschen und dem jüdisehen Wesen" (p. 23), and of the "Ablenkung des Selbsthasses auf ein Objekt, das man hassen kann" (p. 42).

44. K. Barth: "Uns verdriesst es—und dass nehmen wir dem Juden so übel—dass er wie ein Spiegel ist, in welchem uns vorgehalten wird, wer oder was, d.h. wie schlimm wir alle sind", *Die Juden und wir Christen*, 13.

45. Maritain, op. cit., 144.

46. M. Buber, *Der heilige Weg*, 1920, 18: "Es ist des Menschen Sache Gottes Macht in der Erdenwelt zu begründen". Man is here understood to be a fellow-worker in God's task of creation; cf. ibid., 20; cf. also *Two Types of Faith*, 29: "realization in the totality of life" is Buber's recurring theme.

47. Tillich lays special emphasis upon the category of time in the significance of Jewish existence: "Die Juden sind und müssen bleiben das Volk der Zeit"; *Die Judenfrage*, etc., p. 37.

NOTES TO CHAPTER 7

1. Cf. John McConnachie, *The Significance of Karl Barth*, 76: "Dialectic thinking, thinking in question and answer, so that the answer contains always again a question, is, according to Barth, the only thinking open to us in dealing with the relation of God to man."

2. Cf. R. Eisler, *Philosophen-Lexikon*, 1912, 851 f.

3. John Scotus, *Div. nat.*, I, 27.

4. Cf. A. Liebert, *Die geistige Krisis der Gegenwart*, 1923, 181 ff.

5. "Kritisch-Krisenhafte Lage" he calls it.

6. A. Liebert, *Die Krise des Idealismus*, 1936, 47, 176, 235, etc.

7. For Plato's approach to dialectic see Windelbrand-Heimsoeth, *Lehrbuch der Geschichte der Philosophie*, 1948, 99.

8. Cf. Windelband, op. cit., 461.

9. Cf. J. O. Wisdom, "Hegel's Dialectic in Historical Philosophy", *Philosophy*, Journ. Brit. Inst. of Phil., July 1940.

10. Cf. A. Liebert, op. cit., 59 n.

11. Luther, *Comm. on Gal.*, E.T., 1953, 99.

12. So Luther, quoted by H. H. Kramm, *The Theology of Martin Luther*, 1947, 61.

13. Luther, *The Freedom of a Christian*, E.T., Bertram Lee Woolf, *Reformation Writings of Martin Luther*, I, 1952, 375.

14. Luther, op. cit., 369.

15. Cf. Augustine, *De duabus animabus*, 14.

16. Augustine, *De praedest. sanct.*, 3.

17. Kierkegaard's famous parable graphically expresses the believer's position: seventy thousand fathoms of water—man lying constantly out upon the deep—in dependence upon God—trying to swim without being a swimmer.

18. Cf. W. Lowrie, *Kierkegaard*, 1938, 577.

19. Paul Tillich, op. cit., 32 ff. Professor Tillich makes a definite distinction between the Jewish people and the nations: the people of time and the people of space. Polytheism he connects with "space", Monotheism with "time".

20. Cf. *Die Lehren des Judentums*, 1929, III, 215.

21. *Maḥsheve ḳezim*; for sources, see *J.E.*, V, 210 a.

22. Cf. W. Sanday, *Christologies, Ancient and Modern*, 1910, 54; cf. also Loofs, op. cit., 924.

23. Sanday, with the characteristic confidence of the rationalist at the beginning of this century, explains the "hearing" as "insight into principle", thus explaining away the "secret" (cf. op. cit., 229 ff.).

24. As an example we would quote Ezekiel, who spends seven days waiting in silence upon God (Ez. 3. 15). It is the loneliness of the figure of Job as he sits in the Presence of God which gives to the book of Job its prophetic character.

25. Cf. G. F. Moore, *Judaism*, II, 95.

NOTES TO CHAPTER 8

1. For the reason why the name "Hebrew Christian" is more acceptable than "Jewish Christian" see J. Jocz, "The Significance of the Hebrew Christian Position", *The Hebrew Christian* quarterly, April 1945, p. 11: "Had the word 'Jew' no religious but only an ethnic connotation, he (i.e. the Hebrew Christian) would have called himself a *Jewish* Christian, but by reason of his opposition to rabbinism . . . he calls himself a *Hebrew* Christian." But in German-speaking lands the name *Judenchrist* is universally accepted; cf. Gerhard Jasper, "Der Judenchrist als Zeichen Gottes", *Judaica*, III, 1955, 134.

2. Cf. Franz Werfel, *Zwischen Oben und Unter*, 94.

3. Joy Davidman, *Smoke on the Mountain*, 1955, 8.

4. Gerhard Jasper expresses it in the following sentence: "Er [i.e. der Judenchrist] will also mit der Bezeichnung 'Judenchrist' die heilsgeschichtliche Linie bejaht wissen" (op. cit., p. 137).

5. Cf. Carl Becker, *Ja; die Juden haben wirklich Jesum gekreuzigt*, Berlin, 1872, specially pp. 154 ff.

6. Goppelt understands "camp" to stand as "an allegorical symbol of this world", cf., op. cit., 236; but this seems to us a forced interpretation.

7. Cf. H. J. Schoeps: "Weiteres zur Auserwählung Israels", *Judaica*, III, 1946, 190 ff.

8. Cf. Otto Weber, *Jahwe der Gott und Jahwe der Götze.*

9. Cf. Werfel, op. cit., 290; also ibid., 281, 282.

10. Cf. James Parkes, *Judaism and Christianity*, 1948, pp. 18, 21, etc.; J. Jocz, op. cit., 320 f.

11. K. Barth, *Dogmatik*, II, 2, 251: "Die Existenz christlicher Juden wird als Zeichen der unaufhebbaren Kontinuität des göttlichen Weges, als unmittelbare Erinnerung an die Auferweckung des Lazarus oder vielmehr: an die Auferweckung des Menschen Jesu von den Toten ihnen ein besonderes Gnadenzeichen bleiben. Und nur ein trostloses ungeistliches Denken könnte einen Judenchristen veranlassen, sich seiner Herkunft aus Israel zu schämen, oder einen Heidenchristen, sie jenem nachzutragen. Es bedeutet eine höchste und unverwischbare Ehre, ein christlicher Jude zu sein!"

12. The term "convert" is frequently used by Jews and Gentiles, but they give it a different connotation. To the Jew it usually means a "turn-coat", to the Gentile it means a "newcomer". That the Gentile can be a Christian without being a convert is the most revealing fact about "Christianity".

13. K. Barth, op. cit., II, 2, 264: "Sie wird vor Augen haben und halten, dass ihre eigene Existenz als Kirche nur auf dem Grund Israels . . . unter Voraussetzung des Hörens der Verheissung möglich und legitim ist und bleiben kann."

14. Ibid., 256.

NOTES TO CHAPTER 9

1. H. P. Tappan, *A Treatise on the Will*, Glasgow, 1857, 544. This book is chiefly a controversy with an opponent called Edward, but it is a fine example of the *impasse* into which speculative theology can land when it tries to reason *theoretically* on election and free-will.

2. Sanday and Headlam, op. cit., 216 f., 347 ff.

3. K. Barth points out the aberration of the classical doctrine of predestination which places "einen unbestimmten Gott" *vis-à-vis*, "einem umbestimmten Menschen", op. cit., II, 2, 246.

4. We read ἄχρις here in reference to subject rather than to time.

5. The philosophical question of prescience and free-will is outside the scope of this work. We concur, however, wholeheartedly with Sanday and Headlam, that there is no solution to this problem this side of history; cf. op. cit., 350, para 3.

6. Barth, op.cit., II, 2, 345.

7. Sanday and Headlam, op. cit., 218.

8. "Die Erwählung der Gemeinde" is an important phrase in Barth's *Dogmatik*, and is the title of a whole chapter. On the question of sequence: individual—community, or *vice versa*, see ibid., II, 2, 340.

9. Isaiah's question echoes down the centuries: "Who is blind but my servant? or deaf, as my messenger that I send?" (Isa. 42. 19).

10. It is noteworthy that Barth, who was so emphatically Calvinistic on the question of "double predestination" in his earlier work, has now changed its meaning to imply universal salvation: God elects man and condemns himself on man's behalf. Cf. op. cit., II. 2, 177.

BIBLIOGRAPHY

A Minority in Britain, ed. by M. Freedman, 1955.

Ante-Nicene Fathers.

Asch, Sholem, *The Nazarene*, 1939; *The Apostle*, 1943; *Mary*, 1950; *My Personal Faith*.

Augustine, various works.

Barth, Karl, *Die Kirchliche Dogmatik*, Vol. II, 2; *Teaching of the Church regarding Baptism*, E.T., 1948.

Becker, Carl, *Ja; die Juden haben wirklich Jesum gekreuzigt*, 1872.

Belloc, Hilaire, *The Jews*, 1922.

Bevan, E., *Sibyls and Seers*, 1928.

Bistrizki, Nathan, *Jesus of Nazareth*, 1950.

Boman, Thorleif, *Das hebräische Denken im Vergleich mit dem griechischen*, 1952.

Bonsirven, Joseph, *On the Ruins of the Temple*, E.T., 1931.

Bornkamm, Heinrich, *Luther und das Alte Testament*, 1948.

Brown, F., G. R. Driver, and C. A. Briggs, *A Hebrew and English Lexicon of the Old Testament*, 1906.

Brunner, E., *Revelation and Reason*, E.T., 1947.

Buber, Martin, *Der Heilige Weg*, 1920; *I and Thou*, E.T., 1937; *Jewish Mysticism*, E.T., 1931; *The Two Types of Faith*, 1951.

Buber, Martin, and Franz Rosenzweig, *Die Schrift*, *Das Buch Reden* (no date).

Castle, W. T. F., *Syrian Pageant*, 1948 (?).

Chorin, Shalom ben, *Kritik des Estherbuches*, 1948.

Chwolson, D., *Das letzte Passamahl Christi und der Tag seines Todes*, 1892.

Cohen, A., *Everyman's Talmud*, 1949.

Cohen, Philip, *The Hebrew Christian and his National Continuity* (no date).

Cullmann, Oscar, *Christ and Time*, E.T., 1951.

Daiches, S., *Aspects of Judaism*, 1928.

Daube, D., *The New Testament and Rabbinic Judaism*, 1956.

Davidman, Joy, *Smoke on the Mountain*, 1955.

Davies, W. D., *Paul and Rabbinic Judaism*, 1948.

Dembitz, L. N., *Jewish Services in Synagogue and Home*, 1898.

(Denny J.) *Hastings Dictionary of the Bible.*

Die Juden und wir Christen, ed. by Hans Kallenbach, 1950.

Die Lehren des Judentums, ed. by S. Bernfeld and F. Bamberger, 3 vols., 1928–29.

Diestel, Ludwig, *Geschichte des Alten Testaments in der christlichen Kirche*, 1869.

Eckhardt, A. R., *Christianity and the Children of Israel*, 1948.

Edersheim, A., *The Temple*, 1874; *The Life and Times of Jesus the Messiah.*

Eisler, R., *Philosophen-Lexikon*, 1912.

Ellison, H. L., "Jesus and the Pharisees", *Journal of Trans. of Victoria Institute*, 1953.

Encyclopædia Biblica, 1914.
Expositor, The, 3rd series.
Eyth, Max, *Die Brücke über die Ennobucht*, 1955.

Farrar, F. W., *Lives of the Fathers*, 1889.
Feldman, A., *Parables and Similes of the Rabbis*, 1927.
Fishberg, M., *The Jews, a study of Race and Environment*, 1911.
Fleg, Edmond, *Jesus, told by the Wandering Jew*, 1934.
Friedländer, G., *Laws and Customs of Israel*, 1921.
Fülop-Miller, *Leaders, Dreamers and Rebels*, 1935.

Golding, Louis, *The Day of Atonement*, 1945.
Gollancz, Victor, *My dear Timothy*, 1952; *More for Timothy*, 1953.
Goppelt, L., *Christentum und Judentum*, 1954.
Gore, Charles, *The Philosophy of the Good Life*, 1930.
Gowan, H. H., *The History of Religion*, 1934.

Halevi, Jehuda, *Kuzari*, with German transl. by Zifrinowitsch, 1911.
Hanson, R. P. C., *Origen's Doctrine of Tradition*, 1954.
Harnack, A. v., *Dogmengeschichte*, 1883.
Harnack, Theod., *Luthers Theologie*, 1927.
Heppe, H., *Reformed Dogmatics*, E.T., 1950.
Hertz, J. H., *Affirmations of Judaism*, 1927; *The Pentateuch and Haftorah*, 1938.
Hirschell, Solomon, *Prayer Book for German and Polish Jews in England*, Hebr. and Engl.
Hunter, S. J., *Outlines of Dogmatic Theology*, 3 vols., 1909.

Inge, W. R., *God and the Astronomers*, 1933.
Isaac ben Abraham of Troki, *Ḥizzuḳ Emunah*, with German transl. by David Deutsch, 1873.

Jastrow's *Dictionary of the Talmud*, etc.
Jewish Caravan, ed. by L. W. Schwartz, 1935.
Jewish Encyclopedia, 1906.
Jewish Encyclopedia, Vallentine's, 1938.
Jocz, J., *The Jewish People and Jesus Christ*, 1954.
Judaica, various articles, ed. by Robert Brunner, Zürich.
Judaism and Christianity, 3 vols., 1937–38.

Kittel's *Wörterbuch zum N.T.*
Klausner, J., *Jesus von Nazareth*, German, 1934; *From Jesus to Paul*, E.T., 1946; *The Messianic Idea in Israel*, E.T., 1956.
Kosmala, Hans, and R. Smith, *The Jew in the Christian World*, 1942.
Kramm, H. H., *The Theology of Martin Luther*, 1947.

Liebert, A., *Die geistige Krisis der Gegenwart*, 1923; *Die Krise des Idealismus*, 1936.
Lightfoot, J. B., *Galatians*, 1902.
Loofs, F., *Dogmengeschichte*, 1906.
Lowrie, W., *Kierkegaard*, 1938.
Luther, M., *Grosser Katechismus* von G. Holz, 1933; *The Freedom of a Christian*, E.T., Bertram Lee Woolf, 1952.

Machen, J. Gresham, *The Origin of Paul's Religion*, 1921.
Maimonides, M., *Guide for the Perplexed*, E.T., 1947; *Yad ha-ḥazaḳah.*
Maritain, Jacques, *Redeeming the Time*, E.T., 1946.
Marmorstein, A., *The Old Rabbinic Doctrine of God*, 1927.
Matthews, R., *English Messiahs*, 1936.
Mattuck, I. I., *What are the Jews?*, 1939.
Maybaum, I., *Man and Catastrophe*, 1941; *The Jewish Mission*, 1949.
McConnachie, J., *The Significance of Karl Barth*, 1931.
McLoughlin, Emmett, *People's Padre*, 1955.
Minear, P. S., *Eyes of Faith*, 1948.
Montefiore, G. C., *The Old Testament and After*, 1923; *The Synoptic Gospels*, 2 vols., 1909.
Montefiore, G. C., and H. Loewe, *A Rabbinic Anthology*, 1938.
Moore, G. F., *Judaism*, 3 vols., 1930.
Murray, R. H., *Erasmus and Luther*, 1920; *Science and Scientists.*

Newman, L. I., *Jewish Influence on Christian Reform Movements*, 1925.

Oepke, A., *Das neue Gottesvolk*, 1950.
Oesterley, W. O. E., and G. F. Box, *Religion and Worship of the Synagogue*, 1911.
Otto, R., *The Philosophy of Religion*, E.T., 1931.

Parkes, James, *Judaism and Christianity*, 1948.
Pick, Seligman, *Die auf Jesus gedeuteten Stellen des Alten Testaments*, 1923.
Propper, Felix, *Zum Leben berufen*, 1955.

Ramsay, W. M., *Historical Commentary on Galatians*, 1899.
Religion in Geschichte und Gegenwart, 1931, ed.
Riehm, E., *Die messianische Weissagung*, 1885.
Rosadi, G., *The Trial of Jesus*, 1904.
Rosenzweig, Franz, *Der Stern der Erlösung*, 1921.
Rowley, H. H., *Israel's Mission*, 1939.
Rubinstein, H. F., *Hated Servants*, 1944.
Russell, Lord, *The Scourge of the Swastika*, 1954.

Sanday, W., and A. C. Headlam, *Commentary on Romans*, 1900.
Schlatter, A., *Geschichte Israels*, 1925.
Schoeps, H. J., *Aus frühchristlicher Zeit*, 1950; *Jüdisch-christliches Religionsgespräch*, 1949.
Singer, S., *Annotated Prayer Book*, Hebrew and English, 1912.
Söderblom, N., *The Nature of Revolution*, 1933.
Standard Dictionary of the Bible, ed. by A. C. Zenos, 1909.
Strack, H. L., and P. Billerbeck, *Kommentar zum N.T. aus Talmud und Midrash*, 4 vols., 1922–8.
Streeter, B. H., *The Four Gospels*, 1924.
Süssman, Cornelia, and Irving, *Marc Chagall, Painter of the Crucified*; *The Bridge*, ed. by John M. Oesterreicher, 1955.

Tappan, H. P., *A Treatise on the Will*, 1857.
Tillich, Paul, *Die Judenfrage*, 1953.
Torrance, T. F., *The Doctrine of Grace in the Apostolic Fathers*, 1948.
Troeltsch, E., *Glaubenslehre*, 1925.

Weber, F., *Die Lehre des Talmud*, 1880.
Weber, Otto, *Jahwe der Gott und Jahwe der Götze*, 1933.
Werfel, F., *Paul among the Jews*, E.T., 1928; *Zwischen Oben und Unten*, 1946.
Widengren, G., *Sakrales Königtum im Alten Testament*, 1955.
Williams, Lukyn, *Christian Evidences for Jewish People*, 2 vols., 1911–19; *Talmudic Judaism and Christianity*, 1933.
Windelbrand-Heimsoeth, *Lehrbuch der Geschichte der Philosophie*, 1948.
Woodhouse, H. F., *The Doctrine of the Church in Anglican Theology, 1547–1603*, 1954.

Ysander, T., *Studien zum B'eṣ̌tschen Ḥasidismus*, 1933.

INDEX OF SUBJECTS

INDEX OF NAMES